DATA CENTER MANAGEMENT

Nastaran Nazar Zadeh

TAP

Toronto Academic Press

Data Center Management

Nastaran Nazar Zadeh

Toronto Academic Press
224 Shoreacres Road
Burlington, ON L7L 2H2
Canada
www.tap-books.com
Email: orders@arclereducation.com

ISBN: 978-1-77469-787-0

ABOUT THE AUTHOR

Nastaran Nazar Zadeh is a highly experienced computer engineer, researcher, and advisor in the fields of robotics, artificial intelligence and computer science. She holds a Master of Science in Computer Engineering from Mapua University of the Philippines and pursed her Ph.D. in Electronic Engineering at the same institution. With over seven years of teaching experience, Nastaran has taught electronic and computer engineering programs at several reputable academic institutions, where she has also led numerous thesis studies. Her research focuses on developing robotics systems with A.I. and machine learning, which enables her to stay up-to-date with the latest advancements in the field and implement cutting-edge technologies.

Contents

3 Security and Compliance in Data Protection 63

4 Monitoring and Management Tools 97

List of Figures

List of Tables

List of Abbreviations

APEC	Asia Pacific Economic Cooperation
ASHRAE	Refrigerating and Air-Conditioning Engineers and the American Society of Heating
AWS	Amazon Web Services
CCPA	California Consumer Privacy Act
CMS	Configuration Management Software
CORD	Central Office Re-architected as a Datacenter
COTS	Commercial Off-the-Shelf
CRM	Customer Relationship Management
DAS	Direct-Attached Storage
DCIM	Data Center Infrastructure Management
DPP&S	Data Security, Confidentiality, and Security
e-PHI	Electronically-Protected Health Information
ECMP	Equivalent Cost Multipath Routing
EDC	Edge Data Center
EDI	Electronic Data Interexchange
EoR	End-of-Row
ER	Entrance Room
ERM	Enterprise Risk Management
ERP	Enterprise Resource Planning
GDPR	General Data Protection Regulation
HIPAA	Health Insurance Portability and Accountability Act

HPC	High-Performance Computing
ICT	Information Communication Technology
ICT4D	Information and Communication Technology for Development
IoT	Internet of Things
IT	Information Technology
LAN	Local Area Network
MAC	Moves, Adds, and Changes
MAM	Mobile Application Management
MC	Main Cross-Connect
MDC	Modular Data Center
MDM	Mobile Device Management
MoR	Middle-of-Row
MTDC	Multitenant Data Centers
NAS	Network-Attached Storage
NGOs	Non-Governmental Organizations
NMS	Network Management Software
NPM	Network Performance Monitor
OCHA	Coordination of Humanitarian Affairs
OECD	Organization for Economic Cooperation and Development
PCI DSS	Payment Card Industry Data Security Standard
PHI	Personal Health Information
PII	Personally Identifiable Information
PIPEDA	Personal Information Protection and Electronic Documents Act
PMS	Performance Management Software
POP	Point-of-Presence
QoS	Quality-of-Service
SAN	Storage Area Network
SCM	Supply Chain Management

SDS	Software-Defined Storage
SFA	Sales Force Automation
SIEM	Security Information and Event Management
SLAs	Service Level Agreements
SRM	Storage Resource Management
UN	United Nations
VLAN	Virtual LAN
VMs	Virtual Machines
VR	Virtual Reality
WAN	Wide Area Network
WDM	Wavelength Division Multiplexing
WVI	Organizations International

PREFACE

Data centers are the heart of modern technology, supporting the critical infrastructure that powers our digital world. As the reliance on technology continues to grow, the demand for effective and efficient data center management has never been greater. Managing a data center requires a deep understanding of the complex architecture, security protocols, compliance requirements, and power and cooling management. It also requires staying up-to-date with emerging trends and technologies that can improve data center operations and support business growth.

However, managing a data center can be a complex and challenging task, requiring a deep understanding of the various components and processes involved. This book is a comprehensive guide to data center management, providing a detailed overview of the critical concepts and practices involved in managing a data center. The book is divided into eight chapters, each focusing on a different aspect of data center management.

Chapter 1 provides an introduction to data center management, exploring the importance of effective management and the role of data centers in supporting business operations. Chapter 2 delves into data center architecture, providing a thorough overview of the components and systems that make up a data center, including servers, storage, and networking.

Chapter 3 focuses on security and compliance in data protection, highlighting the critical importance of data security and the regulatory requirements that must be met to ensure compliance. Chapter 4 explores the monitoring and management tools used in data center management, including performance monitoring, capacity planning, and incident management.

Chapter 5 covers virtualization and cloud computing, examining the benefits and challenges of these technologies and their impact on data center management. Chapter 6 discusses the importance of power and cooling management, examining the challenges of maintaining a stable and efficient data center environment.

Chapter 7 focuses on the challenges of data center management, including operational challenges, staffing challenges, and budget constraints.

Chapter 8 provides insights into future trends in data center management, including the use of artificial intelligence and machine learning, the growth of edge computing, and the increasing importance of sustainability and energy efficiency.

This book is written for professionals, students, and scholars seeking to improve their understanding of data center management. It is a valuable resource for IT professionals, data center managers, and business leaders seeking to optimize data center operations and support business growth. By reading this book, you will gain a deeper understanding of data center management's critical concepts and practices, enabling you to make informed decisions confidently.

—Author

CHAPTER 1

INTRODUCTION TO DATA CENTER MANAGEMENT

UNIT INTRODUCTION

Managing and sustaining a company's infrastructure for data centers is a component of data center management. It involves overseeing the programming, hardware, and network assets required to operate the organization's programs and services. For an organization's IT network to be available, dependable, and secure, efficient data center administration is essential (Basmadjian et al., 2016).

The management of data centers involves various important tasks, such as:

- **Capacity management:** This entails estimating the number of assets, such as processing power, storage space, and network bandwidth, required to support an organization's programs and services (Gandhi et al., 2012).
- **Resources management:** This comprises keeping track of and maintaining the processors, storage units, network interface, and application resources in the data center.
- **Performance supervision:** This entails keeping an eye on the architecture of the data center, notably server usage, network activity, and storage space.
- **Security monitoring:** To do this, security mechanisms like firewalls, systems for intrusion detection, and network access must be put in place to safeguard the data center network and the data kept inside.

Disaster maintenance entails creating and implementing plans to rebuild from catastrophes like power failures and natural catastrophes while ensuring that crucial systems and data can be recovered quickly (Sari & Akkaya, 2015).

Support and maintenance: This includes assisting consumers and IT personnel and doing routine maintenance on the data center framework as hardware and software updates and network improvements.

For efficient data center administration, technical understanding, strategic thinking, and good communication are necessary. It necessitates strong collaboration with other IT teams, including system administrators, network engineers, and security specialists to guarantee that the data center framework aligns with the company's objectives and goals (Jiadi et al., 2020) (Figure 1.1).

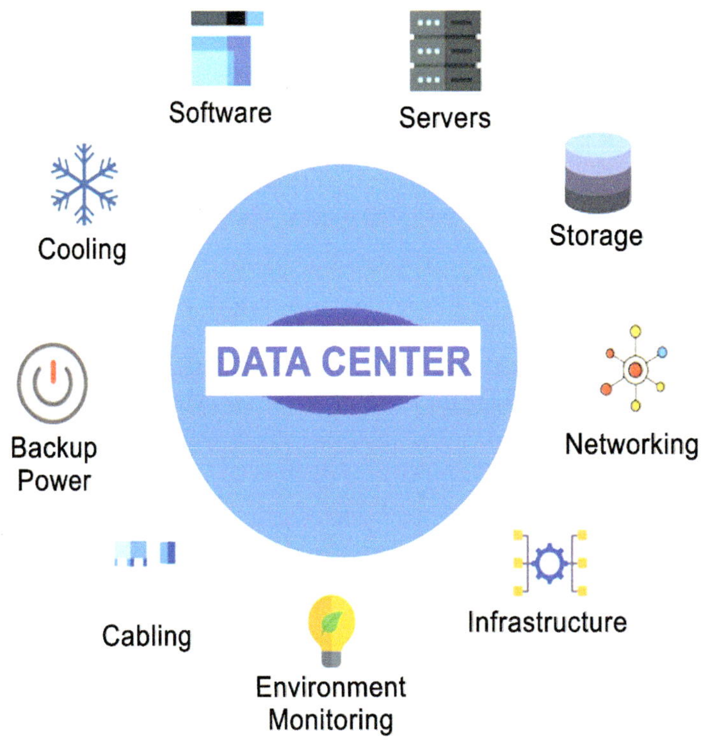

Figure 1.1. Representation of data center (Source: Temok, Creative Commons License).

Learning Objectives

At the end if this chapter, the reader will be able to understand:

1. The concept of data center management
2. The significance of functional domains of data center

3. The factors affecting data center architecture
4. The importance of management of data center
5. The components of data center management
6. The important software of data center management

Key Terms

1. Information Communication Technology (ICT)
2. Electronic Data Interexchange (EDI)
3. Enterprise Resource Planning (ERP)
4. Customer Relationship Management (CRM)
5. Sales Force Automation (SFA)
6. Supply Chain Management (SCM)
7. Multitenant Data Centers (MTDC)
8. Moves, Adds, and Changes (MAC)
9. Wavelength Division Multiplexing (WDM)

1.1. A CONCEPT OF DATA CENTER

According to ANSI/TIA-942, a data center is a structure, or section of a structure, whose main use is to contain a computer room and the rooms that serve it. Consolidating, managing, and distributing information technology (IT) or information communication technology (ICT) assets are a data center's primary duties. As part of this, an infrastructure for data acquisition and administrative hosting that offers services like software and internet connectivity, database administration, data transmission, data storage, and data backup must be housed and supported. Collectively, these services enable e-Business between diverse enterprises, customers, and other government organizations (e.g., government agencies). A few examples of common software services are (Jouppi et al., 2017) (Figure 1.2):

1. Electronic Data Interexchange (EDI)
2. Enterprise Resource Planning (ERP)
3. Customer Relationship Management (CRM)
4. Sales Force Automation (SFA)
5. Supply Chain Management (SCM)

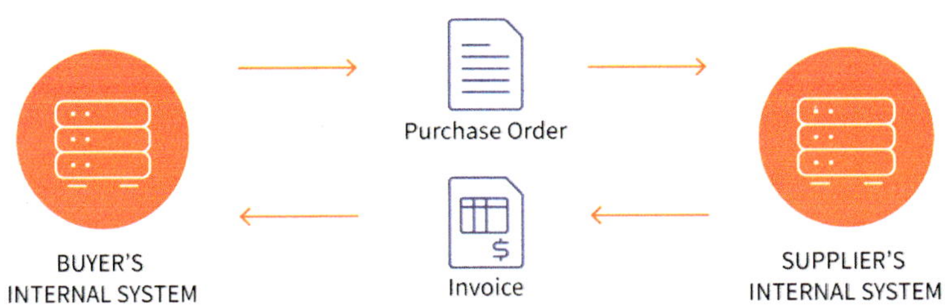

Figure 1.2. Illustration of EDI (Source: Open text crop, Creative Commons License).

Advanced data centers are the major competitors in social media, e-commerce, mobile applications, and conventional data center services. These services go beyond typical on-premises services and may be found in the broader realm of "cloud computing," defined by Infrastructure, Platform, and Applications (IaaS, PaaS, and SaaS). Figure 1.3 illustrates the degree of administration that each type of e-Business service demands from its potential customer. This wide range of services includes programs, information management, real-time performance, networking, operating systems, hypervisor, server management, storage, and full networking (Weerasinghe et al., 2016).

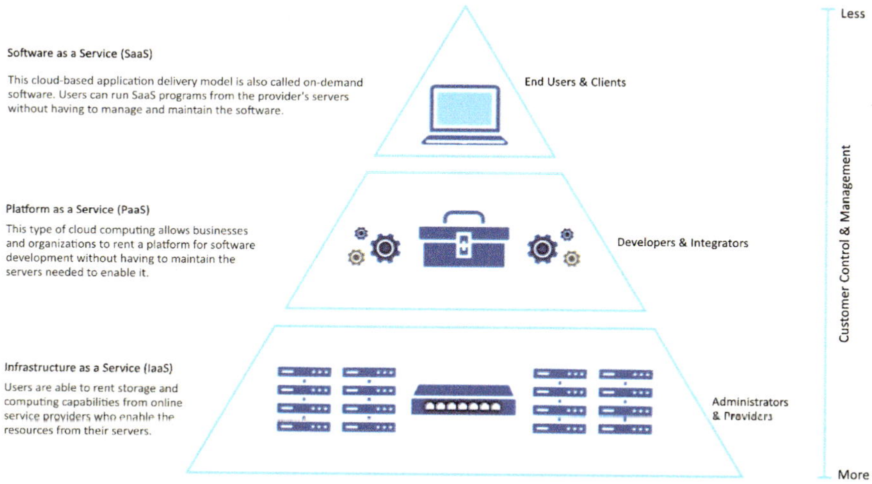

Figure 1.3. Schematic to represent the level of control and management (Source: Plesk, Creative Commons License).

In addition to providing information services, data centers are physically safe locations where mission-critical processes can continue without interruption. Data centers must therefore make the following provisions to ensure the whole system's dependability, resilience, and duplication: Continuous network accessibility

1. Fail-safe power
2. Environmental controls (like HVAC)
3. Fire repression
4. Error maintenance
5. Security, access control, and surveillance
6. An efficient fiber optic cabling network

Based on whether they supported the public or private zone, data centers were previously classified as either business (e.g., corporate) or service (e.g., internet) serving resources.

Businesses, organizations (like colleges), governments, or other commercial enterprises and associations autonomously owned run enterprise data centers. Business facilities include private data handling and interactions and web-based services through extranets or intranets, all backed and overseen by internal IT assistance (Anthony et al., 2018).

Conventional "TELCOs," telephone companies or telecommunications service vendors, or uncontrolled competing service vendors offering the general public and outsourced IT operations through an internet connection typically own and run carrier data centers. Typically, these services are colocation (co-lo) or multitenant data centers (MTDC). The room is rented out to different customers to host services and/or supply networking equipment to link to a network operator. Depending on the requirements, the room can be provided for a single server cabinet, functional cage, or data hall (Malla & Christensen, 2019).

A unique facility type called Hyperscale Data Centers (HDCs), which are significantly larger than their ancestors, has developed along with the two conventional designations. These operators comprise conventional carriers, but they are mostly made up of the leading cloud and e-commerce network operators of the modern day (like Microsoft, Amazon, IBM, Apple, Google, and Facebook). A single firm may use these facilities exclusively, where adaptability is just as important as capacity, or they might have thousands of servers to serve a range of external clients. In addition, cloud service companies are now the main suppliers of demand for global broadband. As per TeleGeography's "The Status of the Network" 2020 edition, they currently comprise more than half of all utilized international capacity (Ding et al., 2019) (Figure 1.4 and Table 1.1).

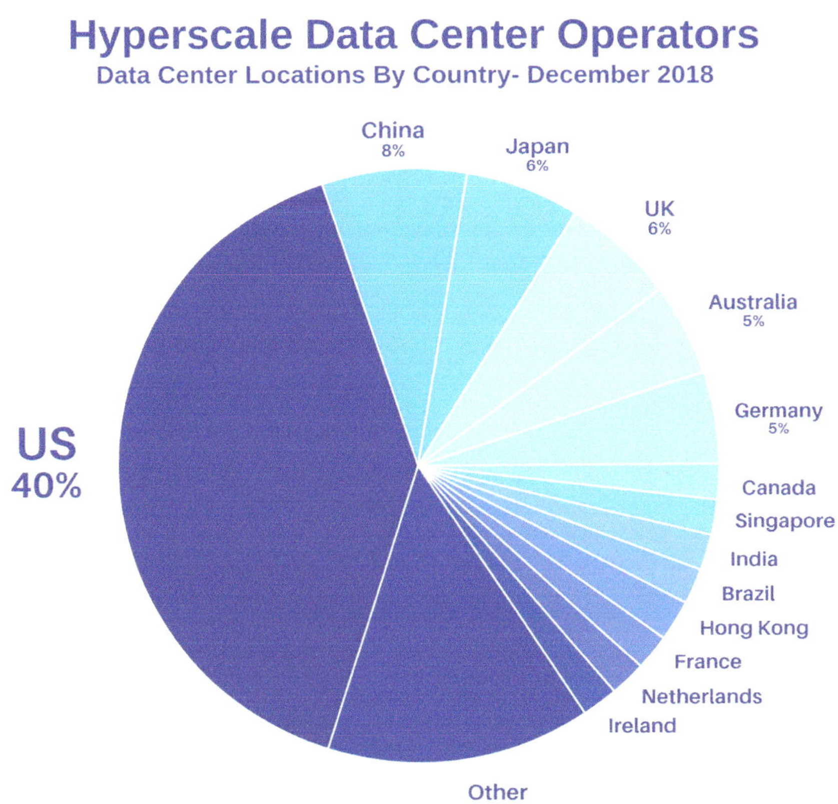

Figure 1.4. A hyperscale representation of data center (Source: Dp facilities, Creative Commons License)

Table 1.1. Types and Services of Data Center (Source: Corning Optical Communication, Creative Commons License)

Enterprise	In-House	• Private ownership • Enterprise large organizations	Organizations can design, build, and operate their facilities
	Colocation "co-lo"	• Customers own hardware • Outsource facility and internal systems maintenance	In a multitenant data center, colocation space can be sold to enterprises by the rack, cabinet, or cage
	Wholesale Data Center	• Sell large space • Supplies facilities maintenance	The provider can sell data center space in larger capacities vs. co-lo
Cloud	Dedicated Hosting	• Servers are **not** shared • Customer controls server	The provider operates and/or rents server capacity to single customers
	Managed Hosting	• Hardware owned by customer or provider • Many services provided	The provider operates servers and storage for its customers
	Shared Hosting	• Multitenant Applications	Customers share server capacity

The expanding Edge Data Center (EDC) market represents a divergent and, at first glance, conflicting approach to HDC growth. Suppliers interact with their consumers at conventional operator networks' "edge," like TELCO main office or MSO headend. Advanced telecommunication networks' "edge" refers to areas where more data is placed near end customers and users to reduce the delay, capacity, and quality-of-service (QoS) problems. Cell building and radio rescue installments, availability and clustering points (such as single OSP closets and connector packaging), business, commercial, sales, economic, distribution (e.g., railroad) locations, linked district nearby places (e.g., light poles), and of course conventional multi-rack matchups in basic or cloud facilities could all be included in this (Aghdai et al., 2013) (Figure 1.5).

By 2025, Bell Laboratories projects that 60% of servers will be housed in EDCs. Furthermore, Gartner said 75% of business data would be generated and handled at the border by 2025.

Among the factors influencing these developments will be the growth in border deployments of Internet of Things (IoT) devices and machine-generated data, primarily device-to-device communications. Service providers must enhance network capability to enable faster and more extensive data processing for innovations like virtual reality (VR), telemedicine, linked vehicles, immersive media, and comprehensive smart city projects. In actuality, cloud service providers are viewed as gates to border assets or as expansions of border computing (Puthal et al., 2018).

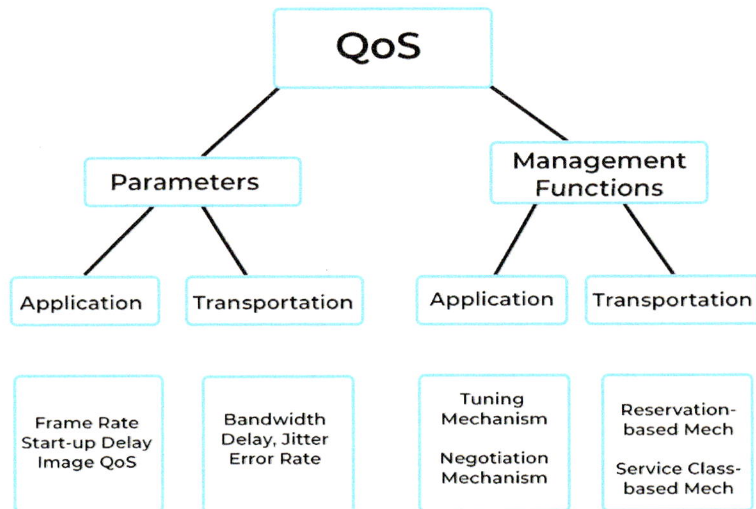

Figure 1.5. Diagram of Quality of Services (Source: Chiradeep BasuMallick, Creative Commons License).

The dispersed and regionally connected mobile network that 5G currently represents, which is a first-generation edge program, will be complemented by EDCs. See the TIA policy paper "Edge Data Centers" and associated TIA and AFCOM white papers on the motivations for and benefits of EDCs for additional details on this subject. Relate to the CORD (Central Office Re-architected as a Datacenter) system for details on initiatives to convert the network edge into a flexible service delivery system. This platform aims to use NFV, SDN, and cloud platforms to upgrade existing central office frameworks into edge data centers.

The demand for such services will increase worldwide, increasing expenditure on public, hyperscale, and edge data centers. There are still millions of data centers in that range, varying from modest business server rooms to corporate MTDCs and today's larger HDC sites, even though these patterns indicate reduced spending for on-premise IT. The long-term growth pattern is clear-cut regarding data center vendors and growing markets (Filani et al., 2008).

The dispersed and regionally connected mobile network that 5G currently represents, which is a first-generation edge program, will be complemented by EDCs. See the TIA policy paper "Edge Data Centers" and associated AFCOM and TIA white papers on the motivations for and benefits of EDCs for additional details on this subject. Relate to the CORD (Central Office Re-architected as a Datacenter) system for details on initiatives to convert the network edge into a flexible service delivery system. This platform aims to use NFV, SDN, and cloud platforms to upgrade existing central office frameworks into edge data centers.

The demand for such services will increase worldwide, increasing expenditure on public, hyperscale, and edge data centers. There are still millions of data centers in that spectrum, varying from modest business server rooms to corporate MTDCs and today's larger HDC sites, even though these patterns indicate reduced spending for on-premise IT. Regarding data center vendors and growing markets, the prolonged growth pattern is clear-cut (Liu et al., 2009).

1.2. FUNCTIONAL DOMAINS OF DATA CENTER

Regarding the architectural features of a data center, the following zones may be applied to categorize its domains and common components, along with the responsibilities that each play in both logical and physical network communication (Cruz & Joshi, 2015).

1.2.1. Wide Area Network (WAN) Connectivity

- Physical: Service/access provider network demarcation
- Logical: Network ("internet") packet routing

1.2.2. Local Area Network (LAN) Connectivity

- Physical: Customer/client-server front-end access
- Logical: Data link frame switching and routing

1.2.3. Storage Area Network (SAN) connectivity

- Physical: Data volume device back-end access
- Logical: Data link frame switching and block-level transfers

1.3. ACCESS TO ENTRANCE DOMAIN

The "point-of-presence" (POP) or "meet-me" room" are two terms that may be used to describe this part of the data center. Moreover, the location of the connection between the service provider's interbuilding cable and the customer-owned intrabuilding cabling is more particularly an entrance room (ER), as specified by ANSI/TIA-942. Accessibility to the service vendor's communications system is made possible by this doorway accessibility area. In addition to conventional PBX or voice gateways and T-3 multiplexers, this section may also house the vendor's boundary hardware and equipment, such as internet gateways and routers. This zone, hence, has traditionally been connected to the "core" network layer design. For reliability or to satisfactory cable length constraints imposed by access providers, data centers may feature numerous entrance rooms. For administrative and security reasons, this area is frequently located further than the main computer room; however, in small data centers, it may also be located in the primary computer room (Schuster et al., 2016) (Figure 1.6).

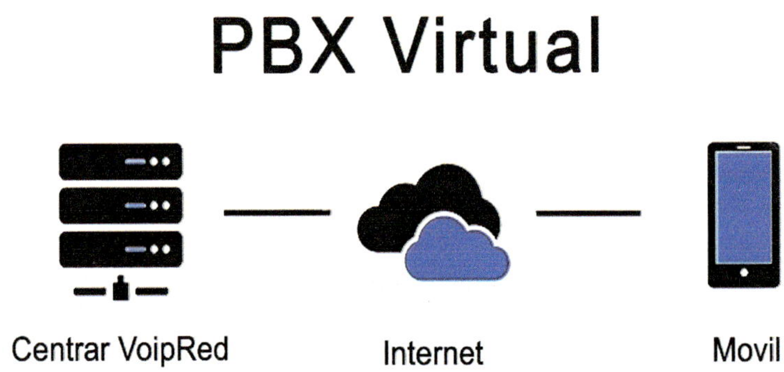

Figure 1.6. Image of virtual PBX (Source: Voipred, Creative Commons License).

1.4. DISPERSION NETWORK DOMAIN

The Main Supply Area is the ER's connection with the remaining information center, or the "computer room" (MDA). The MDA could be close by or integrated into the ER. The servers, the data center's main functioning components, are connected to the outside world through this region (Song et al., 2022).

Catalog, program, application, gaming, document, email, entertainment, virtual, and server software are just a few examples of server kinds. Basic routers, SAN or LAN switches (with "spine" and "interconnection," or "leaf"), high-performance computing (HPC) switches, and software-based virtual machines (VMs) make up the network hardware found in the MDA. The main cross-connect (MC), the hub for circulation for the building's cabling infrastructure, is also located in this area. The MC could also be referred to as the primary patching site for this purpose.

The MDA can link to a lower-layer dispersion site, creating a network to establish communication between all the data center subsystems quickly and efficiently. In TIA-942- these additional dispersion zones and significant components are also described (Kyono et al., 2018).

1.5. STORAGE ZONE

If it is there, the back-end link is provided to data by this section of the data center. Storage Area Networks (SANs) are a staple of the infrastructure found in most data centers because they provide the following benefits:

1. Managing flexibility.
2. Administration, consolidation, and scaling benefits.
3. Back-up, access, automation, movement, virtualization, and software-defined storage (SDS) adaptations.

For these reasons, SANs may be preferred over conventional direct-attached storage (DAS) and network-attached storage (NAS) file-based devices (Lu et al., 2011).

Across storage devices and servers, SANs create switches and directors, allowing thorough network connectivity such that servers can utilize one storage resource (that might be located remotely).

Devices that use block-level storage, like tape, disk (JBOD/RAID), and optical storage drives, are frequently seen in storage spaces. Newer SANs also consider the idea of object storage3, where data communicates at the software level by an API instead of directly through the operating system. Devices for object storage function as modular components that may be combined to create huge storage pools over different locations. HTTP is used to reach object-based storage arrays, the same kinds of disk units as those used in traditional SANs (Singh et al., 2008).

1.6 CONSIDERATIONS OF DATA CENTER ARCHITECTURE

Each of the following factors affects common criteria for data centers:

- Architectural design
- Environmental response
- Electrical
- Physical security access
- Water infiltration
- The overall efficiency of energy may be the single-most crucial factor in efficient data center infrastructure
- Fire protection

Consider the ANSI/TIA-942-B Telecom Infrastructure Standard for Data Centers and other industry assets, like BICSI's data center design and execution standards and best practices, to comprehend these factors further (Hammadi & Mhamdi, 2014).

A general perspective on energy requirements and licensing for data centers can also be obtained from organizations like ASHRAE (Refrigerating and Air-Conditioning Engineers and the American Society of Heating). ASHRAE offers validation and verification methods to ensure that the structure and its systems and components are designed, developed, assembled, verified, serviced, and maintained per the owner's requirement.

Did you Know?

A recent study by Cisco predicts that by 2021, global data center traffic will reach 20.6 zettabytes per year, up from 6.0 zettabytes in 2016, highlighting the need for scalable and efficient data center architectures.

The Uptime Institute, Leadership in Energy and Environmental Design, and AFCOM are other resources for designing data centers, deployment, and operation-related information.

This manual is not meant to serve as an all-inclusive reference to facility development and building or the layout and upkeep of pertinent systems. These professional engineering and thorough project management initiatives touch on numerous industrial norms, codes, and laws (Agyapong et al., 2014).

Instead, this manual emphasizes relevant telecommunications components, such as the common fiber optic cabling systems, spaces, data center channels, and associated topologies. Proper planning and attention during facility building or refurbishment are essential to cost-effectively enable expansion and alterations in the data center telecommunications infrastructure.

Finally, the goal of this manual is not to direct a data center's full cost analysis. Users can add physical infrastructure elements into data center cash flow calculators to explore various cost possibilities. These technologies consider the load, reliability, complexity, elemental power, and cooling systems to calculate the number of racks, floor area, and overall capital costs. Generally, the computations are done to determine how different architectures will function in multiple locations and combinations. At the design documentation fulfillment levels, such evaluations are often completed through the standard bidding procedure by contractors, subcontractors, and equipment suppliers. Cost is the most important factor for those involved in data center projects and the construction and design teams (Curtis et al., 2012).

With the preceding caveat in mind, it should be noted that several design factors are essential for the crucial design, installation, and long-term administration of a data center. They include parameters like capacity, productivity, complexity, and other standards like accessibility, dependability, manageability, and adaptability. Of course, investment and operating costs are also included.

Quantifiable features can be produced to offer some anticipated management over tolerable service interruption concerning facility resources in today's every-time, always-connected world of e-commerce. The rest of this guide will delve deeper into these qualities.

While assessing infrastructure for data centers, the following four factors are crucial to take into account:

1. Manageability
2. Scalability
3. Reliability
4. Availability
5. Flexibility

These factors are connected in various ways. And though it's helpful to set limitations when arranging the design strategy for particular difficulties and modifications that invariably happen during any data center's life cycle. Also, in contemporary data centers, the term "MAC" (Moves, Adds, and Changes) is frequently used to refer to the constantly evolving to reconfigure data center structure and design (Bakshi, 2012) (Figure 1.7).

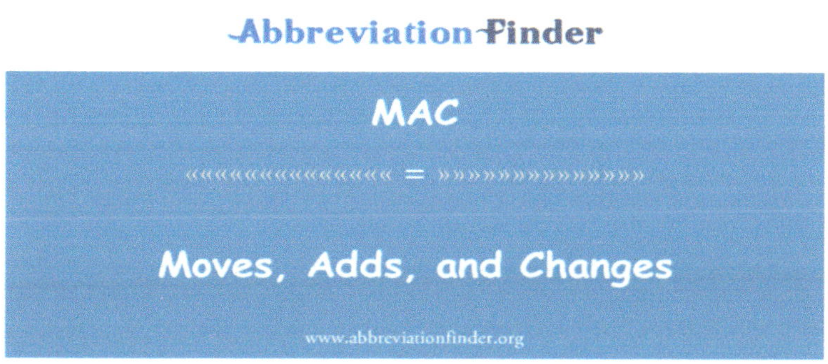

Figure 1.7. Picture of Mac abbreviations (Source: Abbreviation Finder, Creative Commons License).

1.6.1 Manageability

Final users prefer a high-performance discrete solution for the network's smooth operation. It is important to note that the information contained in this chapter, is for informational purposes only and is not intended to be a substitute for professional advice. Structured cabling must be implemented to give administrators more access to the information center architecture. "structural cabling" refers to telecom equipment found in buildings or campuses that comprises several predefined, smaller components known as subsystems. Structured cabling should be arranged so individual fibers can be easily found, MACs can be maintained, and there is enough circulation around the cable to make it efficient (Watson et al., 2009).

The data center may be the place that needs excellent structured cabling the most. The managers and owners of data centers constitute the major users of training materials for structured cabling since they have a low threshold for disruption or network breakdown. The explanation is simple: even though conventional data centers are being decommissioned in place of cloud-based services, the cloud still requires physical infrastructure, which needs to be cabled. The main advantage of a cabling network is that the user gets asses to the infrastructure instead of being confronted with a mess of unorganized and patched wires (Lin et al., 2013).

1.6.2 Flexibility

Although flexibility covers a wide range of data center cable systems, its main focus is on the services that the data center will provide. Changes may be made quickly and easily without much disruption to the regular operations of the data center thanks to flexible cabling architecture. Furthermore, it lessens the chance that the internet infrastructure may become outdated due to advanced technology.

For network engineers and managers, network turnover is a real concern. The network is under more stress by moving workstations and reconfiguring the network. A flexible facility can adapt to changes in the data flow, fiber efficiency, facility area, tenant population, electronics, and equipment, and updates over the cabling's service life. It should be flexible enough to accommodate additional requirements that might call for readjusting the communication between client computers and the owner's network infrastructure (Basmadjian, 2019).

The ANSI/TIA-942-promoted star topology, the forerunner of flexible design, satisfies various application needs. Negotiation between MAC reduction and signal deterioration for passive systems is another aspect of flexibility. A growing trend toward overhead cable trays hung straight from the ceiling for cable management infrastructure to make it easier to add and remove cupboards and stackers of different heights and to make room below elevated tiles for ventilation and cooling demands. Another method of introducing flexibility in the data center is redundant cable connections. A facility can be constructed to accommodate several tiers of reliability to suit various requirements. Of course, adopting a single type of cable (ideally fiber optic) in a modern data center can improve administration and provide versatility for handling new applications (Greenberg et al., 2011).

1.6.3 Scalability

The data center must be scalable to upgrade to greater data rates and add capacity without disrupting business. The primary data center needs to be built to scale up and down quickly and effectively as needs change. The primary point for network storage and data processing was always the data center. Much data would be needed to be transported, stored, and processed by the data center as cloud technology and hybridization become more commonplace. To ensure that the data center can develop and scale to handle new systems and data speeds, it is crucial to comprehend these new applications and the systems they generate, especially for data transfer speeds.

Also, the word "hyper-scale" emphasizes scalability's importance to contemporary data centers. The potential of the computer system to scale in response to rising workload needs is eventually referred to as hyper-scale. This can show up as either vertical or horizontal scaling. While horizontal scaling typically requires increasing the number of machines in the computing system or across different application domains, vertical scaling involves adding additional computing power to already-existing machines. The amount of data rates offered on transmission systems is directly impacted by both forms of scaling (Soundararajan & Govil, 2010).

The data transfer rate in data centers generally deploys multiples of 10 and 100 gigabits. With the connections two-fiber, these installations can expand to hundreds or even thousands of terminals. As a result, each server contains hundreds or even thousands of fibers that need to be controlled by a rack-mountable network cabling system. Installing 400 Gb and 800 Gb systems will require more fibers to be supported in a single chassis. Moreover, parallel optics often replace existing duplex transmission as data rates rise. Configurations of wavelength division multiplexing (WDM) could be an exception to various transmission methods. However, high data rates typically translate to the need for extra optical fibers in advanced dual-layer-mesh or "spine-and-leaf" systems, wherein network switches are completely cross-linked to provide increased data capacity and resilience (Ghosh et al., 2013).

The data transfer rate in data centers generally deploys multiples of 10 and 100 gigabits. With the connections two-fiber, these installations can expand to hundreds or even thousands of terminals. As a result, each server contains hundreds or even thousands of fibers that need to be controlled by a rack-mountable network cabling system. Installing 400 Gb and 800 Gb systems will require more fibers to be supported in a single chassis. Moreover, parallel optics often replace existing duplex transmission as data rates rise. Configurations of WDM could be an exception to various transmission methods. However, high data rates typically translate to the need for extra optical fibers in advanced dual-layer-mesh or "spine-and-leaf" systems, wherein network switches are completely cross-linked to provide increased data capacity and resilience (Niranjan Mysore et al., 2009).

1.6.4 Availability and Reliability

Solutions for cabling structures in data centers must be stable and operate continuously. High availability Association and requirements are divided into categories based on the "tier" grade used in the data center, which ranges from Tier 1 to Tier 4. The required uptime for Tier 4 data centers is 99.995% and less than one half-hour annually. According to BICSI, durability is the likelihood that a machinery component or a system will carry out its assigned task for a predetermined period without experiencing a malfunction. Using average (MTBF) data related to electronics or other auxiliary equipment, durability can be represented by a percentage (Nguyen et al., 2019).

Similarly, average (MTTR) data, which measures the likelihood that an element can be fixed in a specific time, can be used to characterize the supportability of the data center elements. Total data center accessibility, which can be stated in hours per year or comparable percentages, is frequently correlated with the probability that facility systems and accessible at given periods. Hence, evaluating the risks associated with data center outages and developing the infrastructure appropriately is possible (Cheung & Wang, 2019).

In addition to the system's existing resilience and durability, the total data center assets must be adaptable to the business needs that are always fluctuating and may involve unexpectedly fast growth, advancements, and other technological advances.

1.6.5 Efficiency of a Network

Often, "efficiency" refers to how much energy is used. In this regard, the architecture of telecommunications cables, passageways, and spaces can considerably impact overall effectiveness, particularly regarding airflow dispersion. Yet, in this case, the efficiency of a network refers to how quickly and easily MACs can be integrated gradually at the least expensive operational and capital costs. The number and scope of data centers have significantly increased during the last few decades. Data centers must continue to experience rapid expansion in the future as networks develop and evolve toward 100, 200, and 400-gigabit data rates. Owing to the significant expansion of data centers, there is a demand for basic, effective cabling solutions that make the most of available space and enable decreased deployment time and expenses (Alagoz & Gur, 2011).

1.6.6 Product Solutions

The four levels of usefulness that Corning's data center solutions offer are shown in Figure 1.8. Predefined solutions are the best option since they provide a larger fiber volume, quicker deployment, and simple MAC facilitation. Predefined optical fiber wiring options make installing an optical network in the data center easier. A modular structure ensures consistency and adaptability for all-optical communication and is easily scalable and flexible as needs grow. In addition to managing fiber polarization, the predefined solutions practically eliminate it as a factor in the design process, deployment, or configuration (Krishnan et al., 1999).

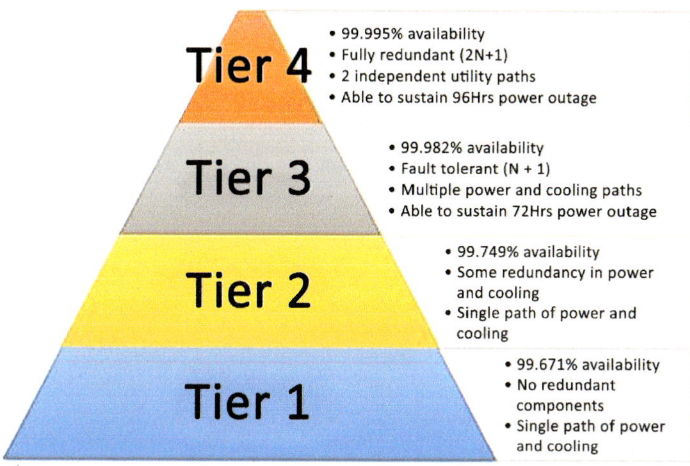

Figure 1.8. Picture of four levels of usefulness that Corning's data center solutions (Source: Charith Hettige, Creative Commons License).

As previously mentioned, the technology map illustrates that connectivity options based on either 2 or 8 fibers will support transmission speeds varying from 10G to 400 G. Base-8 predefined options, including Corning EDGE8® options, boost system density while maximizing system scalability, enhancing connection performance, and fully using the fiber. Predefined components allow quicker MACs and deployment, whereas custom-engineered elements enable easy incorporation into standard SAN directors and switches. A Base-8 solution can also boost network effectiveness in the following ways in the data center:

- High utilization of resources, with lower jumper complexity and removal of stranded cabling resources.

- Adoption of Technology because of 100% fiber utilization without the requirement for conversion modules results in cost and loss savings.
- Risk prevention, giving a basic pathway to 40G, 100G, and even 400G (Mathieu, 2001).

1.7 MANAGEMENT OF DATA CENTER

Remember

Effective management of a data center involves ensuring efficient resource usage, regular equipment monitoring and maintenance, robust security measures, and a comprehensive disaster recovery plan.

Data center management is the set of duties and operations carried out by a company to meet the ongoing needs of running a data center.

The control of hardware, programming, applications, and physical networks is required to run data centers, which are becoming progressively more complicated. Data centers contain various hardware comprising computation and storage systems, which must be regulated for continued operations. Data center management activities frequently include cover software and artificial operations executed on stacks of server hardware (Moshref et al., 2013).

Another important duty falling under the purview of data center administration is overseeing the physical network of a data center. The physical network consists of the necessary cooling and energy for ongoing operations, access, and security control measures for the data center's grounds and backup generators for backup and power outages. All data center managers, including businesses and cloud service vendors, must have human IT personnel on board to perform administration tasks related to the physical software and hardware. Operating companies can better prepare for present and upcoming demands using capacity management, a business service organization (Chu & Wang, 2019).

1.8 COMPONENTS OF DATA CENTER MANAGEMENT

1. The administration of service or product delivery applications.
2. The IT infrastructure to support software.
3. Technology networks to support service capabilities.
4. Modern people support programs and networks.
5. The manual or automated practices to support business and client issues.

Some data centers concentrate their assets, including

employees, on data center the management of application services. The advent of cloud data centers that provide business solutions is the only explanation for this. Many businesses today don't want to concentrate all their efforts on basic IT components. Businesses still desire the results these components bring to their clients' programs and services. Cisco Data Center Network Manager, which offers businesses an operating system for managing network access and regulations, is one illustration of this (Shah et al., 2005) (Figure 1.8).

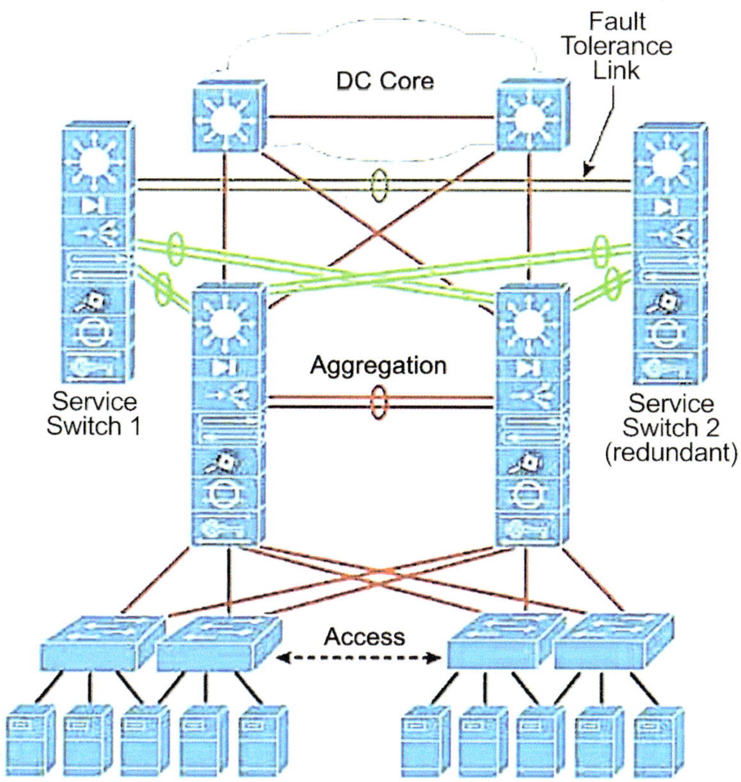

Figure 1.8. Illustration of Cisco Data Center network (Source: Cisco, Creative Commons License).

Cloud service suppliers handle data center networks, particularly in the cloud. By using the monitoring tools of the data center network managed solutions offered, the customer of these services can control the elasticity of the infrastructure components as needed to support the business. This makes it possible to concentrate less on IT and more on the service that IT offers.

Network management and data center platform administration in the cloud is essentially the same. Clients select platforms based on desired results, considering the overall cost and capabilities inserted. Generally speaking, applications and services are managed internally. To enable the services and applications required to assist the end user, the cloud platform and infrastructure options have become more commonplace (Rojanala, 2016).

1.9 DATA CENTER CAPACITY MANAGEMENT

One of the key components of data center administration is capacity management. Knowing how much assets, like hardware and electricity, are utilized at any time is a crucial data center key measure.

Facility design is initiated by data center capacity management. A facility's beginning capacity and the amount that can grow over time to approach a peak capacity must be determined by a manager, along with objectives and projections. The capacity depends on the amount of floor area, computing power, storage room, and the cooling and power abilities that are accessible.

TIPS

To effectively manage data center capacity, regularly assess and plan for future growth, prioritize resource allocation, and adjust plans to optimize resource usage and prevent waste.

Applying virtualization, container, and small services for workflows can improve operations' effectiveness and efficiency, even though hardware and energy resources can frequently be hampered by the physical restrictions of a facility and the regional energy grid (Islam et al., 2019).

1.10 TOOLS OF DATA CENTER MANAGEMENT

There are several tools for managing data centers on the market. Each tool essentially helps in the management of the different data center elements. Tools are typically seen as equivalent to data center software solutions to increase data centers' health, performance, automation, and dependability. Fewer employees are often needed to monitor an ever-expanding IT network located on-premises, in the cloud, and using hybrid, private, and public solutions thanks to the software's assistance in managing the data center in an appropriate, productive, and economical manner (Gupta et al., 2011).

The company views every part of the data center as a resource. Each resource has additional subcategories that include IT assets or abilities for the organization. This categorization makes understanding which resources strategic resources are for controlling as such relative to other assets easier. These resources must be administered, particularly in light of usage requirements. Many businesses discover that they are only using about 40% of their total capacity. This underutilization of the total capacity by the data center results in unnecessary costs. Organizations may transit to cloud solutions to help with cost management and control of total efficiency more elastically if they learn this is the situation in their on-premises data center infrastructures (Barrett et al., 2004).

1.11 SERVICES OF DATA CENTER MANAGEMENT

Data center administration services must assist a company with the data center's present and future conditions. The company should analyze each data center resource's current and previous state, accompanied by crucial success criteria and key performance measures. This will benefit the data center's general health and the provision of essential goods and services to support consumers.

Several cloud services offer various services to control a cloud data center's off-prem, public, hybrid, and private platforms. Many companies have requests for such services because they are not willing to engage professional staff to carry out the specific activities necessary to run a cloud data center. Consider Cloudflare Data Centers, which provides services to assist businesses in over 100 nations (Putnam et al., 2015).

1.12 DATA CENTER MANAGEMENT SOFTWARE

Software for managing the data center infrastructure offers the capabilities and tools managers need to oversee current operations.

Managers of data centers get real-time management insight into the IT infrastructure thanks to DCIM technologies.

DCIM provides a thorough management perspective by taking a holistic approach to all systems in a data center instead of only focusing on one IT resource. DCIM doesn't simply involve observing, though. Operators can also manage data center resources using properly designed DCIM solutions, which can foresee and avoid outages.

A well-implemented DCIM installation promises improved availability, reduced energy usage, issue resolution, and capacity management (Dai et al., 2017).

1.13 PROBLEMS OF DATA CENTER MANAGEMENT

Data center management challenges regarding the security of all aspects of the data center rank among the most important ones. Services, platforms, and application infrastructure all need to be protected. Every component is vulnerable to attacks from several origins, both within and outside. Data is vulnerable to theft, refusal assaults, deletion, manipulation, and abuse. Based on the lifespan and level of data utilization, the information can be found in applications, systems, and platforms. All elements have to be secured for the data center to be private.

Due to malicious intentions, data center security challenges are always changing. Organizations must keep up with the current risks as rapidly as possible as criminals become more inventive. Harmful threats are prevalent; some people think it is only a brief period before all companies are hacked or can be hacked. We frequently get news reports, but there are also reports about security issues with data center administration that we rarely hear (Tang & Pan, 2015).

Numerous more concerns could arise in addition to security in data center management. It is necessary to monitor and keep up with many technological assets. These resources, like a server or network shift, could become problematic for the business and its clients. Organizations must promptly update their IT resources since sometimes assets have reached their lifespans and are no longer maintained by the appropriate operator. If they do not seem to, assistance for service resumption may be at risk when the asset breaks. When a part of the IT architecture is disrupted purposefully or accidentally, doing an impact analysis might be hampered by a lack of awareness of connections across assets. Data Center Management issues must be managed with appropriate risk, impact analysis, and extensive planning techniques and strategies because no data center is ideal (Mann, 2015).

1.14 CHALLENGES IN DATA CENTER MANAGEMENT

Every discipline that is necessary for a data center has its own set of issues in terms of management. In addition to the technical hurdles, it is challenging to be sure that the data center supports the business results. Many businesses occasionally become preoccupied with operating the data center and lose sight of why it is necessary commercially. This leads to initiatives that do not support business objectives, such as individuals working too hard or on tasks that are not directly tied to improving the efficiency and effectiveness of the company's operations and those of its clients. Ensuring the total ownership cost consistently maintains the economic return is one of the data center's concerns; if it does not, the company risks going out of business. Financial difficulties are serious; businesses must constantly concentrate on cost-cutting and revenue expansion. Together with the financial difficulties, there are other difficulties, like managing the platforms' overall administration of the infrastructure and applications. Data management, storage, privacy, accessibility, consistency, efficiency, general performance, and many other challenges are included (Schmidt et al., 2005).

1.15. DATA CENTER MANAGEMENT PRACTICES

Businesses may develop and sustain effective data center management techniques using the best standards.

1.15.1 Measurement

Whatever needs to be managed must first be carefully measured. Having data calculations and records for all resources in a data center.

1.15.2 Effective energy Usage

PUE is one of the most important indicators for managing data centers since it gives controllers insight into how effectively electricity can be used.

1.15.3 Cooling Consideration

One of the energy-intensive parts of managing a data center is cooling. Using diffuse cooler air and improved airflow control methods might reduce expenditures in some regions.

1.15.4 Major Backups

An essential recommended approach is to have redundant and operational system backups.

1.15.5 Proactive and Predictive Maintenance

It is dangerous and may reduce reliability to delay until a specific data center resource breaks without fixing it. Thanks to proactive and predictive maintenance and replacement plans, resources can be fixed and restored before they break down (Appel et al., 2014).

1.15.6 Embrace DCIM

Organizations must be knowledgeable about and equipped with the appropriate DCIM technology for installation to maximize the efficiency of data center protocols.

1.16 DATA CENTER MANAGEMENT IN THE FUTURE

The development of hybrid data centers, including private and public cloud components, is one of the major trends in data center operations. It may be a standard on-premises data center installation, a private or public cloud, or both; organizations want to control all data center resources using just one set of applications.

Another emerging area is the expansion of data center network access. Data centers are expected to be run through remote management and monitoring through DCIM technology, even though local management control centers may still exist.

With an AIOps strategy, there will also probably be more AI-based abilities in data center control operations. A data center might be controlled with minimal human involvement thanks to AI optimization and enhanced remote monitoring when AIOps are used (Rambo & Joshi, 2007).

ACTIVITY 1.1

What are the key factors that need to be considered when designing a data center, and how can these factors impact the overall efficiency and effectiveness of the data center? Provide a real-world example to illustrate your answer.

SUMMARY

The chapter provides an overview of the concept of data center management, the significance of functional domains within a data center, the factors affecting data center architecture, and the importance of management in ensuring the efficient functioning of a data center. The chapter also highlights the components of data center management, which include power and cooling management, security management, and network management. Additionally, the chapter discusses the important software used in data center management, such as data center infrastructure management (DCIM) software and monitoring tools. Overall, this chapter serves as a foundational introduction to the field of data center management, providing a broad understanding of the key concepts and practices involved in this area.

REVIEW QUESTIONS

1. What is the concept of data center management, and why is it essential for organizations?
2. What are the functional domains of a data center, and how do they contribute to the overall functioning of a data center?
3. What are the factors that influence the architecture of a data center, and how can organizations address these factors?
4. Why is effective management of a data center crucial, and what are the consequences of poor management?
5. What are the key components of data center management, and how do they contribute to the overall management process?
6. What are some of the important software used in data center management, and how do they support the management process?
7. How can organizations ensure that their data centers are efficiently managed, and what are some best practices for data center management?

MULTIPLE CHOICE QUESTIONS

1. Which of the following best describes data center management?

a) The process of designing and implementing hardware and software systems to support data processing and storage

b) The practice of optimizing energy efficiency in data centers

c) The maintenance of physical infrastructure in a data center

d) The development of data center policies and procedures

2. What are the functional domains of a data center?

a) Network, hardware, software, and security

b) Operations, management, engineering, and support

c) Storage, compute, virtualization, and automation
d) Infrastructure, facilities, applications, and services

3. **Which of the following is a factor that affects data center architecture?**
   a) Availability of open-source software
   b) Location of the data center
   c) Type of hardware used in the data center
   d) Number of users accessing the data center
4. **Why is management of data center important?**
   a) To ensure the efficient operation of IT infrastructure
   b) To maximize profits for the organization
   c) To minimize security risks and ensure data privacy
   d) To comply with regulatory requirements
5. **What are the components of data center management?**
   a) Hardware, software, facilities, and security
   b) Planning, provisioning, monitoring, and maintenance
   c) Storage, compute, network, and virtualization
   d) Power, cooling, lighting, and ventilation
6. **Which of the following is an important software for data center management?**
   a) Microsoft Excel
   b) Adobe Photoshop
   c) VMware vSphere
   d) Google Chrome

Answers to Multiple Choice Questions

1. (b) 2. (b) 3. (a) 4. (b) 5. (c) 6. (d)

REFERENCES

1. Aghdai, A., Zhang, F., Dasanayake, N., Xi, K., & Chao, H. J. (2013, July). Traffic measurement and analysis in an organic enterprise data center. In 2013 IEEE 14th International Conference on High Performance Switching and Routing (HPSR) IEEE. (Vol.1, pp. 49–55).
2. Agyapong, P. K., Iwamura, M., Staehle, D., Kiess, W., & Benjebbour, A. (2014). Design considerations for a 5G network architecture. IEEE Communications Magazine, 52(11), 65–75.

3. Alagoz, F., & Gur, G. (2011). Energy efficiency and satellite networking: A holistic overview. Proceedings of the IEEE, 99(11), 1954–1979.
4. Anthony Jr, B., Abdul Majid, M., & Romli, A. (2018). A collaborative agent based green IS practice assessment tool for environmental sustainability attainment in enterprise data centers. Journal of Enterprise Information Management, 31(5), 771–795.
5. Appel, S. U., Botti, D., Jamison, J., Plant, L., Shyr, J. Y., & Varshney, L. R. (2014). Predictive analytics can facilitate proactive property vacancy policies for cities. Technological Forecasting and Social Change, 89, 161–173.
6. Bakshi, K. (2012, March). Considerations for big data: Architecture and approach. In 2012 IEEE aerospace conference IEEE. (Vol. 1, pp. 1–7).
7. Barrett, R., Kandogan, E., Maglio, P. P., Haber, E. M., Takayama, L. A., & Prabaker, M. (2004, November). Field studies of computer system administrators: analysis of system management tools and practices. In Proceedings of the 2004 ACM conference on Computer supported cooperative work (Vol. 3, pp. 388–395).
8. Basmadjian, R. (2019). Flexibility-based energy and demand management in data centers: a case study for cloud computing. Energies, 12(17), 3301.
9. Basmadjian, R., Botero, J. F., Giuliani, G., Hesselbach, X., Klingert, S., & De Meer, H. (2016). Making data centers fit for demand response: Introducing GreenSDA and GreenSLA contracts. IEEE transactions on smart grid, 9(4), 3453–3464.
10. Cheung, H., & Wang, S. (2019). Reliability and availability assessment and enhancement of water-cooled multi-chiller cooling systems for data centers. Reliability Engineering & System Safety, 191, 106–110.
11. Chu, W. X., & Wang, C. C. (2019). A review on airflow management in data centers. Applied Energy, 240, 84–119.
12. Cruz, E., & Joshi, Y. (2015). Coupled inviscid-viscous solution method for bounded domains: Application to data-center thermal management. International Journal of Heat and Mass Transfer, 85, 181–194.
13. Curtis, L. H., Weiner, M. G., Boudreau, D. M., Cooper, W. O., Daniel, G. W., Nair, V. P., ... & Brown, J. S. (2012). Design considerations, architecture, and use of the Mini-Sentinel distributed data system. Pharmacoepidemiology and drug safety, 21, 23–31.
14. Dai, B., Xu, G., Huang, B., Qin, P., & Xu, Y. (2017). Enabling network innovation in data center networks with software defined networking: A survey. Journal of Network and Computer Applications, 94, 33–49.
15. Ding, Z., Cao, Y., Xie, L., Lu, Y., & Wang, P. (2019). Integrated stochastic energy management for data center microgrid considering waste heat recovery. IEEE Transactions on Industry Applications, 55(3), 2198–2207.
16. Filani, D., He, J., Gao, S., Rajappa, M., Kumar, A., Shah, P., & Nagappan, R. (2008). Dynamic data center power management: Trends, issues, and solutions. Intel Technology Journal, 12(1), 1–05.

17. Gandhi, A., Harchol-Balter, M., Raghunathan, R., & Kozuch, M. A. (2012). Autoscale: Dynamic, robust capacity management for multi-tier data centers. ACM Transactions on Computer Systems (TOCS), 30(4), 1–26.

18. Ghosh, A., Ha, S., Crabbe, E., & Rexford, J. (2013). Scalable multi-class traffic management in data center backbone networks. IEEE Journal on Selected Areas in Communications, 31(12), 2673–2684.

19. Greenberg, A., Hamilton, J. R., Jain, N., Kandula, S., Kim, C., Lahiri, P., ... & Sengupta, S. (2011). VL2: a scalable and flexible data center network. Communications of the ACM, 54(3), 95–104.

20. Gupta, S. K., Gilbert, R. R., Banerjee, A., Abbasi, Z., Mukherjee, T., & Varsamopoulos, G. (2011, July). Gdcsim: A tool for analyzing green data center design and resource management techniques. In 2011 International Green Computing Conference and Workshops IEEE. (Vol. 1, pp. 1–8).

21. Hammadi, A., & Mhamdi, L. (2014). A survey on architectures and energy efficiency in data center networks. Computer Communications, 40, 1–21.

22. Islam, R. U., Ruci, X., Hossain, M. S., Andersson, K., & Kor, A. L. (2019). Capacity management of hyperscale data centers using predictive modelling. Energies, 12(18), 3438.

23. Jiadi, L., Yang, H., Huan, L., Xinli, Z., & WenJing, L. (2020, March). Research on Data Center Operation and Maintenance Management Based on Big Data. In 2020 International Conference on Computer Engineering and Application (ICCEA) IEEE. (Vol. 1, pp. 124–127).

24. Jouppi, N. P., Young, C., Patil, N., Patterson, D., Agrawal, G., Bajwa, R., ... & Yoon, D. H. (2017, June). In-datacenter performance analysis of a tensor processing unit. In Proceedings of the 44th annual international symposium on computer architecture (Vol. 1, pp. 1–12).

25. Krishnan, M. S., Ramaswamy, V., Meyer, M. C., & Damien, P. (1999). Customer satisfaction for financial services: the role of products, services, and information technology. Management science, 45(9), 1194–1209.

26. Kyono, T., Otsuka, Y., Fukumoto, Y., Owaki, S., & Nakamura, M. (2018, September). Computational-complexity comparison of artificial neural network and Volterra series transfer function for optical nonlinearity compensation with time-and frequency-domain dispersion equalization. In 2018 European Conference on Optical Communication (ECOC) IEEE. (Vol. 1, pp. 1–3).

27. Lin, J., Zha, L., & Xu, Z. (2013). Consolidated cluster systems for data centers in the cloud age: a survey and analysis. Frontiers of Computer Science, 7, 1–19.

28. Liu, L., Wang, H., Liu, X., Jin, X., He, W. B., Wang, Q. B., & Chen, Y. (2009, June). GreenCloud: a new architecture for green data center. In Proceedings of the 6th international conference industry session on Autonomic computing and communications industry session (Vol. 1, pp. 29–38).

29. Lu, L., Hildebrand, D., & Tewari, R. (2011). Zone-based data striping for cloud storage. IBM Journal of Research and Development, 55(6), 1–11.
30. Malla, S., & Christensen, K. (2019). A survey on power management techniques for oversubscription of multi-tenant data centers. ACM Computing Surveys (CSUR), 52(1), 1–31.
31. Mann, Z. Á. (2015). Allocation of virtual machines in cloud data centers—a survey of problem models and optimization algorithms. Acm Computing Surveys (CSUR), 48(1), 1–34.
32. Mathieu, V. (2001). Product services: from a service supporting the product to a service supporting the client. Journal of Business & Industrial Marketing, 16(1), 39–61.
33. Moshref, M., Yu, M., Sharma, A. B., & Govindan, R. (2013, April). Scalable rule management for data centers. In NSDI (Vol. 13, pp. 157–170).
34. Nguyen, T. A., Min, D., Choi, E., & Tran, T. D. (2019). Reliability and availability evaluation for cloud data center networks using hierarchical models. IEEE Access, 7, 9273–9313.
35. Niranjan Mysore, R., Pamboris, A., Farrington, N., Huang, N., Miri, P., Radhakrishnan, S., ... & Vahdat, A. (2009, August). Portland: a scalable fault-tolerant layer 2 data center network fabric. In Proceedings of the ACM SIGCOMM 2009 conference on Data communication (Vol. 2, pp. 39–50).
36. Puthal, D., Obaidat, M. S., Nanda, P., Prasad, M., Mohanty, S. P., & Zomaya, A. Y. (2018). Secure and sustainable load balancing of edge data centers in fog computing. IEEE Communications Magazine, 56(5), 60–65.
37. Putnam, A., Caulfield, A. M., Chung, E. S., Chiou, D., Constantinides, K., Demme, J., ... & Burger, D. (2015). A reconfigurable fabric for accelerating large-scale datacenter services. IEEE Micro, 35(3), 10–22.
38. Rambo, J., & Joshi, Y. (2007). Modeling of data center airflow and heat transfer: State of the art and future trends. Distributed and Parallel Databases, 21, 193–225.
39. Rojanala, R. (2016). Components of Data Mining and Big Data Analytics in Intra-Data Center Networks. International Journal of Advanced Research in Electrical, Electronics and Instrumentation Engineering. 5(7), 11–20.
40. Sari, A., & Akkaya, M. (2015). Security and optimization challenges of green data centers. International Journal of Communications, Network and System Sciences, 8(12), 492.
41. Schmidt, R. R., Cruz, E. E., & Iyengar, M. (2005). Challenges of data center thermal management. IBM Journal of Research and Development, 49(4.5), 709–723.
42. Schuster, S., Vavra, M., & Kern, W. V. (2016). Evidence of a substrate-discriminating entrance channel in the lower porter domain of the multidrug resistance efflux pump AcrB. Antimicrobial Agents and Chemotherapy, 60(7), 4315–4323.
43. Shah, A. J., Carey, V. P., Bash, C. E., & Patel, C. D. (2005, January). Exergy-based optimization strategies for multi-component data center thermal management: Part

I—analysis. In International Electronic Packaging Technical Conference and Exhibition (Vol. 42002, pp. 205–213).

44. Singh, A., Korupolu, M., & Mohapatra, D. (2008, November). Server-storage virtualization: integration and load balancing in data centers. In SC'08: Proceedings of the 2008 ACM/IEEE conference on Supercomputing IEEE. (Vol. 1, pp. 1–12).
45. Song, W., Feng, X., Zhang, G., Gao, L., Yan, B., & Chen, X. (2022). Domain adaptation in automatic picking of phase velocity dispersions based on deep learning. Journal of Geophysical Research: Solid Earth, 127(6), 1–15.
46. Soundararajan, V., & Govil, K. (2010). Challenges in building scalable virtualized datacenter management. ACM SIGOPS Operating Systems Review, 44(4), 95–102.
47. Tang, M., & Pan, S. (2015). A hybrid genetic algorithm for the energy-efficient virtual machine placement problem in data centers. Neural processing letters, 41, 211–221.
48. Watson, B. J., Shah, A. J., Marwah, M., Bash, C. E., Sharma, R. K., Hoover, C. E., ... & Patel, C. D. (2009, January). Integrated design and management of a sustainable data center. In International Electronic Packaging Technical Conference and Exhibition (Vol. 43604, pp. 635–644).
49. Weerasinghe, J., Polig, R., Abel, F., & Hagleitner, C. (2016, December). Network-attached FPGAs for data center applications. In 2016 International Conference on Field-Programmable Technology (FPT) IEEE. (Vol. 1, pp. 36–43).

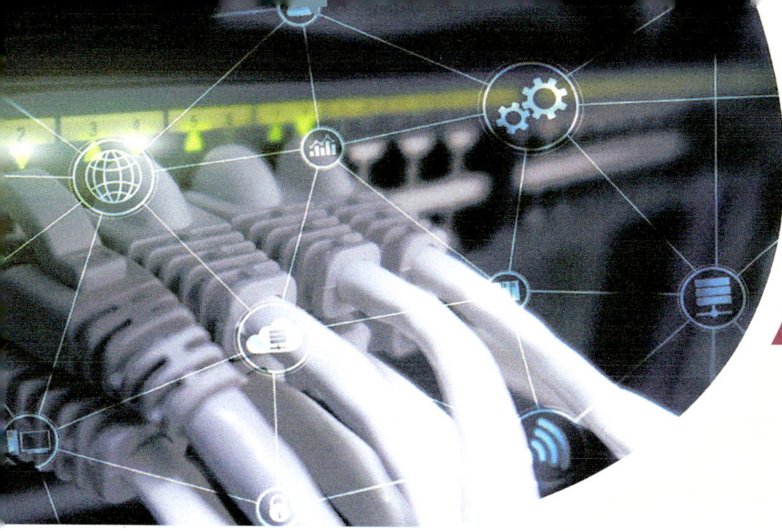

CHAPTER 2

DATA CENTER TOPOLOGIES AND NETWORK ARCHITECTURE

UNIT INTRODUCTION

Datacenter topologies describe the physical architecture of such a data center's networking equipment, whereas network architecture describes the network's general structure and layout. These two are inextricably linked since the topology of a network of data centers substantially influences its overall design (Xia et al., 2017).

Among the most prevalent data center, topologies are:

- **Two-Tier Topology:** This topology comprises first-tier accessibility switches that connect to the hosts and second-tier distribution switches that connect to the core switches.
- **Three-Tier Topology:** The first tier of this topology consists of access switching, the second of aggregating switches, and the third of core switches (Lin et al., 2012).
- **Spine-and-Leaf Topology:** Each leaf device is connected to every spine switching in this design, leading to a non-blocking, increased network (Popa et al., 2010).
- **Mesh Topology:** This architecture connects every network device in a complete mesh arrangement, giving great redundancy with fault tolerance (Singla et al., 2010).

A data center's network infrastructure could be configured to serve several kinds of traffic, including storing, computational, and controlling traffic. Among the most frequent network designs used during data centers are:

- **Layer 2 Network:** The Ethernet protocol is used in this design to build a flat network that allows devices to communicate within a single network segment.
- **Layer 3 Network:** This design routes traffic across various network segments using the IP protocol, allowing for more effective usage of network resources (Gyarmati & Trinh, 2010).
- **Converged Network:** This design consolidates storage and data traffic into a single network backbone, reducing the number of physical connections required in the data center.
- **Software-Defined Networking (SDN):** This design allows centralized network administration and automation by separating the networking control plane from the data plane (Couto et al., 2012).

The final decision regarding the data center topology and network architecture would be based on the company's requirements, considering cost, performance, and scalability.

According to Costa et al. (2009), Tens of thousands of computers are housed in data centers managed by Microsoft, Google, Yahoo, and Amazon to deliver services throughout the Internet, and also the networking remains the only element that has remained constant during the enormous rise of data centers (Figure 2.1).

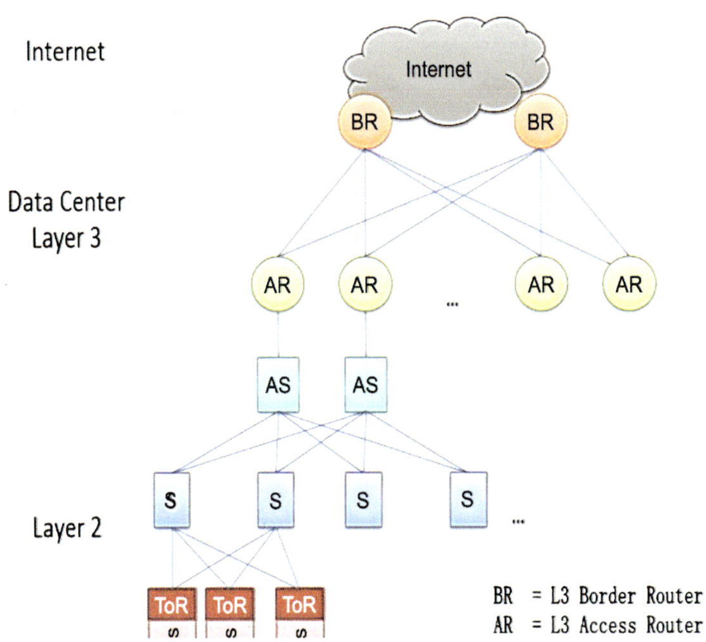

Figure 2.1. Typical data center network architecture illustration (Source: Boyd-Wickizer et al., Creative Commons License).

Typically, routers and switches are arranged in a two- or three-tier hierarchy for data center networks. Using three levels of design is seen in Figure 2.1. Based on the studies, the following explanation for the figure (Greenberg et al., 2009–2011). The hierarchy with top-layer base routers linking to the servers within racks at the bottom may be seen in the figure—data center layer 3, layer 2, including top-of-rack switches, link servers within the hierarchy. Layer 3 of the data center comprises queries coming through IP from the Internet. Traffic entering and leaving the data center is controlled by Layer 3 access and border routers. Layer 3 access routers (AR) connections are aggregated by aggregation switches (AS), which also offer redundancy. Virtual LAN (VLAN) partitioning separates the hundreds of servers comprising a Layer 2 domain into server groups. 20–40 servers are often connected by a 1 Gbps link using a Top of Rack (ToR) switch. Moreover, Ethernet is the physical layer protocol used on all links (Vahdat et al., 2010).

Learning Objectives

At the end of this chapter, reader will be able to understand:

1. The topologies of data center management
2. The importance of centralized and zoned topology
3. The significance of architectures of data center management
4. The concept of enterprise and cloud service data centers
5. The importance of cost structure in data center management

Key Terms

1. Local Area Network (LAN)
2. Storage Area Network (SAN)
3. Top-of-Rack
4. End-of-Row (EoR)
5. Middle-of-Row (MoR)
6. Mesh Network Architecture
7. Multi-Tiered Model
8. Modular Data Center (MDC) Architecture

2.1 TOPOLOGIES

Three basic data center topologies are being used today, each with benefits and drawbacks. Moreover, 2 or 11 topologies are frequently deployed inside a single facility in some bigger data centers (Haddadi et al., 2008).

2.1.1 Centralized

The centralized approach is good for small data centers (under 5,000 square feet). As depicted, there are distinct local area network (LAN)/storage area network (SAN) settings, with home run wiring connecting all server cabinets and zones. Every server is related to the core switches in the major distribution area (Dewatripont & Maskin, 1995).

It allows for more effective port switching and simplifies maintaining and adding components. The centralized architecture performs well for smaller data centers yet fails to scale effectively, making expansion problematic. The large number of elongated cable lines required in bigger data centers generates congestion on cable paths and cabinets and raises costs. While some bigger data centers employ zonal or top-of-rack architectures for LAN traffic, SAN systems may adopt a centralized design. It is particularly true when SAN network switch costs are high, but port usage is critical (Sah & Stiglitz, 1991).

Did you Know?

According to a report by Grand View Research, the global market size for centralized data center topology is expected to reach $26.1 billion by 2027, growing at a compound annual growth rate (CAGR) of 12.5% from 2020 to 2027.

A basic example of a central topology would be many PCs in an office linked to a single hub or switch, subsequently linked to a Wi-Fi router. In this arrangement, the switching or hubs acts as the main node, directing data between PCs or the router (Besley & Coate, 2003).

There are various advantages to central topologies, including:

1. Easy to set up and manage

   Setting up and operating the network with only a central node monitoring all network traffic is simple (Davies et al., 1999).

2. Scalability

   More devices could be added to a single point even as the network expands without needing substantial modifications to the overall design (Bondi, 2000).

3. Cost-effective

Centralized topologies often need fewer connections and network equipment, which can help save money (Lewis, 2007).

Nevertheless, centralized topologies have several drawbacks, such as:

a. Single point of failure

The entire network may be impacted if a central node fails (Silva et al., 2008).

b. Limited bandwidth

All network data should flow via the central node, which can cause bottlenecks and decrease total capacity (Burger et al., 1997).

c. Security concerns

Because all data flow travels through a single point, central topologies are prone to security risks.

In conclusion, centralized topologies might be an excellent choice for small and medium-sized networks which demand a straightforward and cost-effective solution. On the other hand, complex systems or ones with more sophisticated needs may necessitate a more resilient architecture, like a mesh or ring topology (Goodhue & Straub, 1991) (Figure 2.2).

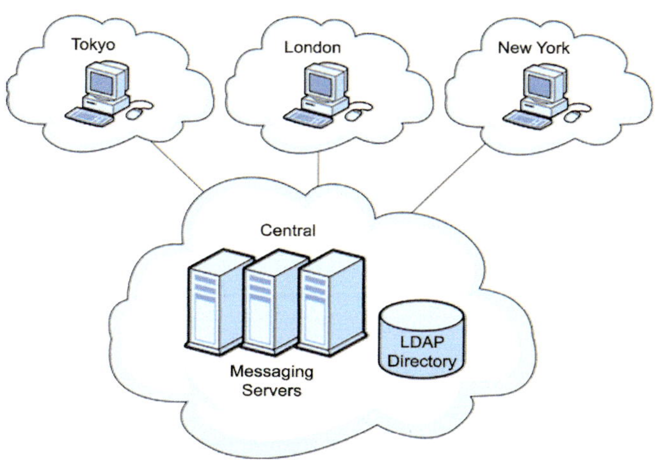

Figure 2.2. Illustration of a centralized model (Source: Oracle Corporation, Creative Commons License).

2.1.2 Zoned

The zoned topology is made up of dispersed switch resources. These switches could be distributed to end-of-row (EoR) or middle-of-row (MoR) locations, as indicated below, having chassis-based switches commonly utilized to handle numerous server cabinets. The ANS/TIA-942 Data Center Standards, propose this approach because it is highly repeatable, scalable, and predictable. One of the most cost-effective architecture is zoned architecture, which provides maximum switch or port usage while reducing cabling expenses (Petrie & Zúñiga, 2007).

End-of-row switching delivers performance benefits in some cases. For example, the LAN connections of two servers (which exchange huge amounts of data) can be put on a single end-of-row switch enabling low-latency port-to-port switching. The requirement to extend the wire back to an end-of-row switch is one possible downside of end-of-row switching. Such cabling could surpass what is necessary for top-of-rack design if each server is linked to redundancy switches (Kahl et al., 2017). A zonal topology divides the network into zones according to predetermined parameters, including function, geography, or level of security. For instance, a business may segment its network by zones for its many divisions, like sales, advertising, and finance. In addition to having network connections, every zone will have its collection of hardware, including PCs, printers, or servers (Halliday et al., 1980) (Figure 2.3).

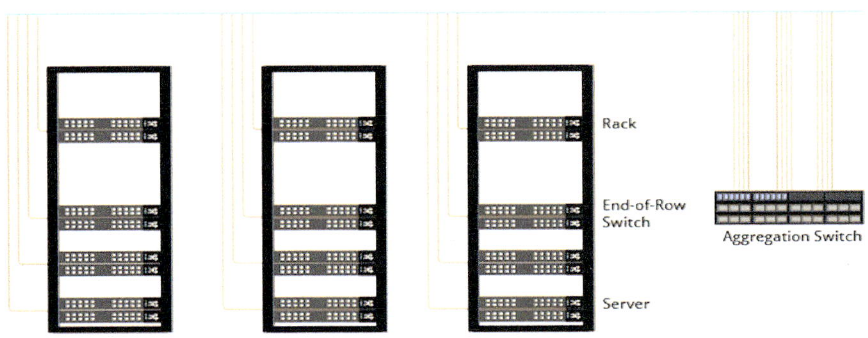

Figure 2.3. End-of-row switching diagram (Source: Community FS, Creative Commons License).

There are various advantages to zonal topologies.

1. Improved Security

Zoned topologies, which divide the network into zones, can increase security by limiting access across zones and managing data flow (Bellare et al., 2005).

2. Scalability

Scaling zoned topologies is simple by introducing new zones or broadening existing ones (Bondi, 2000).

3. Fault Tolerance

Other devices within this zone can continue to communicate with one another even if a device or link inside that zone fails (Randell, 1975).

Zoned topologies do, however, have several drawbacks, such as:

a. Complex Design

Since each zone needs to be properly defined and controlled, zoned topologies could be difficult to design and implement (Clarkson et al., 2004).

b. Increased Latency

Zoned topologies can generate significant latency and delay because devices in various zones should pass via a router or gateways to interact (Henry & Rogers, 1960).

c. Cost

Zoned topologies could require more expensive network hardware, including routers and gateways.

In conclusion, zoned topologies might be a smart choice for businesses that need extreme safety measures or have several departments or services that need network availability. Zoned topologies may cause greater latency and be more difficult and expensive to build than other topologies (Demsetz, 1968).

2.1.3 Top of Rack

As seen below, top-of-rack (ToR) switching often entails two or more switches positioned at the top of a rack in every server cabinet. This topology may be suitable for setups with many of one rack unit (1RU) servers. For redundancy, two switches are cabled to each server inside the rack. Uplink ports to the following switching layer are available on the top-of-rack switching. The top of the rack considerably reduces the need for cable containment and simplifies network cables. This method also offers predicted uplink oversubscription and quick port-to-port switching of servers inside the rack (Cheng et al., 2017).

A top-of-rack design makes better use of the cabling. The costs of underutilizing ports and rising switch prices are frequent trade-offs. Large installations may make top-of-rack switching challenging, and server racks' local area network (LAN) switch equipment risks overheating. To better use switch ports and employ fewer switches overall, some data centers install top-of-rack switches inside a middle-of-row or end-of-row design (Zhang et al., 2008). Every rack in such a typical ToR architecture has several servers linked to a switch just at the top of a rack. The switch connects to a bigger core network to link to certain other racks and the outside globe. Because of the servers' direct connection to the switches, this design offers high bandwidth and minimal latency (Lee et al., 2005) (Figure 2.4).

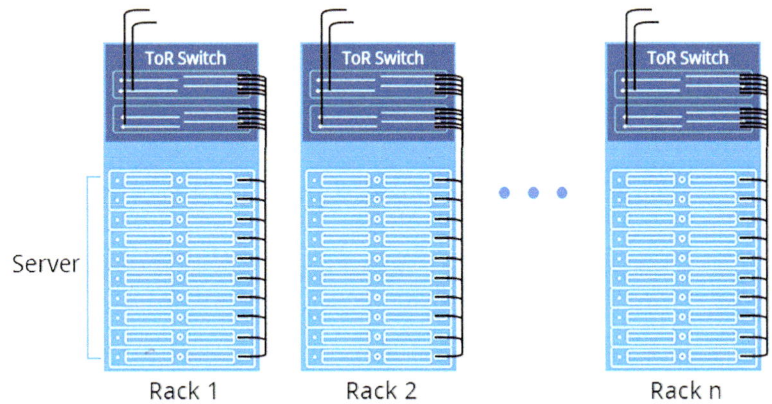

Figure 2.4. Picture of top of rack switch (Source: Fiber optic share, Creative Commons License).

The ToR topology provides several benefits, including:

1. Simplified Cabling

While each rack is linked directly to a switch instead of needing to route cables to a central location, the ToR architecture lowers the complexity of the cabling system (Shen et al., 2021).

2. Improved Performance

ToR architecture can offer high bandwidth and minimal latency by connecting every host directly to a switch (Wang et al., 1999).

3. Scalability

ToR topology is very scalable since new switches may be added to a network and connected to the network infrastructure to add extra racks (McSherry et al., 2015).

ToR topology, however, has significant drawbacks, such as:

a. Limited Reach

ToR topology is made for data centers with a few racks since switches may never reach huge data centers, so at the top of every rack (Brownlee, 2017).

b. Cost

Since each rack has its switch, ToR topology may be more costly than other network designs (Cohen, 1983).

c. Complexity

Because each switch needs to be configured and controlled separately, managing a ToR network could be difficult (Horgan, 1995). In conclusion, ToR topology is a well-liked option for data centers needing great scalability and performance. Still, it might not be appropriate for big data centers or those with tight budgets.

2.2 ARCHITECTURES

2.2.1 Mesh Network Architecture

Every device or node in the network has links to each other as a node, establishing a mesh-like structure. It is known as a mesh network architecture. As several pathways connect any two nodes in this design, redundancy and fault tolerance are provided (Shahdad et al., 2016).

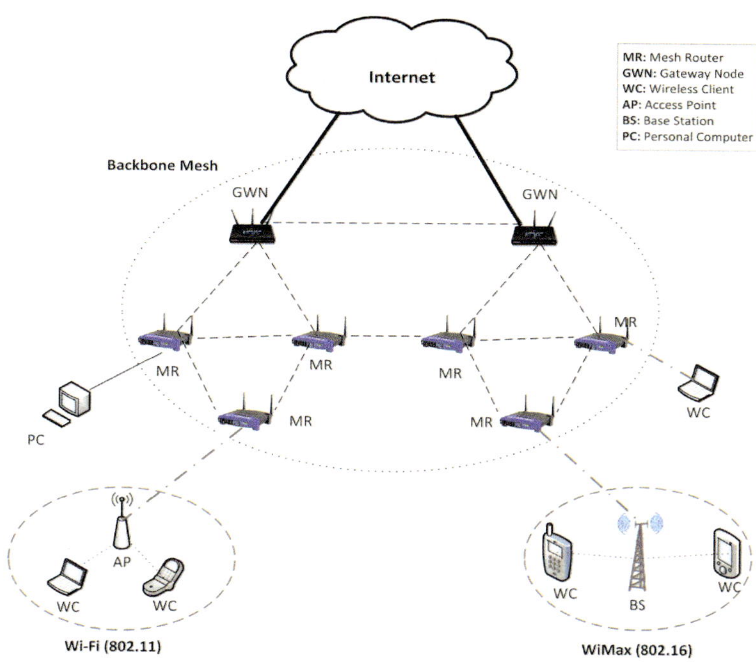

Figure 2.5. Mesh network architecture illustration (Source: Andrey Krendzel, Creative Commons License).

Every node in a mesh network is linked to several other nodes, resulting in an extremely interconnected network. Several pathways can be used between these two nodes in this design, offering redundancy and fault tolerance. If such node or link fails, data may continue to be sent through alternative pathways with in-network (Raniwala & Chiueh, 2005) (Figure 2.5).

Mesh networks provide several benefits, like as:

1. Reliability

Mesh networks offer high levels of dependability because many pathways and redundancy guarantee that information can be delivered even if a node or link fails (Roberts & Priest, 2006).

2. Scalability

Adding extra nodes to a mesh network makes it simple to scale it up since every new node gives the network more pathways and redundancy (Cecchet et al., 2002).

3. Flexibility

Data centers, Wireless networks, and industrial applications are just a few of the uses for mesh networks (Olsson, 2006).

Mesh networks, however, also have several drawbacks, such as:

a. Complexity

Due to the requirement that each node is linked with each other node, mesh networks could be difficult to build and operate (Lloyd, 2001).

b. Latency

Mesh networks may generate significant latency or delays since data must pass through numerous nodes to reach its destination (Padmanabhan & Mogul, 1995).

c. Cost

As each node needs many connections to those other nodes, mesh networks may be more costly than other kinds of network designs. In conclusion, mesh networks are a viable choice for applications that demand high reliability with fault tolerance. Still, their implementation could be more difficult and costly than other network topologies (Shugan, 1980).

2.2.2 Three-Tier or Multi-Tier Model

Data centers and business networks frequently employ tier and multi-tier network design paradigms. It separates the network into several levels or tiers, each offering a different service or function (Averill et al., 2011) (Figure 2.6).

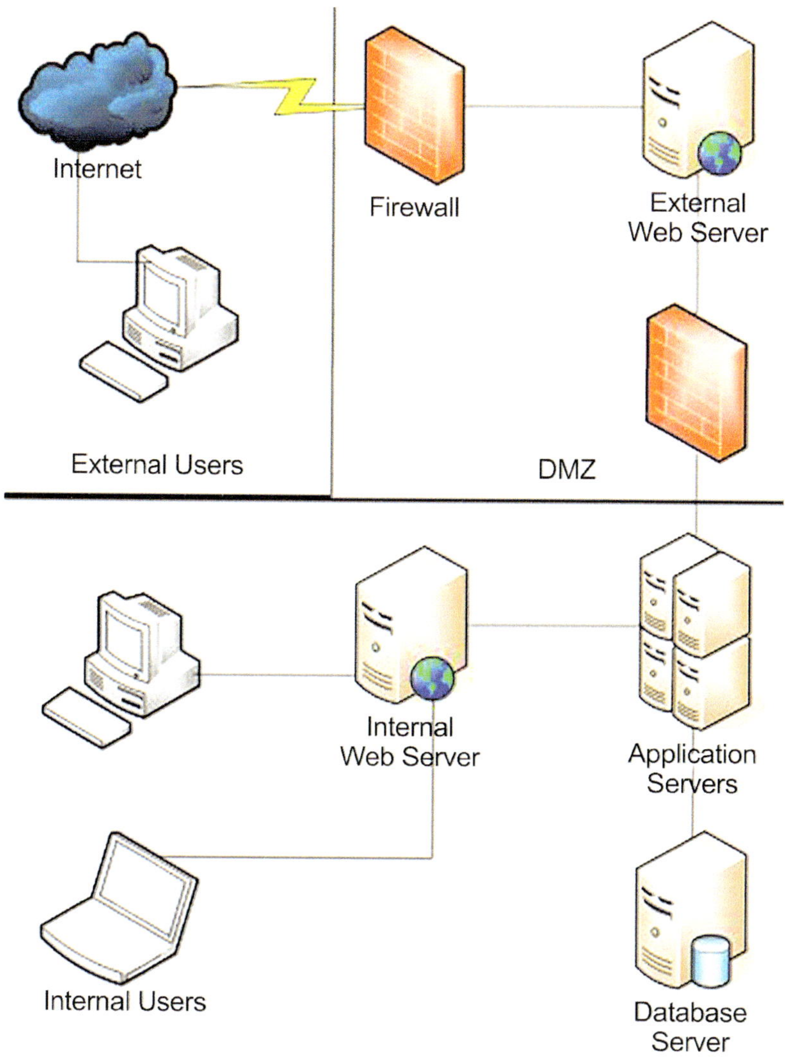

Figure 2.6. An example of a multi-tiered model (Source: Science Direct, Creative Commons License).

The three-tier model, containing the following levels, is the most popular multi-tier model.

1. Access Layer

Connection to end devices, including printers, computers, and other network devices, is provided by this layer. Normally, it is linked to a distribution layer (Wu et al., 2005).

2. Distribution Layer

This tier provides connectivity between the core layer and switches at the access layer. It oversees enforcing regulations and directing traffic between VLANs (Zarifi et al., 2016).

3. Core Layer

This layer oversees sending traffic toward its destination and supplying high-speed communication between switches at the distribution layer. It is the network's foundation (Dhar et al., 2006).

The multi-tier concept provides several benefits, such as:

a. Scalability

The multi-tier paradigm may be expanded as even the network expands by adding extra devices to an access layer or new levels, and it is very scalable (Boyd et al., 2010).

b. Manageability

The multi-tier model's ability to handle each layer independently simplifies deploying changes and addressing issues (Tucker & Melewar, 2005).

c. Security

The multi-tier approach enhances network security by enabling the execution of security controls at each layer (Miller, 2001).

The multi-tier concept, however, also has significant drawbacks, such as:

i. Complexity

Especially in big networks, the multi-tier concept can be challenging to design and implement (Goldenfeld & Kadanoff, 1999).

ii. Cost

The multi-tier approach could be more expensive than other network topologies since it calls for more hardware, like routers and switches (Conlisk, 1988).

iii. Latency

The various data tiers that should pass through during a multi-tier approach to reach their destination might cause additional latency.

In conclusion, the tier and multi-tier architecture is a widely used network design that offers scalability, management, and security but may be difficult and costly to deploy (Parrish et al., 1998).

2.2.3 Mesh Point of Delivery (PoD)

Wireless mesh networks frequently employ the network architecture known as Mesh Point of Delivery (PoD). Several wireless access points (APs) are interconnected to form a mesh network in such a wireless mesh network. The point about which data is transmitted to a mesh network is called the Mesh PoD architecture (Fox et al., 1991).

Every access point function as a PoD in a mesh PoD design and is in charge of providing data to a mesh network. The data is transmitted to the PoD when one client device is connected to an AP, and the PoD then routes the data across the mesh network toward its destination. Given that various routes may be used to connect every two network nodes, this design offers redundancy with fault tolerance (Ferro et al., 2019).

A Mesh PoD architecture provides several benefits, such as:

1. Scalability

The network's capacity and coverage may be increased by adding more access points, making the Mesh PoD design very scalable.

2. Fault Tolerance

Due to the various pathways that may be taken between any two sites in the network, the Mesh PoD design offers redundancy and fault tolerance.

3. Flexibility

Applications for the Mesh PoD architecture include campus networks, outdoor wireless networks, and industrial applications.

The Mesh PoD design, however, has additional drawbacks, such as:

a. Complexity

The Mesh PoD architecture could be complicated to build and administer, as every access point should be linked with each additional access point in the network.

b. Latency

The Mesh PoD design might generate significant latency or delays since data must pass through several access points to reach its destination.

c. Cost

Given that every access point needs many connections to certain other access points, any Mesh PoD architecture may be more costly than other network topologies.

In conclusion, the Mesh PoD design is an excellent choice for wireless mesh networks, which demand great scalability with fault tolerance. At the same time, constructing it could be more difficult and expensive than other network topologies (Grimberg et al., 2021).

2.3 ENTERPRISE AND CLOUD SERVICE DATA CENTERS

Major corporations like Microsoft, Google, and Yahoo have reportedly invested heavily in data centers that serve cloud services, according to Greenberg et al., (2008). According to the same authors (Greenberg et al., 2009), cloud service data centers differ from regular business data centers. Secondly, unlike enterprise data centers wherein automation may only be partially implemented, cloud service data centers must be automated. Data centers for cloud services must also offer significant economies of scale. 100 000 servers, for instance, may be true. Finally, data centers for cloud services should expand rather than contract. Scaling out spreads workload to less expensive systems instead of upgrading expensive gear. Enterprise data center examples are Ethane (Casado et al., 2007) and SEATTLE (Kim et al., 2008) (Figure 2.7).

Figure 2.7. Image of google (Source: Brecorder, Creative Commons License).

In contrast to the existing ones, the business networking designs were initially created by Greenberg et al., (2011) for considerably smaller data centers. To meet the increased demands of data centers, various patches and workarounds for the protocols have been developed due to the restrictions of the conventional design (Chi, 2018).

According to Greenberg et al., (2009), the issue with agility and cloud services' relationship to data centers. The introduction of agile thinking into data centers by cloud services has been a key driver of data center innovation. Cloud services enable mass deployments with flexible server reallocation to various services.

These upgrades do, however, have an economic effect. The monthly cost of a global data center with 100,000 servers is $12 million. The lack of mobility in the present data center designs prevents them from becoming extremely profitable and inexpensive. In a data center, agility is reacting to varying needs more quickly rather than trying to anticipate fluctuations in demand by reallocating resources. Elegant design for data centers promises cost reductions and greater risk management (Beloglazov et al., 2012).

2.4 COST STRUCTURE

Greenberg et al. present data concerning the pricing structure in such a data center. According to table 2.1, networking accounts for 15% of all expenditures in data centers. Nevertheless, networking affects the entire system more broadly. Innovating networking is the secret to lowering overall expenses (Russell et al., 1993) (Table 2.1).

Remember

Effective management of enterprise and cloud service data centers involves ensuring high availability and performance, optimizing resource usage, implementing robust security measures, and employing specific management strategies for cloud-based applications and services.

Table 2.1. Typical Data Center Costs (Source: Bondi, Creative Commons License)

Amortized Cost	Component	Sub-Components
45%	Servers	CPU, memory, storage
25%	Infrastructure	Power distribution, cooling
15%	Power draw	Electrical utility costs
15%	Network	Links, transit, equipment

By Greenberg et al., (2008), the greatest portion of total costs belongs to the servers. To allow efficient use of the hardware and high utilization, the data centers should provide a method to grow the number of servers dynamically and allow focusing resources on optimal locations. Now the fragmentation of resources prevents server utilization.

However, according to Greenberg et al. (2008), permitting scale-out models of inexpensive servers may be necessary to cut infrastructure expenses. In a data center, scaling out could entail transferring ownership of expensive server characteristics, including failure rate, from such a central server to the entire system. By enabling the network architecture that scales out, it is possible to assure low failure rates by using many inexpensive servers instead of just a few expensive ones.

Costs associated with power are comparable to network expenses. For every watt given, IT equipment uses 59%, 8% for distribution losses, and 33% for cooling. By enabling the data centers to operate cooling, hotter-related expenses might be decreased, thus necessitating a more robust and mesh-like network.

Moreover, networking equipment accounts for a sizeable portion of network-related expenditures, according to Greenberg et al. (2008). Wide area networking is responsible for additional expenditures associated with the network, such as traffic towards end users and traffic within data centers and local facilities. Optimizing the traffic with data center location is the main emphasis of networking cost reduction.

The issues and solutions related to data center network topologies are the only ones we address in this article. This essay's second section addresses the primary issues with network designs. Section 3 then analyzes several alternatives that have been presented. We summarize the important points (Fritsch et al., 2004).

2.5 PROBLEMS WITH NETWORK ARCHITECTURES

2.5.1 Scalability and Physical Constraints

As a data center scales up, more costly components are updated and replaced to meet the demand, whereas scaling out involves adding more affordable components (Greenberg et al., 2011).

Utilizing commodity hardware is said to result in a more appealing performance-to-price ratio since the cost of each port is lower than with more technologically sophisticated ones, according to Guo et al. (2009).

The intricacy of the cabling may hinder scalability. For example, in the modular data center (MDC) architecture, the lengthy cables linking the containers become problematic as the container count rises.

Physical limitations like rack layouts with high densities, may result in extremely high-power densities at the room level. Also, the dependability and uptime of the data center depend on an effective cooling system. Air handling units and rack configurations further impact the data center's energy usage (Sharma et al., 2004).

2.5.2 Resource Oversubscription and Fragmentation

As seen in Figure 2.1, when one moves up the usual network architectural hierarchy, this oversubscription ratio quickly rises. Based on those authors, the oversubscription ratio is the proportion of subscriptions that exceed the amount available. Twenty different 1 Gbps servers might be subscribed to one 1 Gbps router, resulting in a 1:20 oversubscription ratio. If the ratio is 1:1, the subscriber can use the entire available bandwidth for communication. For the pathways traversing the top layer in a typical network configuration, the oversubscription ratio could be 1:240. Since unused assets cannot be allocated where required, a server pool with limited server-to-server ability restricts data center efficiency and splits the server pool. These applications must be placed thoughtfully and with consideration for the effect of traffic to prevent this issue. Yet, in reality, this isn't easy.

Given the limited server-to-server capacity architects cluster the servers close to one another in the hierarchy since hierarchy distance influences communication in terms of cost and performance. Moreover, access routers allocate IPs for layer 2 in a topological manner; thus, adding applications outside the scope of layer 2 requires different settings. Today's data centers reserve resources to prevent the extra setup, squandering those resources. Even reservations can't anticipate when a service will require more resources than are reserved, forcing the allocation of those resources from those other services. Resources are split and separated because of reliance (Greenberg et al., 2011).

2.5.3 Reliability, Utilization, and Fault Tolerance

Data centers have low usage and dependability (Greenberg et al., 2009). There should be a means of maintaining the data center operation if one of its components fails. For example, when an access router malfunctions, counterpart pieces typically take over to carry the burden. Yet, as a result, the components only operate at 50% of their potential. Several pathways are not exploited properly in the network topologies of today's data centers. The maximum in typical network topologies is two routes.

Several pathways can be employed by employing Equivalent Cost Multipath Routing (ECMP) (Hopps, 2000). (Al-Fares et al., 2008) While switches presently enable ECMP, several issues still need to be fixed. For example, routing tables expand multiplicatively with the number of pathways utilized, likely increasing search latency and cost.

Links in the middle of data centers are used more frequently than links on edge, on aggregate, according to Benson et al. (2010), while those on edge have larger losses. Depending on the SNMP data of 19 various data centers, this study.

Fault tolerance and smooth performance decline are considered particularly significant because of space and operational restrictions in some systems. With only a typical network design, it may be difficult to guarantee a graceful performance decline. For example, in one event, a core switch failure resulted in performance concerns with ten million active users over several hours.

2.5.4 Cost

Cost is a significant issue influencing decisions concerning data center network design, claim (Al-Fares et al., 2008). The same authors suggest oversubscribing data center network components is one way to cut expenses. Yet, as was already mentioned, oversubscription causes issues. Secondly, we provide the findings of research that looked at how maintaining a 1:1 subscription ratio affects costs when using various network designs. The largest cluster size permitted by the most cutting-edge 10 GigE and common GigE switches throughout a given year is shown in Table 2.2. According to Al-Fares et al., (2008), the table is separated into two distinct topologies:

1. Advanced 10 GigE switches are included in hierarchical designs on layer 3 and as aggregated switches on layer 2. With hierarchical architecture, the edge uses generic GigE switches. Until recently, the port's density of modern switches constrained the largest cluster size. Also, until recently released new devices, aggregation switches could not provide 10 GigE uplinks. When compared with the Fat-tree design, there is a sizable price difference.
2. In contrast to establishing a standard hierarchical network utilizing pricey sophisticated switches, fat-tree is an architecture that permits building a large-scale commodity network with commodity switches. The fat tree is one example of these commodity networks in this table. All tiers of the network design use commodity GigE switches, a feature of the fat tree. Considering the cost distinction between fat-tree design and hierarchical architecture is important. Due to the commodity hardware's declining price trend over the years, Fat-tree design's overall expenses have decreased quickly.

2.5.5 Incast

TCP Throughput Collapse, also called Incast, which results in the under-utilization of connection capacity, was studied by Chen et al., (2009). According to Chen et al., (2009), most data centers employ TCP for interaction between the nodes with Incast, which is distinct from the initial presumptions on which TCP was designed.

In other words, TCP limits the utilization of all available capacity since it is not appropriate for a unique data center setting characterized by low latencies and large bandwidths.

By Fares et al. (2008), a recipient in Incast seeks data from various senders. After receiving the request, the senders send data to the initial recipient and other senders. Yet, there is a bottleneck link during the sender-to-receiver link, which causes the throughput at which the receiver gets the data to drop. The resulting network congestion affects all senders utilizing the same bottleneck link.

	Hierarchical design			Fat-tree		
Year	10 GigE	Hosts	Cost/ GigE	GigE	Hosts	Cost/ GigE
2002	28-port	4,480	$25.3K	28-port	5,488	$4.5K
2004	32-port	7,680	$4.4K	48-port	27,648	$1.6K
2006	64-port	10,240	$2.1K	48-port	27,648	$1.2K
2008	128-port	20,480	$1.8K	48-port	27,648	$0.3K

Table 2.2. The Biggest Cluster Sizes that Switched with Only An Oversubscription Ratio Can Support 1:1 During 2002–2008 (Source: Bondi, Creative Commons License)

Congestion is delayed when switches and routers are upgraded, and their buffer sizes are increased. However, the buffers can still quickly fill up in environments with high latency and bandwidth, such as data centers. According to Chen et al., (2009), large buffer routers and switches are expensive.

2.6 PROPOSED NETWORK ARCHITECTURES

2.6.1 Fat-Tree

Figure 2.10 depicts the introduction of Fat-tree by Al-Fares et al., (2008), which permits the design of low-cost commodity network components. The network's switching components are all identical. Moreover, some pathways to the final hosts will always take the entire bandwidth. Also, as shown in Table 2.2, the expense of the Fat-tree network is lower than the regular one.

According to Al-Fares et al., (2008), the essence of IP/Ethernet is to create a connection utilizing a single routing channel between the destination and the source. Fat-tree architecture suffers from serious performance problems due to a single routing path. This solution suggests employing two-level routing tables, which may be implemented on hardware that uses Content-Addressable Memory, to address the performance problems (CAM).

Al-Fares et al., (2008) claim that the switch qualities affect the size of the Fat-tree. A switch with 48 ports can handle a network with 27,648 hosts; however, upgrading switches is necessary to scale out to accommodate networks with more than 100,000 hosts. Moreover, wiring with Fat-tree architecture might be a significant obstacle; nevertheless, packaging and placement strategies are suggested for this problem.

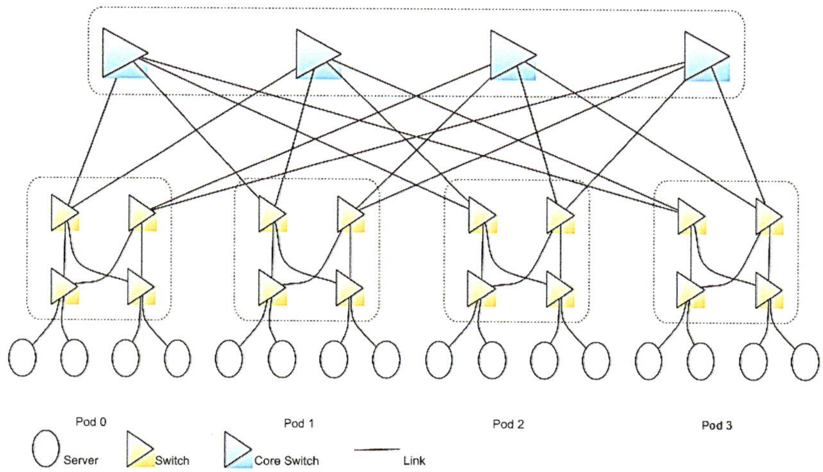

Figure 2.8. Schematic of fat-tree design (Source: Al-Fares et al., Creative Commons License).

According to Al-Fares et al., (2008), the switch attributes impact the Fat-growth. Tree's A switch with 48 ports can manage a network with 27,648 hosts; however, to grow out to support networks with more than 100,000 hosts, switches must be upgraded. Furthermore, wiring in Fat-tree design may be a very difficult challenge; nevertheless, packing and placement techniques are provided to solve this issue.

2.6.2 Monsoon

Monsoon is a mesh-like infrastructure for "cloud" services (Greenberg et al., 2011), using commodity switches to cut costs and enable powerful scalability of up to 100,000 servers. Using Valiant Load Balancing during the monsoon enhances performance (VLB). Although the architecture is split into IP layer 3 and Ethernet layer 2, monsoon concentrates on layer 2. Layer 2 has several advantages, including lower costs, the removal of server fragmentation (all applications may share a vast flat address space), and prevention of IP-layer functionality disruption.

Layer 2 switches must support MAC-in-MAC tunneling, 16K MAC entries, and customizable control plane software to work with the monsoon. Moreover, 20 servers' 1-Gbps connectivity should be handled by a top-of-rack switch on two 10-Gbps uplinks. The 144 10-Gbps ports on the higher layer switches should be plenty. Around 100,000 servers may be supported by this design without any layer 2 links being overloaded. Instead of using specialized and expensive hardware, load balancers (LB) may be constructed using inexpensive servers. Equal Cost MultiPath (ECMP) is used by IP layer 3 to evenly distribute requests from the Internet to access routers (AR) (ECMP).

According to Greenberg et al., (2008), ARP must be replaced by a new virtual Mac interface called Monsoon Agents with an encapsulator, a user-mode process that encapsulates Ethernet messages. The Monsoon networking stack needs to get path information from a directory service. A Directory Service may be installed using a variety of methods. Ingress Server, which functions with Access Routers, is a further service required for the Monsoon architecture (AR). For the VLB's Monsoon load encapsulation dynamic spreading, an Ingress Server is necessary.

TIPS

When implementing a fat-tree network architecture, carefully plan and configure the network to optimize traffic flow, minimize latency, and ensure high availability by employing redundancy and failover measures. Use technologies like QoS and load balancing to optimize performance.

2.6.3 BCube and MDCube

A shipping container called BCube (Guo et al., 2009) is based on the modular data center (MDC) concept. A few thousand servers linked by switches create an MDC crammed into a 20- or 40-foot shipping container. MDC provides quick deployment, cheaper production and cooling, and better system and power densities. Items based on shipping containers are already available from well-known players, including HP, Microsoft, and Sun.

MDCube (Wu, et al., 2009) is a framework for building container-based mega-data centers. The BCube architecture links numerous servers within the container and is used for MDCube containers. MDCube is, in other words, a plan for a mega-data center that uses BCube-based containers as its building pieces.

There are a few network ports on every server, which are connected to mini switches. The server is given control over the routing intelligence. In contrast to BCube, the authors assert that Clos topology-based systems like Monsoon, VL2, and Fat tree don't support one-to-x (one-to-one, one-to-several, and one-to-all) well. Results further demonstrate that BCube provides more smooth performance decline than conventional network designs.

MDCube, which offers high network capacity for mega-data centers, strong fault tolerance, and reasonable cable complexity, is suggested by Wu et al., (2009). The high-speed interfaces for switches in BCube connect BCube containers in MDCube. The MDCube switches serve as virtual interfaces to BCube containers, which operate as virtual nodes in MDCube. Because MDCube has a server-centric architecture, the servers handle the logic. In a server-centric way, MDCube needs networking stack upgrades for load balancing and failure-resistant routing. Switching and servers in BCubes are reserved for external connections to offer to route to other networks.

Compared to mega-data centers built using single-structure designs like BCube or Fat-tree, the number of inter-container cables in MDCube is approximately two orders smaller, according to Wu et al., (2009) (Figure 2.9).

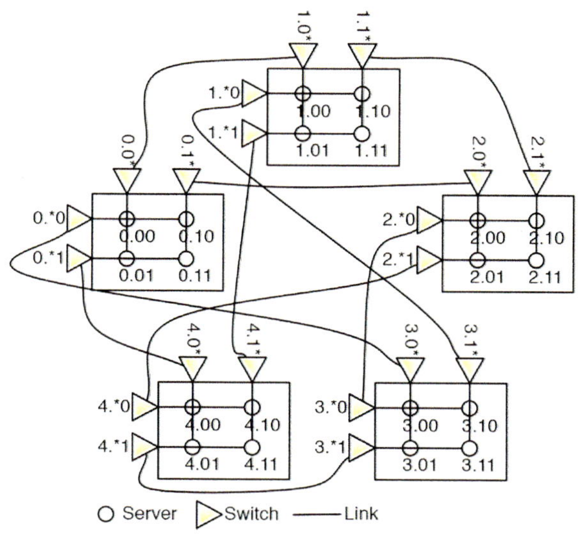

Figure 2.9. Example of MDCube design (Source: Casado et al., Creative Commons License).

2.6.4 VL2

VL2, a network design that employs flat addressing to prevent resource fragmentation, Valiant Load Balancing (VLB) for traffic dispersion, and address resolution enabling huge server pools, is introduced by Greenberg et al., (2009). The real topology provides path variety. As it generates the appearance of a single layer-2 switch that spans the whole data center by generating a virtual layer, VL2 is expected to provide agility and address many present difficulties. Moreover, the network design of VL2 does away with the requirement for over-scribing links in the network.

According to Greenberg et al., (2009), VL2 needs a directory service with a service agent for VL2 addressing and routing, perhaps like monsoon does. Also, it appears that VL2 needs network stack modifications on servers to support VL2 addressing and routing architecture. Application-specific (AAs) and location-specific (LAs), used to isolate server names from locations and provide agility, are fundamental ideas in VL2 addressing and routing. Although AAs are solely utilized in apps, LAs are issued for all switches and interfaces.

According to Greenberg et al., (2009), one VL2 design principle is to allow implementation on existing hardware so that VL2 can be used even today. The authors evaluated VL2 performance with a working prototype. The results indicate that VL2 is efficient and achieves high load-balancing fairness. In addition, rough cost estimates also indicate that a typical network without oversubscribed links costs 14 times more than an equivalent VL2 network.

VL2 design is still costly, according to the authors of MDCube (Greenberg et al., 2009), as they utilize very high-end switches in layer 2. For instance, 448 448-port 10Gbps intermediate and aggregate switches would be needed to establish a network with one million servers.

2.6.5 Fixing Incast

In their study on TCP Incast solutions, (Chen et al., 2009)'s team prioritized TCP-based techniques above developing new technologies. Also, it could be more economical and appealing to the operators of data centers. An example of a non-TCP-based technique is an application-level global scheduler. A universal scheduler would necessitate changes to all of the apps, but as was already said, this sort of solution is not appealing due to its effort and complexity.

In (Chen et al., 2009), tests were carried out, and the dynamics of Incast were investigated. The statistics show discrepancies between the results of the tests and the relevant work in this field. An analytical method was also presented to explain the tendencies that were seen.

ACTIVITY 2.1

Suppose you have been tasked with designing a network architecture for a new data center that will support a variety of workloads, including high-performance computing and cloud-based applications. What factors would you consider when selecting a topology for the network, and how would you ensure that the network is optimized for performance, scalability, and reliability? Provide a real-world example to illustrate your answer.

SUMMARY

In this chapter, we first provide basic information regarding the cost structure and the current development in the data center sector. The issues with current data center network designs were discussed, including physical limitation, scalability, resource fragmentation and oversubscription, utilization dependability, fault tolerance, cost, and Incast. Finally, we presented several newly suggested fixes for the issues. We discussed MDCube, VL2, and Monsoon. All the suggested solutions had advantages and disadvantages. Still, based on our initial assessment, we believe the ones most advantageous to the sector can be deployed immediately and require little modification to the hardware already in place. Using inexpensive, mass-produced gadgets rather than high-end ones seems to be a prevalent theme among the suggested remedies.

REVIEW QUESTIONS

1. What are the different topologies used in data center management?
2. Why is centralized and zoned topology important in data center management?
3. What is the significance of architectures in data center management and how do they affect performance?
4. Explain the difference between enterprise and cloud service data centers.
5. How does cost structure impact data center management, and what are some strategies for managing costs effectively?

MULTIPLE CHOICE QUESTIONS

1. Which of the following is not a common data center topology?

a) Star
b) Mesh
c) Bus
d) Ring

2. What is the main advantage of a centralized data center topology?

a) Higher scalability
b) Lower latency
c) Greater redundancy
d) Easier management

3. What is a zoned data center topology?

a) A topology where servers are organized by function or application
b) A topology where servers are organized by geographic location
c) A topology where servers are organized by power consumption

d) A topology where servers are organized by manufacturer

4. What is the main advantage of a cloud service data center?

a) Lower cost

b) Greater control

c) Higher security

d) Greater scalability

5. Which of the following is a common architecture for data center management?

a) Client-server

b) Peer-to-peer

c) Three-tier

d) Mesh

6. What is an enterprise data center?

a) A data center owned by a government agency

b) A data center owned by a large corporation

c) A data center that provides cloud services

d) A data center that provides co-location services

7. What is a cloud service data center?

a) A data center that provides co-location services

b) A data center that provides cloud services

c) A data center that is owned by a government agency

d) A data center that is owned by a non-profit organization

8. What is the importance of cost structure in data center management?

a) It affects the profitability of the data center

b) It affects the scalability of the data center

c) It affects the security of the data center

d) It affects the performance of the data center

9. Which of the following is not a common network architecture for data centers?

a) Fat-tree

b) Clos

c) Mesh

d) Spine-leaf

10. Which of the following is a key feature of a spine-leaf network architecture?

a) It allows for direct connections between all devices in the network

b) It provides multiple paths between devices for redundancy

c) It organizes devices into tiers based on their function

d) It is a hierarchical architecture with distinct core, aggregation, and access layers

Answers to Multiple Choice Questions

1. (c)	2. (d)	3. (a)	4. (d)	5. (c)
6. (b)	7. (b)	8. (a)	9. (c)	10. (d)

REFERENCES

1. Al-Fares, M., Loukissas, A., & Vahdat, A. (2008). A scalable, commodity data center network architecture. ACM SIGCOMM Computer Communication Review, 38(4), 63–74.
2. Averill, O. H., Rinaldi, C., & Collaborative, U. S. E. L. (2011). Multi-tier system of supports (MTSS). District Administration, 48(8), 91–95.
3. Bellare, M., Pietrzak, K., & Rogaway, P. (2005). Improved security analyses for CBC MACs. In Advances in Cryptology–CRYPTO 2005: 25th Annual International Cryptology Conference, Santa Barbara, California, USA, August 14–18, 2005. Proceedings 25 (pp. 527–545). Springer Berlin Heidelberg.
4. Beloglazov, A., Abawajy, J., & Buyya, R. (2012). Energy-aware resource allocation heuristics for efficient management of data centers for cloud computing. Future Generation Computer Systems, 28(5), 755–768.
5. Benson, T., Anand, A., Akella, A., & Zhang, M. (2010). Understanding data center traffic characteristics. ACM SIGCOMM Computer Communication Review, 40(1), 92–99.
6. Besley, T., & Coate, S. (2003). Centralized versus decentralized provision of local public goods: a political economy approach. Journal of Public Economics, 87(12), 2611–2637.
7. Bondi, A. B. (2000, September). Characteristics of scalability and their impact on performance. In Proceedings of the 2nd International Workshop on Software and Performance (pp. 195–203).
8. Boyd-Wickizer, S., Clements, A. T., Mao, Y., Pesterev, A., Kaashoek, M. F., Morris, R. T., & Zeldovich, N. (2010, October). An Analysis of Linux Scalability to Many Cores. In OSDI (Vol. 10, No. 13, pp. 86–93).
9. Brownlee, J. (2017). The limited reach of authoritarian powers. Democratization, 24(7), 1326–1344.
10. Burger, D., Goodman, J. R., & Kagi, A. (1997). Limited bandwidth to affect processor design. IEEE Micro, 17(6), 55–62.
11. Casado, M., Freedman, M. J., Pettit, J., Luo, J., McKeown, N., & Shenker, S. (2007). Ethane: Taking control of the enterprise. ACM SIGCOMM Computer Communication Review, 37(4), 1–12.
12. Cecchet, E., Marguerite, J., & Zwaenepoel, W. (2002). Performance and scalability

of EJB applications. ACM Sigplan Notices, 37(11), 246–261.

13. Chen, Y., Griffith, R., Liu, J., Katz, R. H., & Joseph, A. D. (2009, August). Understanding TCP incast throughput collapse in datacenter networks. In Proceedings of the 1st ACM Workshop on Research on Enterprise Networking (pp. 73–82).
14. Cheng, Y., Fiorani, M., Lin, R., Wosinska, L., & Chen, J. (2017). POTORI: a passive optical top-of-rack interconnect architecture for data centers. Journal of Optical Communications and Networking, 9(5), 401–411.
15. Chi, Y. (2018). Network system structure design for data centers in large enterprises using cloud computing. International Journal of Enterprise Information Systems (IJEIS), 14(2), 87–97.
16. Clarkson, P. J., Simons, C., & Eckert, C. (2004). Predicting change propagation in complex design. J. Mech. Des., 126(5), 788–797.
17. Cohen, J. (1983). The cost of dichotomization. Applied Psychological Measurement, 7(3), 249–253.
18. Conlisk, J. (1988). Optimization cost. Journal of Economic Behavior & Organization, 9(3), 213–228.
19. Costa, P., Zahn, T., Rowstron, A., O'Shea, G., & Schubert, S. (2009, August). Why should we integrate services, servers, and networking in a data center?. In Proceedings of the 1st ACM Workshop on Research on Enterprise Networking (pp. 111–118).
20. Couto, R. S., Campista, M. E. M., & Costa, L. H. M. (2012, December). A reliability analysis of datacenter topologies. In 2012 IEEE Global Communications Conference (GLOBECOM) (pp. 1890–1895). IEEE.
21. Davies, B., Baron, S., Gear, T., & Read, M. (1999). Measuring and managing service quality. Marketing Intelligence & Planning, 17(1), 33–40.
22. Demsetz, H. (1968). The cost of transacting. The Quarterly Journal of Economics, 82(1), 33–53.
23. Dewatripont, M., & Maskin, E. (1995). Credit and efficiency in centralized and decentralized economies. The Review of Economic Studies, 62(4), 541–555.
24. Dhar, A., Paul, M. C., Pal, M., Mondal, A. K., Sen, S., Maiti, H. S., & Sen, R. (2006). Characterization of porous core layer for controlling rare earth incorporation in optical fiber. Optics Express, 14(20), 9006–9015.
25. Ferro, N., Micheletti, S., & Perotto, S. (2019). POD-assisted strategies for structural topology optimization. Computers and Mathematics with Applications, 77(10), 2804–2820.
26. Fox, J. H., Donegan, T. L., Jacocks, J. L., & Nichols, R. H. (1991). Computed Euler flowfield for a transonic aircraft with stores. Journal of Aircraft, 28(6), 389–396.
27. Fritsch, M., Görzig, B., Hennchen, O., & Stephan, A. (2004). Cost structure surveys for Germany. Journal of Contextual Economics–Schmollers Jahrbuch, (4), 557–566.
28. Goldenfeld, N., & Kadanoff, L. P. (1999). Simple lessons from complexity. science, 284(5411), 87–89.

29. Goodhue, D. L., & Straub, D. W. (1991). Security concerns of system users: A study of perceptions of the adequacy of security. Information & Management, 20(1), 13–27.
30. Greenberg, A., Hamilton, J. R., Jain, N., Kandula, S., Kim, C., Lahiri, P., ... & Sengupta, S. (2009, August). VL2: A scalable and flexible data center network. In Proceedings of the ACM SIGCOMM 2009 Conference on Data Communication (pp. 51–62).
31. Greenberg, A., Hamilton, J. R., Jain, N., Kandula, S., Kim, C., Lahiri, P., ... & Sengupta, S. (2011). VL2: a scalable and flexible data center network. Communications of the ACM, 54(3), 95–104.
32. Greenberg, A., Hamilton, J., Maltz, D. A., & Patel, P. (2008). The cost of a cloud: research problems in data center networks. ACM SIGCOMM Computer Communication Review, 39(1), 68–73.
33. Greenberg, A., Lahiri, P., Maltz, D. A., Patel, P., & Sengupta, S. (2008, August). Towards a next generation data center architecture: scalability and commoditization. In Proceedings of the ACM Workshop on Programmable Routers for Extensible Services of Tomorrow (pp. 57–62).
34. Grimberg, S., Farhat, C., Tezaur, R., & Bou□Mosleh, C. (2021). Mesh sampling and weighting for the hyperreduction of nonlinear Petrov–Galerkin reduced□order models with local reduced□order bases. International Journal for Numerical Methods in Engineering, 122(7), 1846–187
35. Guo, C., Lu, G., Li, D., Wu, H., Zhang, X., Shi, Y., ... & Lu, S. (2009, August). BCube: a high performance, server-centric network architecture for modular data centers. In Proceedings of the ACM SIGCOMM 2009 Conference on Data Communication (pp. 63–74).
36. Gyarmati, L., & Trinh, T. A. (2010). Scafida: A scale-free network inspired data center architecture. ACM SIGCOMM Computer Communication Review, 40(5), 4–12.
37. Haddadi, H., Rio, M., Iannaccone, G., Moore, A., & Mortier, R. (2008). Network topologies: inference, modeling, and generation. IEEE Communications Surveys & Tutorials, 10(2), 48–69.
38. Halliday, A. N., Stephens, W. E., & Harmon, R. S. (1980). Rb-Sr and O isotopic relationships in 3 zoned Caledonian granitic plutons, Southern Uplands, Scotland: evidence for varied sources and hybridization of magmas. Journal of the Geological Society, 137(3), 329–348.
39. Henry, F. M., & Rogers, D. E. (1960). Increased response latency for complicated movements and a "memory drum" theory of neuromotor reaction. Research Quarterly. American Association for Health, Physical Education and Recreation, 31(3), 448–458.
40. Hopps, C. (2000). NextHop Technologies, "Analysis of an Equal-Cost Multi-Path Algorithm," (pp. 1–5). RFC 2992, Informational, Network Working Group.
41. Horgan, J. (1995). From complexity to perplexity. Scientific American, 272(6), 104–109
42. Kahl, M., Viccaro, M., Ubide, T., Morgan, D. J., & Dingwell, D. B. (2017). A branched

magma feeder system during the 1669 eruption of Mt Etna: evidence from a time-integrated study of zoned olivine phenocryst populations. Journal of Petrology, 58(3), 443–472.

43. Kim, C., Caesar, M., & Rexford, J. (2008). Floodless in Seattle: a scalable ethernet architecture for large enterprises. ACM SIGCOMM Computer Communication Review, 38(4), 3–14.
44. Lee, Y. H., Lee, M. H., & Hur, S. (2005). Optimal design of rack structure with modular cell in AS/RS. International Journal of Production Economics, 98(2), 172–178.
45. Lewis, N. S. (2007). Toward cost-effective solar energy use. science, 315(5813), 798–801.
46. Lin, D., Liu, Y., Hamdi, M., & Muppala, J. (2012, December). Flatnet: Towards a flatter data center network. In 2012 IEEE Global Communications Conference (GLOBECOM) (pp. 2499–2504). IEEE.
47. Lloyd, S. (2001). Measures of complexity: a nonexhaustive list. IEEE Control Systems Magazine, 21(4), 7–8.
48. McSherry, F., Isard, M., & Murray, D. G. (2015, May). Scalability! but at what cost?. In HotOS (Vol. 15, pp. 14–14).
49. Miller, B. (2001). The concept of security: Should it be Redefined?. The Journal of Strategic Studies, 24(2), 13–42.
50. Olsson, N. O. (2006). Management of flexibility in projects. International Journal of Project Management, 24(1), 66–74.
51. Padmanabhan, V. N., & Mogul, J. C. (1995). Improving HTTP latency. Computer Networks and ISDN Systems, 28(1–2), 25–35.
52. Parrish, N. M., Dick, J. D., & Bishai, W. R. (1998). Mechanisms of latency in Mycobacterium tuberculosis. Trends in Microbiology, 6(3), 107–112.
53. Petrie, H. T., & Zúñiga-Pflücker, J. C. (2007). Zoned out: functional mapping of stromal signaling microenvironments in the thymus. Annu. Rev. Immunol., 25, 649–679.
54. Popa, L., Ratnasamy, S., Iannaccone, G., Krishnamurthy, A., & Stoica, I. (2010, November). A cost comparison of datacenter network architectures. In Proceedings of the 6th International COnference (pp. 1–12).
55. Randell, B. (1975, April). System structure for software fault tolerance. In Proceedings of the International Conference on Reliable Software (pp. 437–449).
56. Raniwala, A., & Chiueh, T. C. (2005, March). Architecture and algorithms for an IEEE 802.11-based multi-channel wireless mesh network. In Proceedings IEEE 24th Annual Joint Conference of the IEEE Computer and Communications Societies (Vol. 3, pp. 2223–2234). IEEE.
57. Roberts, P., & Priest, H. (2006). Reliability and validity in research. Nursing Standard, 20(44), 41–46.
58. Russell, D. M., Stefik, M. J., Pirolli, P., & Card, S. K. (1993, May). The cost structure

of sensemaking. In Proceedings of the INTERACT'93 and CHI'93 Conference on Human Factors in Computing Systems (pp. 269–276).

59. Sah, R. K., & Stiglitz, J. E. (1991). The quality of managers in centralized versus decentralized organizations. The Quarterly Journal of Economics, 106(1), 289–295.
60. Shahdad, S. Y., Sabahath, A., & Parveez, R. (2016, April). Architecture, issues and challenges of wireless mesh network. In 2016 International Conference on Communication and Signal Processing (ICCSP) (pp. 557–560). IEEE.
61. Sharma, R., Bash, C., Patel, C., & Beitelmal, M. (2004, June). Experimental investigation of design and performance of data centers. In The Ninth Intersociety Conference on Thermal and Thermomechanical Phenomena in Electronic Systems (IEEE Cat. No. 04CH37543) (Vol. 1, pp. 579–585). IEEE.
62. Shen, B., Chen, X., Fu, L., Zhang, M., Chen, Y., Sheng, J., ... & Coombs, T. (2021). A simplified model of the field dependence for HTS conductor on round core (CORC) cables. IEEE Transactions on Applied Superconductivity, 31(8), 1–5.
63. Shugan, S. M. (1980). The cost of thinking. Journal of Consumer Research, 7(2), 99–111.
64. Silva, M. B., Skjødt, M., Atkins, A. G., Bay, N., & Martins, P. A. F. (2008). Single□ point incremental forming and formability—failure diagrams. The Journal of Strain Analysis for Engineering Design, 43(1), 15–35.
65. Singla, A., Singh, A., Ramachandran, K., Xu, L., & Zhang, Y. (2010, October). Proteus: a topology malleable data center network. In Proceedings of the 9th ACM SIGCOMM Workshop on Hot Topics in Networks (pp. 1–6).
66. Tucker, L., & Melewar, T. C. (2005). Corporate reputation and crisis management: The threat and manageability of anti-corporatism. Corporate Reputation Review, 7, 377–387.
67. Vahdat, A., Al-Fares, M., Farrington, N., Mysore, R. N., Porter, G., & Radhakrishnan, S. (2010). Scale-out networking in the data center. IEEE Micro, 30(4), 29–41.
68. Wang, Q. G., Lee, T. H., Fung, H. W., Bi, Q., & Zhang, Y. (1999). PID tuning for improved performance. IEEE Transactions on Control Systems Technology, 7(4), 457–465.
69. Wu, H., Lu, G., Li, D., Guo, C., & Zhang, Y. (2009, December). MDCube: a high performance network structure for modular data center interconnection. In Proceedings of the 5th International Conference on Emerging Networking Experiments and Technologies (pp. 25–36).
70. Wu, Y., Chou, P. A., Zhang, Q., Jain, K., Zhu, W., & Kung, S. Y. (2005). Network planning in wireless ad hoc networks: a cross-layer approach. IEEE Journal on selected areas in communications, 23(1), 136–150.
71. Xia, Y., Sun, X. S., Dzinamarira, S., Wu, D., Huang, X. S., & Ng, T. E. (2017, August). A tale of two topologies: Exploring convertible data center network architectures with flat-tree. In Proceedings of the Conference of the ACM Special Interest Group on Data Communication (pp. 295–308).

72. Zarifi, D., Farahbakhsh, A., Zaman, A. U., & Kildal, P. S. (2016). Design and fabrication of a high-gain 60-GHz corrugated slot antenna array with ridge gap waveguide distribution layer. IEEE Transactions on Antennas and Propagation, 64(7), 2905–2913.
73. Zhang, X., VanGilder, J. W., Iyengar, M., & Schmidt, R. R. (2008, May). Effect of rack modeling detail on the numerical results of a data center test cell. In 2008 11th Intersociety Conference on Thermal and Thermomechanical Phenomena in Electronic Systems (pp. 1183–1190). IEEE.

CHAPTER 3

SECURITY AND COMPLIANCE IN DATA PROTECTION

UNIT INTRODUCTION

Data security and compliance are essential components of data protection in the modern digital era. To prevent legal and financial repercussions, companies must have security procedures to safeguard their data from cyber assaults.

Data protection from illegal access, loss, or destruction is called data security. This covers safeguarding data being used (data being processed by applications or users), in route (transferred between systems), and at rest (data that is stored). Cryptography, security systems, routers, systems for detecting and preventing intrusions, and security information and event management (SIEM) systems are a few examples of data security precautions (Zerlang, 2017) (Figure 3.1).

Contrarily, compliance means abiding by the norms and obligations of laws and regulations. Regulations like the General Data Protection Regulation (GDPR) in the European Union, Health Insurance Portability and Accountability Act (HIPAA) in the United States, and the Personal Information Protection and Electronic Documents Act (PIPEDA) in Canada are examples of compliance in the regard of data security. For businesses dealing with credit card data, compliance involves regulations like the Payment Card Industry Data Security Standard (PCI DSS) (Kalaiprasath et al., 2017).

Figure 3.1. Representation of Security Information and Event Management (SIEM) systems (Source: Wallarm, Creative Commons License).

To meet these laws and requirements, companies must ensure they have the proper data security procedures in place. Failing to comply can lead to severe legal and financial repercussions, reputational harm to the company, and other consequences.

Companies need to have a comprehensive strategy that comprises the following actions to guarantee compliance and data security (Hendre & Joshi, 2015):

- **Risk Evaluation:** A security breach's possible effects, infrastructure risks, prospective dangers, and hazards to an organization's data and systems must all be identified (Shin et al., 2017).
- **Security Procedures and protection:** Data classification, Access controls, incident response, and encryption are just a few of the safety measures and processes that organizations must establish and put into place to handle the threats that have been identified (Stanberry, 1998).
- **Security Training:** To make sure that its personnel, partners, and other parties are knowledgeable about the organization's security policies and processes and can recognize potential security threats, organizations must offer security education to these parties (McCrohan et al., 2010).
- **Supervising and Reporting:** Businesses must keep focusing on abnormalities and security breaches in their networks and notify the proper authorities of such instances (Lavy, 2014).
- **Consistent advancement:** To guarantee that they continue

to be efficient in defending against changing security issues, organizations must regularly examine and upgrade their safety measures and processes.

Organizations can supplement these actions with third-party security products and services to improve data security and compliance. Some of these are threat intelligence, controlled security services, and security consultancies.

In conclusion, enterprises must seriously consider the crucial components of data protection—data security and compliance. In order to safeguard their data from cyber intrusions and to escape financial and legal repercussions, they must put the necessary security precautions in place. An all-encompassing strategy that incorporates risk analysis, procedures and guidelines for security, training courses, reporting and monitoring, and continual improvement is necessary (Kosseff, 2016).

3.1 AUTHORIZED CONCERNS OF DATA SECURITY

Organizations must abide by several legal obligations to secure personal data and prevent financial and legal repercussions, even though data protection rules and regulations continually change. Failing to abide by these regulations may have serious legal and financial penalties and reputational harm to a company. This part will discuss the legal facets of security and compliance in data protection.

In the European Union (EU), the General Data Protection Regulation (GDPR) is one of the main existing legislation for data protection (Hu & Ahn, 2011) (Figure 3.2).

Figure 3.2. Illustration of General Data Protection Regulation (GDPR) (Source: Modern analyst, Creative Commons License).

No matter where a business is located, if it processes the personal information of EU individuals, the GDPR applies. Restrict guidelines for data protection are included in the GDPR, such as the following:

- **Influence of default and design on data security:** Businesses must ensure that data protections are included by default instead of added to their systems and procedures (Dogruel et al., 2017).
- **Rights to data access:** People have the right to gain access, update, and erase their personal information. They also have the right to disagree with its usage and demand to transfer to another organization (Hudson et al., 2020).
- **Data breach notification:** Within 72 hours of breach awareness, organizations must notify the relevant agencies (Peters, 2014).
- **Evaluation of data security impact:** To evaluate the possible impact on people's privacy, companies must complete DPIAs for any large data analysis process.

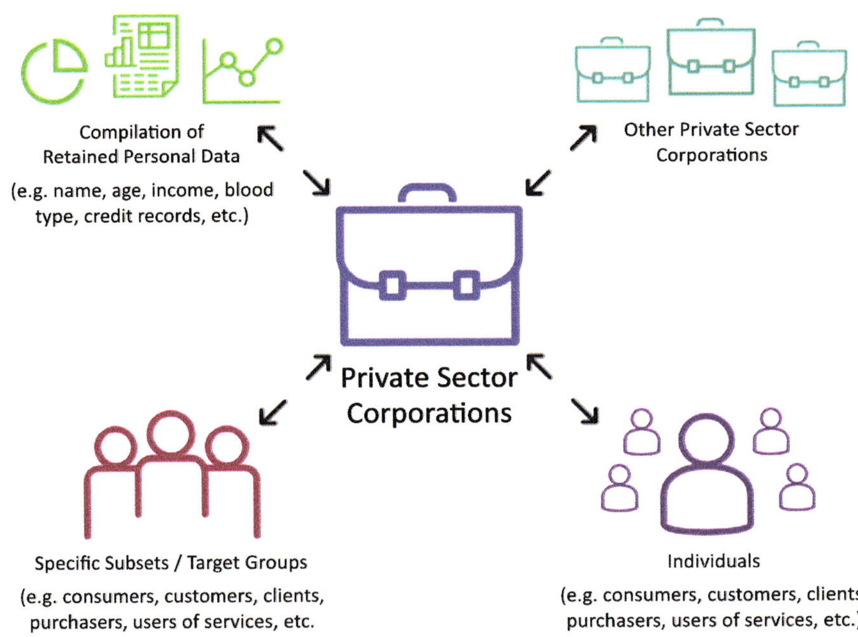

Figure 3.3. Representation of Personal Information Protection and Electronic Documents Act (PIPEDA)

(Source: Cybersrc, Creative Commons License).

The HIPAA is a crucial legislative foundation for data protection in the US. HIPAA imposes stringent rules for securing healthcare companies' personal health information (PHI). HIPAA mandates that businesses place physical, managerial, and technical protections to secure personal health information and notify the proper authorities of any breaches (Fernando et al., 2018).

The California Consumer Privacy Act (CCPA) and the Personal Information Protection and Electronic Documents Act (PIPEDA) in Canada are two more legislative structures for data protection. These rules mandate the protection of personal data and the reporting of data breaches.

Companies should also follow several industry-specific standards regarding these legislative frameworks, including the PCI DSS for businesses that manage credit card data (Figure 3.3).Companies must implement the necessary security precautions, like encryption, access controls, and breach monitoring and avoidance systems, to ensure compliance with these regulatory obligations. Organizations should regularly conduct safety checks and risk evaluations to detect and reduce potential security threats (Shrivastava et al., 2021).

Companies must have incident management strategies to prevent and fix security breaches and notify the proper authorities and any affected parties as needed, per legal requirements.

In conclusion, corporations must abide by several legal obligations to protect personal information and prevent facing financial and legal repercussions. Standards for data breach reporting, data subject rights, data protection, and data protection impact analyses are all covered by these legislative frameworks. Companies must also adhere to standards particular to their industry, such as PCI DSS. Organizations must place the necessary security safeguards, carry out regular security checks and risk monitoring, and have emergency response strategies in place to meet these criteria (Nicol, 2005).

3.2 STRATEGIC POSSIBILITIES AND IMMEDIATE THREATS

Information and communication technology for development (ICT4D) has lately changed from an innovative feature to a catalyst for achieving specific socioeconomic strategic priorities as the development and relief industry has grown over several decades. The inherent advantages and hazards associated with collecting, analyzing, and utilizing data about recipients and subpopulations are becoming more and more clear to ICT4D professionals from both local and international Non-governmental organizations (NGOs), civil society organizations, United Nations (UN) agencies, funding agencies, and businesses in the private sector (Bryant, 2020).

The concept of responsible data is "the obligation to make sure the people's rights to assent, secrecy, security and possession around the information systems of selection, stockpiling, demonstration, and retrieval of data, since honoring the transparency values and its openness" has resulted from community attempts to identify and discuss these possibilities and dangers and has gained some ground all over the ICT4D space. Additionally, several organizations, NGOs, sponsors, for-profit businesses, and others three have already attempted to establish unique remedies to these problems (Roege et al., 2017).

TIPS

To manage immediate threats in a data center, establish and regularly review emergency response plans, define clear roles and responsibilities, conduct training and simulations, have redundant systems in place, and regularly test and maintain backup power and cooling systems.

The United Nations Office for Coordinating Humanitarian Affairs and GovLab at New York University/the Center for Entrepreneurship at Leiden University have recently issued helpful studies and suggestions on ethical data. To guarantee a remarkable degree of compliance with data protection, confidentiality, and safety principles and standards for ICT4D, there is a lack of generally accepted and used standards and principles.

Organizations International (WVI) has been putting into practice a Data Security, Confidentiality & Security (DPP&S) structure that follows Information Technology (IT) industry standards for the past four to five years. Regarding appropriate methods and safety measures, this concept is appropriate to WVI on a worldwide scale and to particular ICT4D initiatives. WVI has conducted desk research on these larger global patterns to comprehend the present state of other structures, regulations, investigations, and adherence. WVI has also recorded the execution of the internal structure and case analysis of its humanitarian supplies, well-being, and nutrition strategy (Wang & Lu, 2013).

3.3 EXISTING GUIDELINES, REGULATIONS, AND NETWORKS

Regarding Digital Development Principle 8, several important paradigms are pertinent. They are all significant criteria that must be evaluated and taken into consideration for execution, even though they all present certain obstacles in terms of implementing humanitarian, advancement, and ICT4D programs.

In 2013, the Organization for Economic Cooperation and Development (OECD) amended its privacy rules to include a risk-management strategy and a consideration of the significance of fostering global connectivity in protecting privacy. Affiliates of the OECD are provided with principles and recommendations for implementing them (Figure 3.4). In these countries, both the private and public sectors are accountable for supplying the following:

1. limitations of Data collection;
2. Confidence in Data quality;
3. Purpose of data collection;
4. Limitation on the purpose of data usage;
5. Confidence of security privacy;
6. Clarity of policies, practices, and developments about the data;
7. Rights for the people from whom information is collected;
8. Reliability of the data controller (Stigler & Chamberlin, 2012).

Figure 3.4. Logo of Organization for Economic Cooperation and Development (OECD) (Source: Ivett Molnar, Creative Commons License).

There are rules governing the flow of data internationally, which demand that limits reflect real concerns and promote minimal limitations on data exchange among members. National privacy policies, data protection breach notification systems, and privacy programs are also included. It is crucial to remember that most OECD members are affluent, advanced technological countries capable of creating reliable regulatory systems. Although just six of the organization's thirty-five affiliates are outside Europe and North America, the OECD maintains relationships and accords with many non-member countries, which may lack regulatory regimes.

The Health Insurance Portability and Accountability Act of 1996 (HIPAA) rules in the United States and the General Data Protection Regulation (GDPR), which will supplant the present Data Protection Directive in May 2018, are two crucial guideposts that have to be taken into account when assessing existing data security, confidentiality, and privacy standards. Organizations in industrialized nations are also worried about their capacity to comply with the GDPR rules because they are far stricter than HIPAA (Urnov, 2003).

The "Privacy Rule," "Security Rule," "Enforcement Rule," and "Omnibus Rule" are the four rules that makeup HIPAA. ICT4D (Information and Communication Technologies for Development) is mainly affected by the Privacy and Security Rule because they protect personally sensitive and electronic health information, respectively.

The Privacy Rule limits the publication of the following and only allows the revelation of "minimum essential" data to protect personally sensitive data.

1. A person identified by the data;
2. The organization's service, payment, and healthcare treatments;
3. Uses and disclosures to which the person has the choice to respond;
4. Auxiliary use and disclosure;
5. Public demand and benefit interests;
6. Limitations on data sets that have been discovered.

Individuals are entitled to review and edit their data as necessary; demand limited access from various bodies to their data, and demand notification when and to whom their sensitive information has been released.

To "protect the privacy of individuals' health data while controlling various businesses to use innovative technology to enhance the standard and effectiveness of patient care," the Security Rule was created. Entities must: concerning electronically-protected health information (e-PHI) (Shen et al., 2019):

a) Guarantee the privacy, confidentiality, and accessibility of all e-PHI they generate, obtain, sustain, or transfer;
b) Identify and protect against risks to the privacy or safety of the data that are anticipated;
c) Guard against reasonably anticipated unauthorized uses or disclosures.

While no specific methods are provided, the Security Rule offers some advice on important factors to consider while formulating protocols. In addition to providing a specific collection of technical, physical, and managerial protections, organizations are expected to conduct continuing risk analyses.

The new General Data Protection Regulation (GDPR), like the present Data Protection Directive of the European Union, imposes restrictions on using any sensitive data. A historical legal justification for using that data is required for "lawful processing," It cannot breach eight important personal rights, which are covered in more detail below. Children need to be able to interpret privacy notifications. Online services for children may only analyze information with a guardian's permission, except when providing preventative or counseling services, according to the GDPR's specific provisions for safeguarding children's rights (Radecka et al., 2018).

Individual rights according to the GDPR include:

a) to be informed
b) to have access
c) to be rectified
d) to erasure
e) to limit processing
f) to information portability
g) to object
h) to self-controlled decision-making and profiling.

The insistence on responsibility is the most notable distinction between the old directive on data protection and the new GDPR. Companies must follow the GDPR and establish their unique governance model to prove compliance and maintain records. There is a checklist of what the records must show, but no uniform governing system must be followed. Although not obligatory, conducting data security impact evaluations is highly recommended.

Few organizations now adhere to the rules, according to the law firm DLA Piper, which advises them to concentrate on doing so before the GDPR is implemented to guarantee that they are fully compliant by May 2018. The life and medical sciences sectors now have a lower compliance level with the new criteria, which is very important for them.

The Asia Pacific Economic Cooperation (APEC) Privacy Policy, designed to enable electronic commerce, attempts to protect data through a dynamic approach that will guarantee privacy but not obstruct data sharing (Matinmikko et al., 2018) (Figure 3.5).

Figure 3.5. Representation of Asia-Pacific Economic Cooperation (Source: APEC, Creative Commons License).

Asia-Pacific Economic Cooperation

The principles privacy framework are as follows.

3.3.1 Preventing Measures

Provisions for personal data should be created to avoid any harm (Hutchings et al., 2013).

3.3.2 Notice

People should be aware of the following facts either before, during, or as early as feasible after data collection:

a) That their data is being collected;
b) The purpose of its collection;
c) To whom the data will possibly be disclosed;
d) The identity of the personal data controller and how to have contact with them;
e) available options for limiting the disclosure of their data (Binkley, 2016).

3.3.3 Limitation of Collection

Only data pertinent to the goal of collecting may be acquired, and data-collecting procedures should be lawful, ethical, and transparent to the subject of the data (Hartzog & Richards, 2020).

3.3.4 Usage Personal Data

If the subject agrees, personal data might only serve the specific objectives it originally obtained and other strongly linked uses. Only the products or services ordered by the person or legal authorities may be provided using the data (Tikkinen-Piri et al., 2018).

3.3.5 Choice

People need mechanisms to exercise control over the collection, use, and disclosure of personal data that are clear, easy to use, and reasonably priced (Wiczorek & Zirk, 2019).

3.3.6 The Integrity of Personal Data

Personal data must be true, comprehensive, and as recent as is required for the intended use (Chen & Zhao, 2017).

3.3.7 Privacy Safeguard

Processors of personal data are required to implement precautions appropriate for the risk's magnitude and level (Kung et al., 2017).

3.3.8 Access and Correction

People shall be capable of reviewing the data that the processor of their data has about them, challenging its correctness, and, if necessary, requesting that it be updated or removed. The person should be informed of the facts if it is decided that it is not suitable (Huang et al., 2018).

3.3.9 Accountability

Compliance with the above guidelines should be the responsibility of the personal data controller (Felici et al., 2013).

3.4 DATA PROTECTION, CONFIDENTIALITY, AND SECURITY STRUCTURE

Data security, confidentiality, and privacy are particular issues in the Organization's purview. We have been employing electronic technology to increase the effect and caliber of our programs in our development and humanitarian efforts for several years, with ICT4D project activity recorded as recently as 2003.

Figure 3.6. A framework of data security protection (Source: Bank info security, Creative Commons License).

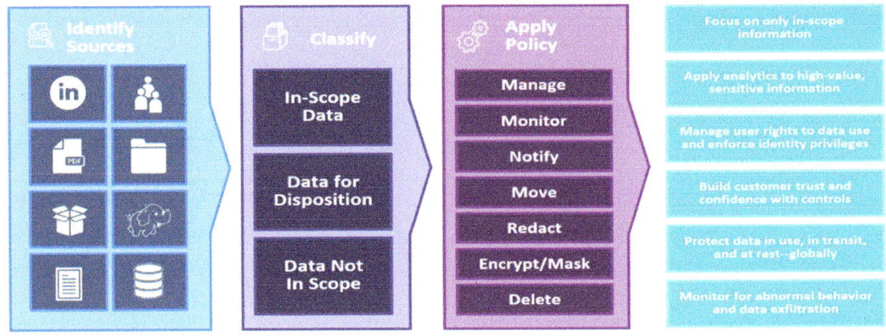

Did you Know?

According to a report by Gartner, global spending on information security and risk management technology and services is forecast to reach $170.4 billion in 2022, representing a 12.4% increase from 2021.

We employ electronic technology in agriculture, risk management, healthcare, nutrition, food stamps, campaigning, education, and industrial progress. Due to their scale, safe data practices for our funders, recipients, staff, and associates are a critical concern. In the past few years, efforts have been made to create organizational frameworks for data privacy and security. Discussions on what data security must entail in humanitarian instances have been ongoing. To get agreement on international norms regarding information security, confidentiality, and privacy, there remains great work to be done because ICT4D is a relatively new field in the developing sector (Ali et al., 2021) (Figure 3.6).

3.4.1 Security and Privacy of Data

We think that all data security, confidentiality, and legal parties need to agree if sensitive data is guaranteed to be safe and confidential.

Companies have made progress in recent years in formally uniting the security and data privacy units with tight ties to the legal department. This includes improving the organization's data privacy and security posture and creating international standards and evaluation procedures (Clifton & Marks, 1996).

Although this method is challenging to master, organizations concentrate on its most important programs:

1. Horizon (Organization's integrated system with design, monitoring and evaluation, project budgeting, sponsorship monitoring, child well-being outcome reporting, and rich media capacities);
2. Our People (Organization's centralized employee HR system);
3. Sponsorship (Organization's sponsored-child database);

4. Sun6 (Organizations Partnership's global financial system).

The Enterprise Risk Management (ERM) team collaborates with the data Security team when analyzing risk to guarantee that both teams view and categorize risk from the same perspective.

By weighing the risks associated with each organizational system and considering the organization's overall functions, ERM develops a standardized list of the most significant ten operational risks. These dangers have been internationally linked with their appropriate risk areas. Although WVI now contributes to the risk management systems used by the campaigning offices (internally known as Support Offices SOs), specific goals call for merging these systems (Weber, 2010) (Figure 3.7).

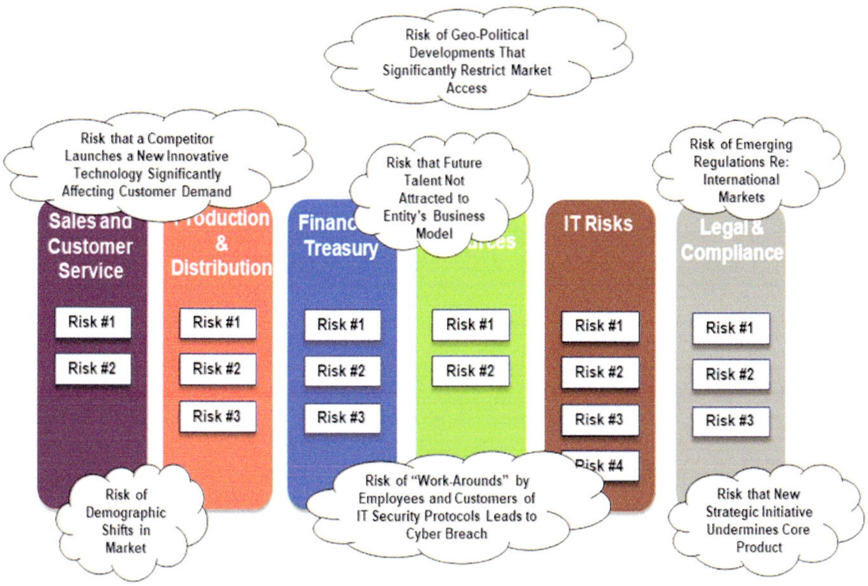

Figure 3.7. Enterprise Risk Management (ERM) (Source: NC State University, Creative Commons License).

3.4.2 Current Policies

Global data privacy and security rules have been an ongoing endeavor for the corporation for many years. The International Organization for Standardization (ISO) has recently been used by Data Security, Administrative, and the ERM to build a list of rules based on global norms. Three principles were created as a result of this effort, and they apply to all Organizational units, such as microfinance banks (Aldossary & Allen, 2016).

3.4.2.1 Partnership Policy on International Information Confidentiality and Privacy

To guarantee uniformity in data security and privacy, adherence with relevant data security and privacy legislation, common practice, security of Personally Identifiable Information (PII), and risks minimization of regulatory adherence failures and adverse harm for the Organization, this strategy offers a general structure for global data security and privacy at Organizations. All other information securities and privacy-related rules are housed under this main policy (Shiraz & Aldrich, 2019) (Figure 3.8).

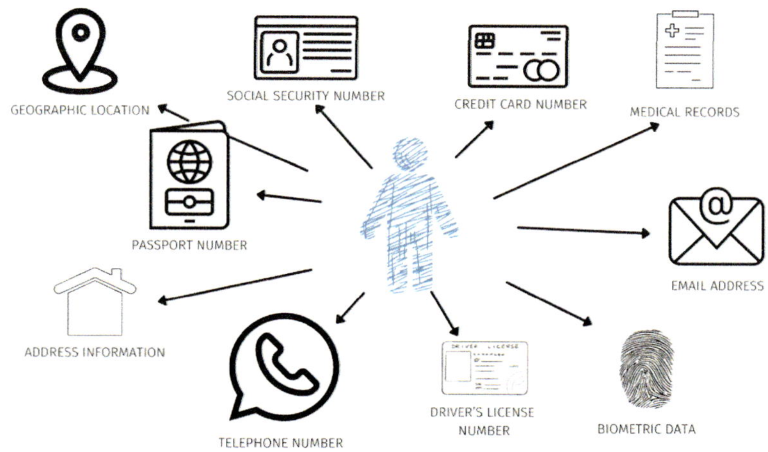

Figure 3.8. Representation of Personally Identifiable Information (PII) (Source: Data privacy manager, Creative Commons License).

3.4.2.2 Partnership Policy on Data Security

The data security standards and practices necessary to guarantee the privacy, authenticity, and reliability of the organization's resources, information, and IT systems are documented by this policy, which serves as a general concept for data security at companies. All other technological and access control standards are subsumed under this main policy (Steinhart, 2006).

3.4.2.3 Administrative Policy on Data Security

The partnership's issues, objectives, and targets for global data security are addressed in this strategy. The Partnership Strategy on Data Security, which was authorized by the council, supports and is consistent with it. Offices may increase their rules' level of depth or rigor, but they must adhere to the same minimum requirements as this policy. The next approach will be to make this policy and current policies compatible.

The creation of a management approach to global security and confidentiality and different data protection and privacy standards is now being assessed. These regulations are a wonderful beginning and are the industry norm for all businesses (Culhane, 2016).

3.4.3 Enforcement Mechanisms

Setting standards is crucial, but enforcing them is frequently challenging. Employee training for data security awareness is one of the current strategies. It aims to empower staff to take ownership of protecting company information from illegal access, to identify possible security risks, and to be capable of reporting events right away. Online training, learning incentives, and phishing evaluations strengthen learning. Employee Training for Global Information Protection and Privacy is currently being developed (Ryutov & Neuman, 2002).

3.4.4 Data Security Assessment Protocol

Companies have created project integration information Final Security Review (FSR) evaluations parallel to policies. Organizations conduct three stages of evaluations to ensure that they are appropriate for a reason (Nardone et al., 2016).

3.4.4.1 Security Lite Assessment (FSR-Lite)

It is employed to evaluate cloud services, foreign web services, commercial off-the-shelf (COTS) programs, and outside suppliers of services (Ezeokoli et al., 2016).

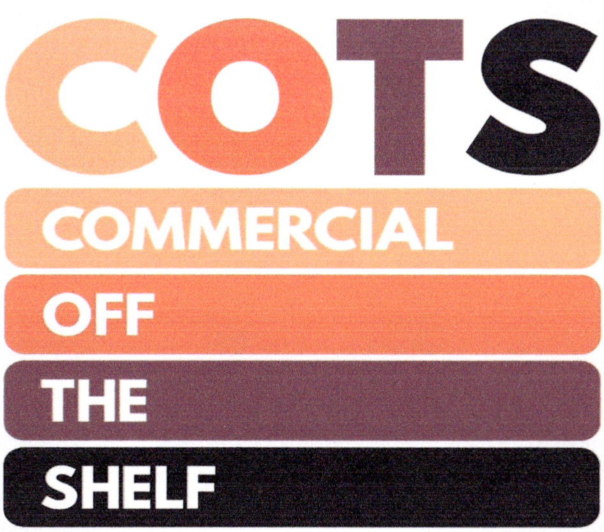

Figure 3.9. Representation of Commercial Off-the-Shelf (COTS) (Source: Dreamstime, Creative Commons License).

3.4.4.2 Basic Security Assessment (FSR-Basic)

It is employed to evaluate small versions of an already-existing program, business, or system that include authorized modifications, new components, or functionality (Wu & Tsai, 1983).

3.4.4.3 Full Security Assessment (FSR-Full)

It evaluates initiatives delivering significant updates, new iterations, or innovative designs for important partnership-wide programs or activities (like Horizon, Sponsorship, Financial Systems, and Our People) (Morison et al., 2004).

Following the determination of the degree of the method, the three main information security method is used:

> **Remember**
>
> In data security and protection, ethical considerations involve protecting privacy and confidentiality, implementing appropriate security measures, ensuring compliance with relevant laws and regulations, and using data in a responsible and transparent manner that aligns with ethical principles.

1. **Questionnaire of Registration:** encompassing the rules, the border, the internet, the data centers, the computer applications, and the information;
2. **The baseline for Minimum security:** comprises application programming review, architectural review, network security assistant, minimum security baseline (MSB) border security, policy review verification and approvals, and MSB information management;
3. **Review of Final security:** This procedure results in the determination of the assessment's final grade. High risk (0%-59%) is not advised for installation, followed by low risk (80%-100%), which is approved and advised for installation, and medium risk (60%-79%), which needs senior execution approval.

After installation, the big four tier 1 apps (Our People, Horizon, Sun6, and Sponsorship) undergo third-party vulnerability examinations and security risk rectification to ensure the project's ongoing data security (Nguyen et al., 2013).

3.5 ETHICAL CONSIDERATIONS

Numerous of the international security and privacy principles that have been detailed so far have been founded on an ethical foundation. Hence, ethical concerns are incorporated into current standards around the world. These standards typically contain the values of ensuring safety, guaranteeing privacy, keeping secrecy during release, and protecting that the benefits associated with information collecting exceed the dangers.

Many organizations and countries have considered the "Fair Information Practice Principles" of the US Federal Trade Commission as a solid set of moral principles for developing their privacy policies. They serve as the foundation for numerous US legislation. The following guidelines apply:

1. An individual should be informed of security practices before the collection of information.
2. The subject must express their consent, which they can withdraw at any time, to use the data gathered precisely.
3. The person must always be able to examine and update their data.
4. Security precautions and controls must be in place, and data integrity must be maintained.
5. A system enabling the person to file complaints against the company collecting the data must be in place to enforce compliance with the abovementioned requirements (Safdar et al., 2020).

According to opponents, the lack of a guiding concept results in an overdependence on self-regulation.

At the UN Headquarters in New York, UN Global Pulse hosted an "Improving Data Security & Privacy in ICT4D" session in May 2015. In this course, a variety of ethical topics were covered with a focus on the following:

a) The requirement to acquire permission from persons whose information is being collected;
b) the significance of security risk assessments and their current absence from any project or program gathering personally sensitive data;
c) the fact that transfer of data is inherently unsafe and the significance of developing secure ways for disclosing de-identified information;

The importance of openness, especially when it relates to winning over individuals and communities.

In a humanitarian context, we have particular difficulties in addressing these problems. Written consent in a critical situation is discussed in the policy paper "Humanitarianism in the Cyberwarfare Era" by the United Nations Office for the Coordination of Humanitarian Affairs (OCHA). Those who need medical care might be physically incapable of giving permission. Saving lives comes first when written consent could make the difference between life and death for a few minutes (Shou, 2012) (Figure 3.10).

In the early stages of a disaster, organizations might not be certain how the information would be utilized, which makes it difficult to tell people appropriately. Even if a statement regarding exposure and use is made, people with low levels of literacy in the language that the declaration is made in might not be capable of giving informed permission. Recipients may also agree to measures that they would not support in a situation other than a disaster. It is challenging to imagine a means to eliminate the threat of compulsion posed by the disaster. Complete security will render humanitarian assistance impracticable by prohibiting data acquisition, and the public release of private data would also put individuals at risk, according to OCHA. Obviously, the obligation not to cause damage should be weighed with the necessity to preserve lives under pressure situations (Kinkela, 2013).

Figure 3.10. Logo of Coordination of Humanitarian Affairs (OCHA) (Source: Cinfo, Creative Commons License).

Risk evaluation is cited in OCHA's policy document as a crucial place to start when getting information about humanitarian disasters. A breakaway session at the UN Global Pulse workshop discussed the key elements of developing rewards, damages, and threats approaches. A risk evaluation offers non-data security officials working in the humanitarian sector a practical means to decide if and to what extent the advantages exceed the risk and damages. The initial evaluation instrument has been finished and is available for download from UN Global Pulse's website. A two-phase evaluation method is now being developed for humanitarian programs. Risk evaluation, however, can be difficult to carry out since humanitarian organizations frequently lack assets like workforce and finance (Prinsloo & Slade, 2013).

Whenever data is exchanged, a security breach could occur. According to a collaborative study by NetHope and Mastercard, few humanitarian professionals believe a security breach is possible. As a result, they are unaware of the significance of removing personally identifiable data and developing private data transmission protocols, and they do not view these as top priorities. Donors frequently share this sentiment and prefer not to use their funds to establish local security protocols.

Since that confidentiality can be seen as a Western concept and that vulnerability is viewed in various cultures, it is possible that even the populations from which data is obtained do not completely appreciate the significance of data security (Rigg, 2018).

In actuality, there are many significant risks associated with using humanitarian information. OCHA defines the most urgent concerns for the humanitarian context as political attacks on marginalized community residents who need relief, assaults on humanitarian associates, threats of illegal activities, and deception. According to the Overseas Security Advisory Council (OSAC) of the U.S. Department of State, "with a lack of assets for cybersecurity programs, humanitarian efforts are more exposed to system breaches, and malicious hackers frequently regard humanitarian organizations as an obvious mark." These ethical concerns must be considered because any of these breaches could damage confidentiality and harm (de Jong et al., 2019) (Figure 3.11).

Figure 3.11. A cybersecurity program (Source: Prescient Solutions, Creative Commons License).

When it relates the humanitarian work ethically, openness is crucial. Organizations have a policy that states that community members own the data they collect from them. For various agencies to have faith in Organizations, they must be confident that we would "disclose" pertinent data when it is suitable, according to Organizations' Open Information Policy.

This can be challenging when information is kept and made available online, especially when it is expressed in a format that is not understood by the people from whom the data was acquired. OCHA advises organizations to establish means by which these populations can freely enjoy their right to receive correct, current data, even if doing so necessitates a "low-tech" solution. Additionally, they must be made aware of the privacy statement and provided information on filing concerns and changing the data (Rivera-Romero et al., 2020).

3.6 ORGANIZATIONS EXPERIENCE

Performing in the humanitarian context is not exempt from data security and confidentiality concerns. Data security is primarily a human issue, despite the temptation to immediately turn to technology as a cure. It includes the collection of human data through human-managed systems. Confidential information, data about a person's sensitivities, and PII have all been gathered by the NGO community for a long time. Still, they frequently have not yet been handled correctly and shared properly. The exposure risk is rising dramatically as more and more information is being collected electronically (Chua et al., 2018).

In development and humanitarian situations, organizations' approaches to data security and protection can be applied in one of two aspects: we can attempt to pin down and take control of everything, or we can collaborate to empower others to make informed decisions and accomplish tasks as safely as feasible. Both possibilities speak to the kind of organization World Vision intends to be and call for clear choices and investments. Organizations endeavor to collaborate with partners for the welfare of our recipients, following our basic values30. Knowing the problems that professionals encounter is crucial to handle moral data protection considerations when providing community-based programs or conducting humanitarian assistance (Haney et al., 2018).

3.6.1 Efficiently Working Within a Regulatory Environment

If one explores the world, one finds a variety of regulatory and legal systems managing the confidentiality and security of data. Yet, basic privacy measures are usually in a place that aligns with human rights standards. WHO said that 73 of the 116 member nations in the healthcare field had established national digital health strategies, which generally consider data safety and confidentiality as well as ethical considerations. However, there are indications that these policies' execution may not be successful. Despite having restrictive laws in place, a new assessment that analyzed present behavior regarding digital reproductive, maternal, and child health records found that preventive measures of data and adherence to fundamental privacy laws were insufficient. Knowing these policy frameworks and operating within them are essential to implementing effective ICT4D, given our joint duty to integrate with national data systems (Mallaburn & Eyre, 2014).

Our current evaluation found that mHealth project teams have various degrees of competence to support government colleagues, identify gaps in regulatory and legal structures, assist in formulating policy, and enhance its execution. Teams with well-developed collaborating capabilities and equitable involvement from IT and healthcare professionals through unofficial engagement protocols (advisory or analytical boards/committees, working groups for developing policy, and active participation at consensus-building events) have the most successful professional relationships (Fabrizio et al., 2007).

3.6.2 Risks Regarding 'Consent'

Recipients of humanitarian assistance are usually questioned before receiving services to collect data. This calls into doubt whether recipients truly provided "permission." Taking permission falls on a scale between uninformed and informed agreement; generally speaking, we are closer to uninformed permission than we would like to be. Humanitarian professionals are discovering this. The issue is defining the essential nature of "consent" that recipients must accept:

a) Acceptance of the usage of data for the intended purpose?
b) Do you have permission to share this information with others, and for what purpose?
c) Who is in charge of selecting the best time and parties with whom to disclose the data?
d) Given the type of information received, what level of risk exists for the recipient (e.g., involves verification of a trait that may be ostracizing, prohibited, or otherwise causes serious issues for that person should data security be compromised)?

We also need to consider the psychological impact of disaster/traumatic events on a person's decision-making ability. How does this influence the process of obtaining consent, and in particular, is some level of coercion unavoidable (Gustafson et al., 1994)?

3.6.3 Different Uses of Information

A growing range of attributes (such as wealth, education, religion, health status, etc.) is included in data sets due to consumer requests for data on an expanding range of indicators. Such data sets can offer useful information to help target programs or humanitarian efforts and safeguard recipients in vulnerable environments. Data could be used to target vulnerabilities legitimately or to be accessible, but it may also be exclusive or discriminatory. In this context, the following difficult questions are posed:

a) Would sharing decrease if we decided to use data exclusively for the reasons it was obtained?

b) How can we ensure that top decision-makers are engaged in using and exchanging information that was originally acquired for one reason but is now being evaluated to be applied in a different way? And how can we accomplish this without micromanaging?

c) How many employees are advised when and how to share information with outside parties? A common request is for data sharing with the local or federal authorities, but it can also include other sorts of collaborators, such as outside academics.

It is crucial for humanitarian Organizations to properly establish which employees (or staff levels or jobs) require access to specific data sets. Very likely, no employee needs access to all the information. Further guidelines should be tailored to the specific country's circumstances regarding data sharing across authorities and borders. Companies should only provide the data elements necessary to fulfill their requirements when transferring information with outside parties. This does not entail concealing all program-level evaluations, analyzing data, and influencing statistics, but it does require being more deliberate regarding when and how to provide this data.

On the contrary, synchronization of information standards is a rising trend that substantially improves data sharing or real compatibility among information systems in the healthcare field, where open access to data is considered as beneficial. In addition to calling for open data standards, the global community has proposed employing fundamental semantic and syntactic norms to implement these norms. A global consensus regarding data privacy and security measures has been hindered by the variety of national settings that influence legislative and ethical structures regarding information privacy and personal rights. Still, recent advancements in this field are promising (Peterson & Pitz, 1988).

3.6.4 Concerns of Data Holder and Privacy

Who do we consider to be the recipient's data holder? Are organizations the owner? If yes, what does it imply, and what obligations does it impose? What data rights do beneficiaries have? Can a recipient come to any of our offices and request to examine all the information we have had on them, including who it has been discussed with? This is currently not an easy thing to do. Recipients will eventually have far more power over who has their personal information, but this won't happen until there is a significant organizational and sectoral shift. On the contrary, the health industry has a rising tendency toward having de-identified data openly accessible for collaboration and exchanging scientific information. The ownership of data and this idea have not yet been fully harmonized (Lwin et al., 2007).

3.6.5 Digital Development in Data Security

The Digital Development Principles program and subsequent global discussion have made it clear that innovators employed by healthcare organizations must consider data privacy and security when developing solutions. According to the EU advice on this, privacy concerns of the application must be taken into account at every development phase and everywhere the consumer is offered a decision (Somani et al., 2010).

3.6.6 Biometrics Usage

Measuring natural human features, such as fingerprints or face detection, is known as biometrics. Regrettably, most NGOs lack an organizational approach to biometrics and are frequently required to deploy the usage of biometrics at the request of donors. In some clearly defined situations, complete personal identity assurance is required by ethics. One such circumstance is the organizations' participation in a Sierra Leonean Ebola vaccine trial. In this instance, ethical guidelines advise that researchers ensure the distribution of a medicine trial to the intended user before it is used. When there are many individuals, biometrics can build confidence and considerably speed up the procedure. It does not necessarily make sense to employ biometrics or any other technical development solely since it is possible. Companies must create their perspectives on biometrics and clarify their use case (Hossain & Al Hasan, 2022).

3.6.7 A Cash-Based Technology

Most programs organizations work on involve data collection, analysis, and production. Yet, the current trend toward more cash-based software forces a company to reconsider the kinds of data we gather and how we use the data. We are working closely with official financial service companies with standardized and strictly controlled systems and processes as cash-based programs age. We frequently need to gather data categorized as personally identifiable information to verify their existence when we send cash to recipients using these systems. We frequently have to transfer all or a portion of the data we gather with other parties. To ensure that practices for shared data conformance with international standards and relevant national policies destined to protect the confidentiality and safety of data, we must completely comprehend this procedure so that we are aware of what information requires to be communicated.

ICT solution development in the humanitarian sector must carefully balance the recipient's privacy rights and the requirement to eliminate deception or, in some situations, to react to information requests submitted under cover of terrorism (Maitland & Boyd, 2001).

3.6.8 Geo-Coded Information: A Specified Set of Problems

The application of geo-coded data is gaining popularity and has established itself as a valuable analytical tool in several development-related fields. Maps can effectively demonstrate intricate designs. But with such a potent weapon come worries about data confidentiality and safety. This is especially true for the health and demographic surveys, where methods have been devised to "de-identify" geo-coded data by adding a small but predictable degree of random spatial variation, only slightly altering statistical models. Organizations have included geo-coded data collecting in some management areas, but only up to now to identify and monitor the location of important local assets, such as improved water sources or basic medical facilities. Geocode descriptors may be used at the home level, although no clear standards exist (Matthews et al., 2005).

3.6.9 Fixing Gaps in Regulations and Guidance

Organizations have several ethical standards concerning the Partnership Policy on Data Security and the Partnership Policy on Global Data Protection and Privacy. Recent updates and dissemination of guidance about the gathering of regular monitoring data:

Ethics Quick Reference Guide: The particular ethical guidelines that should be observed when gathering both quantitative and qualitative information from children are outlined in this manual. These specifications, outlined in the organization's child protection principles, ensure that our procedures don't endanger kids more than they help them. From the perspective of regular assessment and more intensive research, rules that provide guidelines on data-gathering ethics are now being revised (Shneiderman, 2020).

These principles are a good place to start, yet there is potential for development in terms of policy and actual operational advice. Some places for development are as follows:

The need for virtual private networks (VPNs) should be improved and made more regular;

a) Decreasing document sharing on skype;
b) Decreasing the variety of offices by using uncertain wireless internet;
c) Raising the variety of backups, hard drives, and databases that are encoded data;
d) Making the use of security tools to improve the caliber of passwords that Staff members use;
e) policy establishing the conditions under which data should be de-identified, outlining the degrees of user access for de-identified

information for company intelligence purposes, and governing easy accessibility to these datasets;

f) Practical advice on the creation of de-identified datasets, particularly geocoded information, and techniques to record when information use contracts are necessary (e.g., providing data access to other scholars);

g) Defining the agency's perspective on telehealth, juncture diagnostics and other monitoring techniques, epidemic monitoring, and the efficiency of the supply chains for drugs and other goods

h) Improved instruction on how to find and execute country-specific information confidentiality regulations for frontline personnel would include uniformity in how we handle information sharing and retention, taking into account the following:

1. all surveys data with personally identifiable data is stored locally in a local database;
2. storing extremely confidential material locally in secured databases;
3. Personal data and digital identities are kept on the internet under well-maintained barriers.

The International Committee of the Red Cross' Guidelines on Personal Data Security, Oxfam's Data Security Strategy, Oxfam's Data Privacy Policy, and the Data Commissioner's Office's Privacy in Mobile Applications are just a few of the important industrial standards that help to direct our work in along with internal rules and regulations. Lastly, if regulations and recommendations are inadequately conveyed, they can easily end up in the data graveyard, no matter how effective. We must constantly communicate our current policies and seek to make them better. The personnel should be informed of our rules, their details, and how they apply to their jobs (Greenberg, 2020).

3.6.10 Prediction of Tomorrow's Technology

It's crucial to remember that as the developmental and humanitarian communities attempt to deal with the effects of modern new technology, we should also consider the future. Innovations like Blockchain are revolutionizing financial services in the humanitarian sector, but they are also extending outside financial information and will change data management over the next decade or so. Information and communication technologies can revolutionize employment in the health industry through ongoing developments in low-cost, portable diagnostic purposes and quick screening tools.

We must comprehend these technologies, evaluate their possible benefits and risks to our recipients regarding data safety and confidentiality, and always uphold the highest moral standards (Rhoen, 2017).

ACTIVITY 3.1

Suppose you are the Chief Information Security Officer (CISO) for a healthcare organization that manages sensitive patient data. How would you ensure that the organization is compliant with relevant data protection regulations such as the Health Insurance Portability and Accountability Act (HIPAA) and the General Data Protection Regulation (GDPR)? What specific security measures and controls would you implement to protect the confidentiality, integrity, and availability of patient data, and how would you ensure that all personnel involved in the handling of data are trained and aware of their responsibilities? Provide a real-world example to illustrate your answer.

SUMMARY

The chapter "Security and Compliance in Data Protection" explores various aspects related to data security, confidentiality, and compliance with regulations. The chapter begins by discussing concerns related to authorization of data security, highlighting the importance of implementing secure and authorized access controls to protect sensitive data. It then goes on to discuss rules and regulations about data center management, emphasizing the need for organizations to comply with various data protection regulations.

The chapter also highlights the significance of having a robust data protection, confidentiality, and security structure to safeguard sensitive information against unauthorized access, theft, or loss. The concept of ethical considerations in data center management is also discussed, emphasizing the importance of maintaining ethical standards in managing sensitive data.

Finally, the chapter presents real-world examples of organizations' experiences related to data center management, highlighting the challenges they faced and the strategies they implemented to overcome these challenges. Overall, the chapter provides a comprehensive overview of various aspects related to data security, confidentiality, and compliance, offering insights and best practices to organizations for effectively managing their data centers.

REVIEW QUESTIONS

1. What are the concerns related to the authorization of data security?
2. What are the rules and regulations about data center management?
3. Why is data protection, confidentiality, and security structure important?
4. How do ethical considerations play a role in data center management?
5. What experiences have organizations had related to data center management?
6. What measures can be taken to ensure compliance with data protection regulations and standards?

MULTIPLE CHOICE QUESTIONS

1. What are the concerns related to the authorization of data security?

a) Data privacy
b) Unauthorized access
c) Data loss
d) All of the above

2. What are the rules and regulations about data center management?

a) HIPAA
b) GDPR

c) CCPA
d) All of the above

3. **Why is data protection, confidentiality and security structure important?**
   a) To prevent data breaches and leaks
   b) To protect sensitive information
   c) To comply with legal requirements
   d) All of the above
4. **What is the concept of ethical considerations in data center management?**
   a) Adhering to ethical principles and values in data management practices
   b) Providing preferential treatment to certain types of data
   c) Limiting access to certain data for personal gain
   d) None of the above
5. **What is an organization's experience related to data center management?**
   a) The organization's ability to manage and protect data
   b) The organization's financial success
   c) The organization's physical security measures
   d) None of the above
6. **What is the purpose of data protection?**
   a) To ensure the confidentiality of information
   b) To prevent data breaches
   c) To comply with legal requirements
   d) All of the above
7. **What is the difference between confidentiality and data security?**
   a) Confidentiality is the protection of sensitive data, while data security is the protection of all data.
   b) Confidentiality is the protection of data from unauthorized access, while data security is the protection of data from loss or damage.
   c) Confidentiality is the protection of data from loss or damage, while data security is the protection of data from unauthorized access.
   d) None of the above.
8. **What is the purpose of a data protection officer (DPO)?**
   a) To ensure that data processing activities comply with data protection laws
   b) To ensure that data processing activities are profitable
   c) To ensure that data processing activities are efficient
   d) None of the above

9. **Which of the following is an example of a data breach?**
   a) An employee loses a USB drive containing sensitive data
   b) A hacker gains unauthorized access to a database
   c) A customer accidentally deletes an important file
   d) All of the above
10. **Which of the following is not a common data protection regulation?**
   a) HIPAA
   b) GDPR
   c) SOX
   d) LAN

Answers to Multiple Choice Questions

1. (d)	2. (d)	3. (d)	4. (a)	5. (a)
6. (d)	7. (b)	8. (a)	9. (b)	10. (d)

REFERENCES

1. Aldossary, S., & Allen, W. (2016). Data security, privacy, availability and integrity in cloud computing: issues and current solutions. International Journal of Advanced Computer Science and Applications. 7(4), 1–15.
2. Ali, B., Gregory, M. A., & Li, S. (2021). Multi-access edge computing architecture, data security and privacy: A review. IEEE Access, 9, 18706–18721.
3. Binkley, J. W. (2016). Fair notice of unfair practices: Due process in FTC data security enforcement after Wyndham. Berkeley Tech. LJ, 31, 1050–1079.
4. Bryant, J. (2020). Africa in the Information Age: Challenges, Opportunities, and Strategies for Data Protection and Digital Rights. Stan. Tech. L. Rev., 24, 389.
5. Chen, J., Ma, H., & Zhao, D. (2017). Private data aggregation with integrity assurance and fault tolerance for mobile crowd-sensing. Wireless Networks, 23, 131–144.
6. Chua, H. N., Wong, S. F., Low, Y. C., & Chang, Y. (2018). Impact of employees' demographic characteristics on the awareness and compliance of information security policy in organizations. Telematics and Informatics, 35(6), 1770–1780.
7. Clifton, C., & Marks, D. (1996, May). Security and privacy implications of data mining. In ACM SIGMOD Workshop on Research Issues on Data Mining and Knowledge Discovery (Vol. 1, pp. 15–19).
8. Culhane, D. P. (2016). The potential of linked administrative data for advancing homelessness research and policy. European Journal of Homelessness. 10(3), 11–21.
9. de Jong, B. C., Gaye, B. M., Luyten, J., van Buitenen, B., André, E., Meehan, C.

J., ... & Antonio, M. (2019). Ethical considerations for movement mapping to identify disease transmission hotspots. Emerging Infectious Diseases. 25(7), 1–24.

10. Dogruel, L., Joeckel, S., & Vitak, J. (2017). The valuation of privacy premium features for smartphone apps: The influence of defaults and expert recommendations. Computers in Human Behavior, 77, 230–239.
11. Ezeokoli, F. O., Ugochukwu, S. C., Agu, N. N., & Akabogu, S. C. (2016). An assessment of the use, benefits and challenges of the 'cash-lite' policy, for construction projects In Anambra State, Nigeria. European Scientific Journal. 12(16), 1–17.
12. Fabrizio, K. R., Rose, N. L., & Wolfram, C. D. (2007). Do markets reduce costs? Assessing the impact of regulatory restructuring on US electric generation efficiency. American Economic Review, 97(4), 1250–1277.
13. Felici, M., Koulouris, T., & Pearson, S. (2013, December). Accountability for data governance in cloud ecosystems. In 2013 IEEE 5th International Conference on Cloud Computing Technology and Science. IEEE. (Vol. 2, pp. 327–332).
14. Fernando, Y., Chidambaram, R. R., & Wahyuni-TD, I. S. (2018). The impact of Big Data analytics and data security practices on service supply chain performance. Benchmarking: An International Journal, 25(9), 4009–4034.
15. Greenberg, D. (2020). Humpty Dumpty rides again: Using voluntary guidance to fill gaps in legislation. Statute Law Review, 41(3), 3–5.
16. Gustafson, K. E., McNamara, J. R., & Jensen, J. A. (1994). Parents' informed consent decisions regarding psychotherapy for their children: Consideration of therapeutic risks and benefits. Professional Psychology: Research and Practice, 25(1), 16.
17. Haney, J. M., Theofanos, M., Acar, Y., & Prettyman, S. S. (2018, August). "We make it a big deal in the company": Security Mindsets in Organizations that Develop Cryptographic Products. In SOUPS@ USENIX Security Symposium (Vol. 1, pp. 357–373).
18. Hartzog, W., & Richards, N. (2020). Privacy's constitutional moment and the limits of data protection. BCL Rev., 61, 1687.
19. Hendre, A., & Joshi, K. P. (2015, June). A semantic approach to cloud security and compliance. In 2015 IEEE 8th International Conference on Cloud Computing. IEEE. (Vol. 1, pp. 1081–1084).
20. Hossain, M. A., & Al Hasan, M. A. (2022). Improving cloud data security through hybrid verification technique based on biometrics and encryption system. International Journal of Computers and Applications, 44(5), 455–464.
21. Hu, H., & Ahn, G. J. (2011). Multiparty authorization framework for data sharing in online social networks. In Data and Applications Security and Privacy XXV: 25th Annual IFIP WG 11.3 Conference, DBSec 2011, Richmond, VA, USA, July 11–13, 2011. Proceedings 25. Springer Berlin Heidelberg. (Vol. 1, pp. 29–43).
22. Huang, Q., Yang, Y., & Wang, L. (2018). Correction to "secure data access control with ciphertext update and computation outsourcing in fog computing for Internet of Things." IEEE Access, 6, 17245–17245.

23. Hudson, M., Garrison, N. A., Sterling, R., Caron, N. R., Fox, K., Yracheta, J., ... & Carroll, S. R. (2020). Rights, interests and expectations: Indigenous perspectives on unrestricted access to genomic data. Nature Reviews Genetics, 21(6), 377–384.
24. Hutchings, A., Smith, R. G., & James, L. (2013). Cloud computing for small business: Criminal and security threats and prevention measures. Trends and issues in Crime and Criminal Justice, (456), 1–8.
25. Kalaiprasath, R., Elankavi, R., & Udayakumar, R. (2017). Cloud security and compliance-a semantic approach in end to end security. International Journal on Smart Sensing and Intelligent Systems, 10(5), 482–494.
26. Kinkela, K. (2013). Practical and ethical considerations on the use of cloud computing in accounting. Journal of Finance and Accountancy, 14, 1–2.
27. Kosseff, J. (2016). Positive cybersecurity law: Creating a consistent and incentive-based system. Chap. L. Rev., 19, 401.
28. Kung, A., Kargl, F., Suppan, S., Cuellar, J., Pöhls, H. C., Kapovits, A., ... & Martin, Y. S. (2017). A privacy engineering framework for the internet of things. Data Protection and Privacy: (In)visibilities and Infrastructures. 2(3), 163–202.
29. Lavy, S. (2014). Supervisor security provision: Correlates and related mechanisms. Psychological reports, 114(3), 758–783.
30. Lwin, M., Wirtz, J., & Williams, J. D. (2007). Consumer online privacy concerns and responses: a power–responsibility equilibrium perspective. Journal of the Academy of Marketing Science, 35, 572–585.
31. Maitland, G., & Boyd, C. (2001, November). Fair electronic cash based on a group signature scheme. In ICICS (Vol. 1, pp. 461–465).
32. Mallaburn, P. S., & Eyre, N. (2014). Lessons from energy efficiency policy and programmes in the UK from 1973 to 2013. Energy Efficiency, 7, 23–41.
33. Matinmikko, M., Latva-aho, M., Ahokangas, P., & Seppänen, V. (2018). On regulations for 5G: Micro licensing for locally operated networks. Telecommunications Policy, 42(8), 622–635.
34. Matthews, S. A., Detwiler, J. E., & Burton, L. M. (2005). Geo-ethnography: Coupling geographic information analysis techniques with ethnographic methods in urban research. Cartographica: The International Journal for Geographic Information and Geovisualization, 40(4), 75–90.
35. McCrohan, K. F., Engel, K., & Harvey, J. W. (2010). Influence of awareness and training on cyber security. Journal of internet Commerce, 9(1), 23–41.
36. Morison, K., Wang, L., & Kundur, P. (2004). Power system security assessment. IEEE power and energy magazine, 2(5), 30–39.
37. Nardone, R., Rodríguez, R. J., & Marrone, S. (2016, December). Formal security assessment of Modbus protocol. In 2016 11th International Conference for Internet Technology and Secured transactions (ICITST) IEEE. (Vol. 2, pp. 142–147).
38. Nguyen, P. H., Klein, J., Le Traon, Y., & Kramer, M. E. (2013, December). A systematic

review of model-driven security. In 2013 20th Asia-Pacific Software Engineering Conference (APSEC). IEEE. (Vol. 1, pp. 432–441).

39. Nicol, D. M. (2005). Modeling and simulation in security evaluation. IEEE security & privacy, 3(5), 71–74.
40. Peters, R. M. (2014). So you've been notified, now what: The problem with current data-breach notification laws. Ariz. L. Rev., 56, 1171.
41. Peterson, D. K., & Pitz, G. F. (1988). Confidence, uncertainty, and the use of information. Journal of Experimental Psychology: Learning, Memory, and Cognition, 14(1), 85.
42. Prinsloo, P., & Slade, S. (2013, April). An evaluation of policy frameworks for addressing ethical considerations in learning analytics. In Proceedings of the Third International Conference on Learning Analytics and Knowledge (Vol. 3, pp. 240–244).
43. Radecka, A., Loughlin, L., Foy, M., de Ferraz Guimaraes, M. V., Sarinic, V. M., Di Giusti, M. D., ... & Raine, J. (2018). Enhancing pharmacovigilance capabilities in the EU regulatory network: the SCOPE joint action. Drug safety, 41, 1285–1302.
44. Rhoen, M. (2017). Rear view mirror, crystal ball: Predictions for the future of data protection law based on the history of environmental protection law. Computer Law and Security Review, 33(5), 603–617.
45. Rigg, T. (2018). The ethical considerations of storing client information online. Professional Psychology: Research and Practice, 49(5–6), 332.
46. Rivera-Romero, O., Konstantinidis, S., Denecke, K., Gabarrón, E., Petersen, C., Househ, M., ... & Mayer, M. Á. (2020). Ethical considerations for participatory health through social media: healthcare workforce and policy maker perspectives. Yearbook of Medical Informatics, 29(1), 71–76.
47. Roege, P. E., Collier, Z. A., Chevardin, V., Chouinard, P., Florin, M. V., Lambert, J. H., ... & Todorovic, B. (2017). Bridging the gap from cyber security to resilience. In Resilience and Risk: Methods and Application in Environment, Cyber and Social Domains. Springer Netherlands (Vol. 1, pp. 383–414).
48. Ryutov, T., & Neuman, C. (2002, June). The specification and enforcement of advanced security policies. In Proceedings Third International Workshop on Policies for Distributed Systems and Networks. IEEE. (Vol. 1, pp. 128–138).
49. Safdar, N. M., Banja, J. D., & Meltzer, C. C. (2020). Ethical considerations in artificial intelligence. European journal of radiology, 122, 708–768.
50. Shen, F., Sun, R., Yao, J., Li, J., Liu, Q., Price, N. D., ... & Wang, Z. (2019). OptRAM: In-silico strain design via integrative regulatory-metabolic network modeling. PLoS computational biology, 15(3), 23–50.
51. Shin, J., Son, H., & Heo, G. (2017). Cyber security risk evaluation of a nuclear I&C using BN and ET. Nuclear Engineering and Technology, 49(3), 517–524.
52. Shiraz, Z., & Aldrich, R. J. (2019). Secrecy, spies and the global South: intelligence studies beyond the 'Five Eyes' alliance. International Affairs, 95(6), 1313–1329.

53. Shneiderman, B. (2020). Bridging the gap between ethics and practice: guidelines for reliable, safe, and trustworthy human-centered AI systems. ACM Transactions on Interactive Intelligent Systems (TiiS), 10(4), 1–31.
54. Shou, D. (2012). Ethical considerations of sharing data for cybersecurity research. In Financial Cryptography and Data Security: FC 2011 Workshops, RLCPS and WECSR 2011, Rodney Bay, St. Lucia, February 28-March 4, 2011, Revised Selected Papers 15. Springer Berlin Heidelberg. (Vol. 1, pp. 169–177)
55. Shrivastava, U., Song, J., Han, B. T., & Dietzman, D. (2021). Do data security measures, privacy regulations, and communication standards impact the interoperability of patient health information? A cross-country investigation. International Journal of Medical Informatics, 148, 104–110.
56. Somani, U., Lakhani, K., & Mundra, M. (2010, October). Implementing digital signature with RSA encryption algorithm to enhance the Data Security of cloud in Cloud Computing. In 2010 First International Conference On Parallel, Distributed and Grid Computing (PDGC 2010). IEEE. (pp. 211–216).
57. Stanberry, B. (1998). The legal and ethical aspects of telemedicine. 2: Data protection, security and European law. Journal of Telemedicine and Telecare, 4(1), 18–24.
58. Steinhart, G. (2006). Libraries as distributors of geospatial data: Data management policies as tools for managing partnerships. Library Trends, 55(2), 264–284.
59. Stigler, B., & Chamberlin, H. M. (2012). A regulatory network modeled from wild-type gene expression data guides functional predictions in Caenorhabditis elegans development. BMC systems biology, 6(1), 1–15.
60. Tikkinen-Piri, C., Rohunen, A., & Markkula, J. (2018). EU General Data Protection Regulation: Changes and implications for personal data collecting companies. Computer Law & Security Review, 34(1), 134–153.
61. Urnov, F. D. (2003). Chromatin remodeling as a guide to transcriptional regulatory networks in mammals. Journal of Cellular Biochemistry, 88(4), 684–694.
62. Wang, W., & Lu, Z. (2013). Cyber security in the smart grid: Survey and challenges. Computer Networks, 57(5), 1344–1371.
63. Weber, R. H. (2010). Internet of Things–New security and privacy challenges. Computer Law & Security Review, 26(1), 23–30.
64. Wiczorek, R., & Zirk, A. (2019). Using warning systems with adaptable thresholds: Choice of security level, compliance and performance in a simulated computer security task. International Journal of Human-Computer Studies, 125, 32–40.
65. Wu, F., & Tsai, Y. K. (1983). Probabilistic dynamic security assessment of power systems-I: Basic model. IEEE Transactions on Circuits and Systems, 30(3), 148–159.
66. Zerlang, J. (2017). GDPR: a milestone in convergence for cyber-security and compliance. Network Security, 2017(6), 8–11.

CHAPTER 4

MONITORING AND MANAGEMENT TOOLS

UNIT INTRODUCTION

Data centers are complex and delicate environments. They are made of thousands of different components performing different operations, from servers, network devices, storage, virtual machines, to cooling and power units (Hazır, 2015) (Figure 4.1).

All components interconnected through underground or top-of-the-rack cabling and connected to power distribution units. IT managers & NOC Engineers struggle to keep control of every single detail in their data center infrastructure (Rakhmonov & Kurbonov, 2020).

Most of the time, they are running their data centers with tools such as Excel and Visio. But running a sophisticated facility with a spreadsheet is a recipe for disaster.

Here is our list of the best Data Center Management Software for NOC operators:

1. SolarWinds Network Performance Monitor: A platform of services that offer network and device monitoring with specialist modules for different equipment and services on your network. Buy all of the units or just select one or two to provide all your network monitoring needs. Runs on Windows Server.
2. Paessler PRTG Network Monitor: This bundle includes a large number of monitoring tools for networks, servers, and applications. You tailor the package by deciding which sensors to turn on. Runs on Windows Server (Harmel et al., 2009).

3. ManageEngine OpManager: A software package that provides monitoring tools for physical and virtual services on a network. Watch over your network devices and monitor your hypervisors with this package. Available for Windows Server and Linux.
4. NLyte Software: Watch over all of your data center infrastructure with this monitoring package that includes hardware and services performance tracking. This is a SaaS platform.
5. Kaseya VSA: This is a remote monitoring and management package (RMM) aimed at managed service providers that includes all of the technician tools needed to watch over and run the systems of clients. This is a SaaS platform (Jones et al., 2016).
6. Device42: this system monitoring platform is centered around a discovery and mapping module that creates an asset inventory. Get live monitoring of all discovered devices with this virtual appliance that installs on cloud platforms, Citrix, VMWare, or Hyper-V.
7. Zabbix: This free system monitoring package covers networks, servers, and applications. It searches the network for all devices and creates a network topology map and then starts live monitoring. Runs on Linux.
8. Nagios: A monitoring package for networks servers, and applications that can be extended by thousands of free plugins. Available in free and paid versions, this package installs on Linux or on Windows over a hypervisor (Hernantes et al., 2015).

NOC Engineers need software capable of planning for capacity, inventorying, maximizing uptime, unifying visibility, automation, reporting, and more.

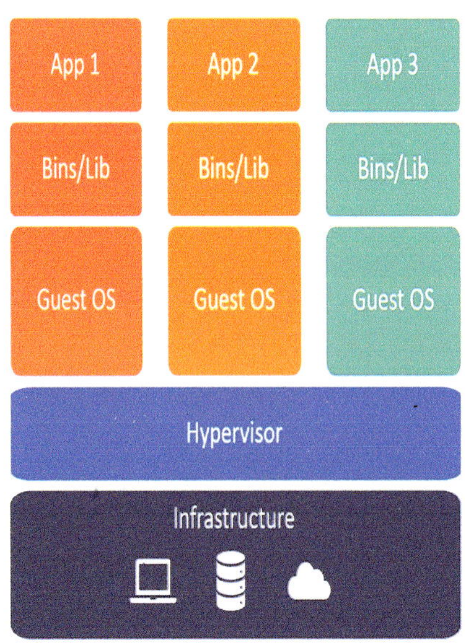

Figure 4.1. Illustration of virtual machines (Source: Weave works, Creative Commons License).

Learning Objectives

At the end of the chapter, the reader will be able to understand:

1. The tools of data center management
2. The advantages/benefits of data center management softwares
3. The concept of server management software, storage management softwares and network management softwares
4. The significance of configuration management softwares
5. The importance of virtualization software
6. The process of selecting best tool of data center management

Key Terms

1. DCIM (Data Center Infrastructure Management)
2. Vendor Lock In
3. Nagios
4. Zabbix
5. PRTG
6. Storage Management
7. Storage Resource Management

4.1 DATA CENTER MANAGEMENT TOOLS

This software is built to provide daily insights into the operations and health of the data center. Advanced management software can perform data center tasks automatically.

The software also provides a centralized platform for easy access and management of the infrastructure and services (Gupta et al., 2011). It can help different IT departments within an organization such as DevOps, Infrastructure, Networking, etc. to collaborate and work from a single platform. The most common type of data center management software is known as the DCIM (Data Center Infrastructure Management), which focuses only on the infrastructure. Other tools can be broader and provide information on other elements such as network, storage, virtual, and applications. These same tools can also give you access to alerting, reporting, automation, and more capabilities (Figure 4.2).

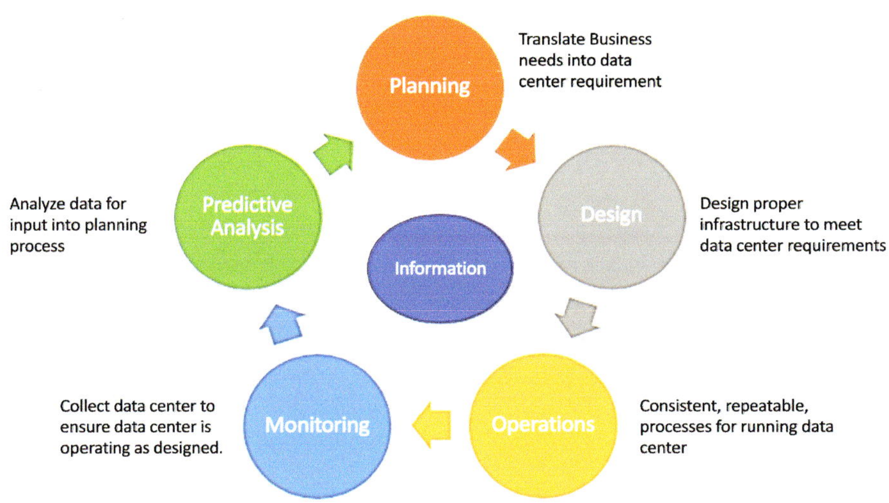

Figure 4.2. Schematic of DCIM (Data Center Infrastructure Management) (Source: my network insights, Creative Commons License).

4.2 DATA CENTER MANAGEMENT SOFTWARE SERVICES

On a basic level, data center management software should be capable of providing the following:

1. Node details: Display device information such as status, vendor, IP, type, system name, etc.
2. Unified visibility: Get a centralized view across all the elements in the data center.

3. Layouts and maps: Get a graphical 2D or 3D representation of the data center room, its cabinet layout, and the cabling.
4. Configuration and change: Document and monitor configuration and changes (Beloglazov & Buyya, 2010).
5. Environment: Manage and monitor the power, and environmental factors of your data center.
6. Automate processes: Automate common processes like scheduling, backups, compliance checks, node discovery, etc.

Other comprehensive data center management software can provide additional information that popular DCIM products cannot, such as:

1. Network management: Monitor and manage different multi-vendor data center network technologies.
2. Compute infrastructure: Manage your entire on-premises physical and virtual computing infrastructure.
3. Manage storage: Keep track and control all your data center storage devices, such as DAS, NAS, or SAN (Putnam et al., 2015).
4. Manage applications: Keep control of your applications deployed in your data center.
5. Reporting and alerting capabilities: Generate reports to gain insights into your data center and get alarms when there is a failure.

Did you Know?

The global data center infrastructure management (DCIM) market size was valued at USD 2.46 billion in 2020 and is expected to grow at a CAGR of 13.3% from 2021 to 2028.

4.3 BENEFITS OF USING DATA CENTER MANAGEMENT SOFTWARE

There are several advantages of using software or tools in data center management. Here are some of the key benefits.

4.3.1 Improved Efficiency

Data center management software can automate many routine tasks such as server provisioning, configuration management, and patch management, freeing up IT staff to focus on more strategic initiatives (Wang et al., 2010). This can lead to improved efficiency and productivity.

4.3.2 Enhanced Visibility

Software tools can provide real-time visibility into the performance of servers, storage, and networking equipment. This can help IT staff identify and troubleshoot issues quickly, before they become major problems.

Remember

Regularly check and update your monitoring and management tools to ensure they are effectively tracking and optimizing your system's performance.

4.3.3 Increased Security

Data center management software can help organizations maintain a secure environment by automating security policies, detecting and alerting on security threats, and ensuring compliance with industry regulations (Greenberg et al., 2008).

4.3.4 Cost Savings

Automation and improved efficiency can lead to cost savings by reducing the need for manual labor and minimizing downtime.

4.3.5 Scalability

As organizations grow and their IT infrastructure expands, data center management software can help ensure that the infrastructure is able to scale to meet changing business needs.

4.3.6 Standardization

Software tools can help enforce standardization across the data center, ensuring that equipment is configured and managed in a consistent manner, which can improve reliability and reduce the risk of errors (Greenberg et al., 2009).

Overall, data center management software can help organizations optimize their IT infrastructure, reduce costs, and improve reliability and security.

4.4 LIMITATIONS OF USING DATA CENTER MANAGEMENT SOFTWARES

While there are many benefits to using software or tools in data center management, there are also some limitations that organizations should be aware of.

4.4.1 Complexity

Data center management software can be complex and require a significant investment in time and resources to implement and maintain (Shende et al., 2015). In some cases, the cost of the software and the resources needed to implement and maintain it may outweigh the benefits.

4.4.2 Compatibility Issues

Data center management software may not be compatible with all hardware and software systems, which can limit its usefulness.

4.4.3 Training Requirements

Staff may need to be trained on how to use the software effectively, which can be time-consuming and costly.

4.4.4 Security Concerns

Data center management software can be a target for hackers and other cyber criminals. Organizations must take steps to ensure that the software is secure and that sensitive data is protected.

TIPS

Investing in a reliable server management software can save your organization both time and money by streamlining processes and improving overall system performance.

4.4.5 False Sense of Security

While data center management software can provide real-time visibility into the performance of servers, storage, and networking equipment, it is not a substitute for human expertise. IT staff must still be trained and knowledgeable in order to effectively manage the data center (Calheiros et al., 2011).

4.4.6 Vendor Lock-In

Organizations that adopt a particular data center management software may find themselves locked into that vendor's ecosystem, limiting their ability to switch to a different software solution if needed (Beloglazov et al., 2012).

Overall, organizations should carefully evaluate the benefits and limitations of data center management software before making a decision to adopt it (Figure 4.3).

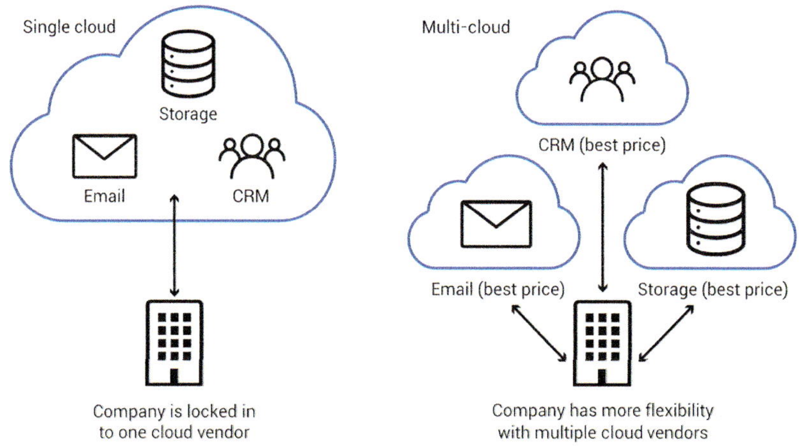

Figure 4.3. Diagram of vendor lock in (Source: The forecast, Creative Commons License).

4.5 SERVER MANAGEMENT SOFTWARE

Server management software is a type of software designed to monitor, manage, and automate the administration of servers within a data center. It provides IT teams with tools to ensure that servers are running efficiently, are secure, and are meeting service level agreements (SLAs) (Sehgal & Ganguli, 2006).

There are several types of server management software, including server monitoring software, server configuration management software, server backup and recovery software, and server virtualization management software (Figure 4.4).

Figure 4.4. Illustration of benefits of Service Level Agreements (SLAs) (Source: Service now, Creative Commons License).

4.5.1 Server Monitoring Software

Server monitoring software is used to monitor the performance of servers in real-time. It provides information on server availability, resource utilization, and application performance (Peng & Wang, 2010). Some popular server monitoring tools include Nagios, Zabbix, and PRTG Network Monitor.

4.5.2 Server Configuration Management Software

Server configuration management software is used to automate the deployment and configuration of servers (White et al., 2005). It allows IT teams to configure servers in a consistent manner, reducing the risk of configuration errors. Some popular server configuration management tools include Puppet, Chef, and Ansible.

4.5.3 Server Backup and Recovery Software

Server backup and recovery software is used to backup server data and recover it in case of a disaster. It ensures that critical data is protected and can be quickly restored in the event of a failure (Moreau, 2006). Some popular server backup and recovery tools include Veeam Backup and Replication, Acronis Backup, and Commvault (Figure 4.5).

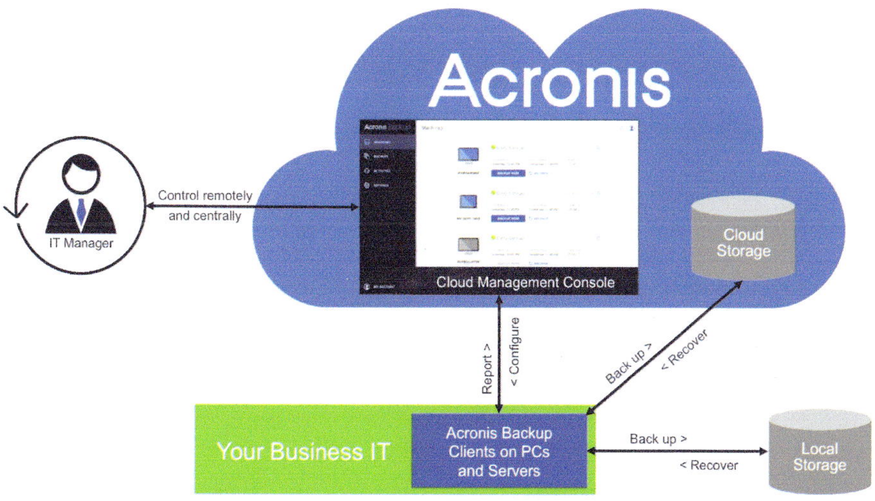

Figure 4.5. Diagram of Acronis Backup (Source: Cloud service, Creative Commons License).

Server management software provides several benefits to IT teams, including improved server performance, automation of routine tasks, improved security, and cost savings. It can help to minimize downtime and ensure that servers are running efficiently. Automation and improved efficiency can lead to cost savings by reducing the need for manual labor (Peifeng et al., 2013). It can also help to ensure that servers are secure by automating security policies, detecting and alerting on security threats, and ensuring compliance with industry regulations.

However, server management software can also present several challenges, including complexity, compatibility issues, training requirements, and security concerns. It can be complex and require a significant investment in time and resources to implement and maintain. It may not be compatible with all hardware and software systems, which can limit its usefulness. Staff may need to be trained on how to use the software effectively, which can be time-consuming and costly. Finally, server management software can be a target for hackers and other cyber criminals. Organizations must take steps to ensure that the software is secure and that sensitive data is protected.

In conclusion, server management software is an essential tool for data center management. It provides IT teams with tools to monitor, manage, and automate the administration of servers. While it presents several challenges, its benefits in terms of improved server performance, automation of routine tasks, improved security, and cost savings make it a valuable investment for any organization.

4.5.4 Benefits of Server Management Software

Server management software provides several benefits to IT teams.

4.5.4.1 Improved Server Performance

Server management software provides real-time monitoring of server performance, allowing IT teams to identify and troubleshoot performance issues quickly. This can help to minimize downtime and ensure that servers are running efficiently (Waters, 2005).

4.5.4.2 Automation of Routine Tasks

Server management software can automate routine tasks such as server provisioning, configuration management, and patch management. This can free up IT staff to focus on more strategic initiatives and improve efficiency.

4.5.4.3 Improved Security

Server management software can help to ensure that servers are secure by automating security policies, detecting and alerting on security threats, and ensuring compliance with industry regulations.

4.5.4.4 Cost Savings

Automation and improved efficiency can lead to cost savings by reducing the need for manual labor and minimizing downtime (Lim et al., 2011).

4.5.5 Challenges of Server Management Software

While server management software provides many benefits, it also presents several challenges.

4.5.5.1 Complexity

Server management software can be complex and require a significant investment in time and resources to implement and maintain (Jammal et al., 2014).

4.5.5.2 Compatibility Issues

Server management software may not be compatible with all hardware and software systems, which can limit its usefulness.

4.5.5.3 Training Requirements

Staff may need to be trained on how to use the software effectively, which can be time-consuming and costly (Weyns, 2017).

4.5.5.4 Security Concerns

Server management software can be a target for hackers and other cyber criminals. Organizations must take steps to ensure that the software is secure and that sensitive data is protected (Hakiri et al., 2014).

Server management software provides many benefits to IT teams, including improved server performance, automation of routine tasks, improved security, and cost savings. However, it also presents several challenges, including complexity, compatibility issues, training requirements, and security concerns. Organizations should carefully evaluate the benefits and challenges of server management software before making a decision to adopt it.

4.6 STORAGE MANAGEMENT SOFTWARE

Storage management software is an essential tool for organizations that require efficient and cost-effective storage of data. It is a type of software that helps manage and optimize the storage of data on computer systems, servers, and other storage devices (Ying & Yong, 2009). In today's digital world, the amount of data generated by organizations is growing at an exponential rate. Therefore, it is crucial to have storage management software to manage data storage efficiently.

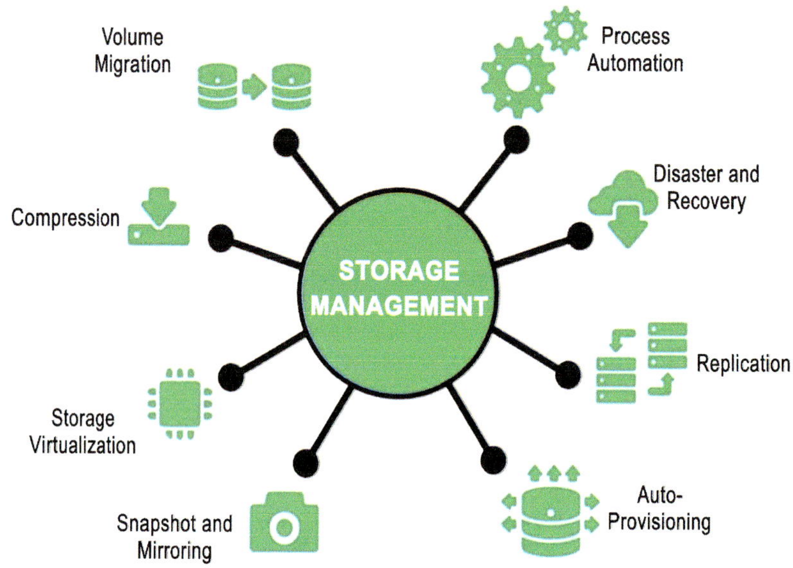

Figure 4.6. Illustration of components of storage management (Source: Marc Wilson, Creative Commons License).

4.6.1 Features of Storage Management Software

The following are the key features of storage management software.

4.6.1.1 Data Backup and Recovery

Data backup and recovery is an essential feature of storage management software (Alba et al., 2014). It allows users to create backup copies of important data and recover it in the event of a disaster or data loss. Backup and recovery software ensures that data is stored safely and can be retrieved quickly when needed.

4.6.1.2 Data Archiving

Data archiving is another feature of storage management software that enables users to store less frequently accessed data on long-term storage devices to free up primary storage resources (Cabrera et al., 1998). Archiving software moves older, inactive data from primary storage to lower-cost secondary storage to reduce costs and free up space.

4.6.1.3 Data Deduplication

Data deduplication is a process that identifies and removes duplicate data to optimize storage space (Kaczmarski et al., 2003).

Deduplication software examines data to identify identical files or blocks of data and stores only one copy, reducing storage requirements.

4.6.1.4 Storage Tiering

Storage tiering is a feature that allows users to assign different types of data to different types of storage devices based on their importance or access frequency. Storage tiering ensures that critical data is stored on faster and more reliable storage devices, while less frequently accessed data is stored on slower and less expensive storage devices.

4.6.1.5 Storage Virtualization

Storage virtualization is a feature that allows users to manage and allocate storage resources across multiple storage devices as a single pool of storage. Virtualization software enables users to allocate storage based on their needs, ensuring that data is stored efficiently and cost-effectively (Ravandi & Papapanagiotou, 2017).

4.6.2 Types of Storage Management Software

There are several types of storage management software available.

4.6.2.1 Backup Software

Backup software is a type of storage management software that creates copies of data to protect against data loss due to hardware failure, cyber-attacks, or natural disasters. Backup software enables organizations to recover data quickly and ensure business continuity (Lakshminarayanan et al., 2013) (Figure 4.7).

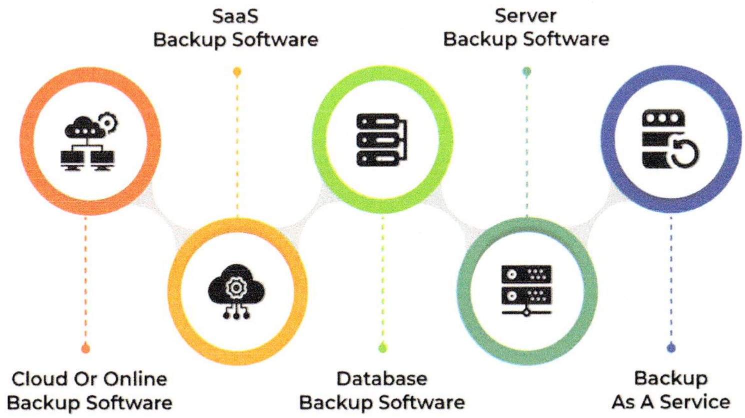

Figure 4.7. Image of types of backup software (Source: Software suggest, Creative Commons License).

4.6.2.2 Archiving Software

Archiving software is a type of storage management software that moves data to lower-cost secondary storage to free up primary storage resources. Archiving software enables organizations to reduce storage costs, improve performance, and ensure compliance with data retention policies.

4.6.2.3 Storage Optimization Software

Storage optimization software is a type of storage management software that optimizes the use of storage resources. This type of software includes data deduplication, compression, and tiering to reduce storage costs and improve performance.

4.6.2.4 Storage Resource Management (SRM) Software

SRM software is a type of storage management software that helps organizations manage storage resources across their entire infrastructure. SRM software provides visibility into storage usage, performance, and capacity, allowing organizations to optimize their storage environment and reduce costs (Waters, 2005).

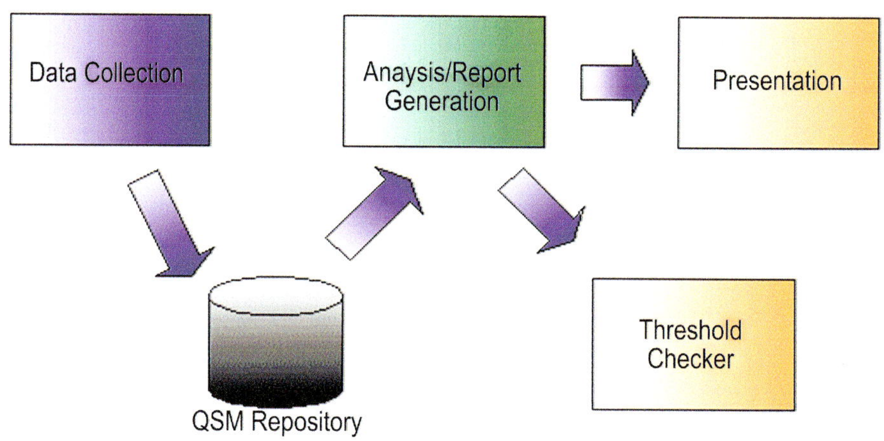

Figure 4.8. Schematic of Storage Resource Management (SRM) (Source: SUPPORT Bull, Creative Commons License).

4.6.3 Benefits of Storage Management Software

The following are the benefits of storage management software.

4.6.3.1 Cost Savings

Storage management software helps organizations save costs by reducing storage requirements, optimizing storage usage, and automating storage management tasks (Lomb et al., 1996).

4.6.3.2 Improved Performance

Storage management software helps organizations improve performance by ensuring that critical data is stored on faster and more reliable storage devices, while less frequently accessed data is stored on slower and less expensive storage devices.

4.6.3.3 Better Data Protection

Storage management software ensures that data is stored safely and can be retrieved quickly when needed, protecting against data loss due to hardware failure, cyber attacks, or natural disasters.

4.6.3.4 Increased Efficiency

Storage management software automates storage management tasks, enabling IT staff to focus on other critical tasks (Brubeck & Rowe, 1996). It also provides visibility into storage usage, performance, and capacity, allowing organizations to optimize their storage environment and reduce costs.

4.6.4 Examples of Storage Management Software

There are many storage management software solutions available in the market.

4.6.4.1 IBM Spectrum Storage

IBM Spectrum Storage is a software-defined storage solution that provides a unified storage platform for organizations. It includes features such as data deduplication, compression, and tiering to reduce storage costs and improve performance (Figure 4.9).

Figure 4.9. Picture of IBM Spectrum storage (Source: Globenet International, Creative Commons License).

4.6.4.2 Dell EMC Unity

Dell EMC Unity is an all-flash storage array that provides high performance and reliability for organizations (Brooks et al., 2006). It includes features such as data deduplication, compression, and tiering to optimize storage usage and reduce costs.

4.6.4.3 NetApp ONTAP

NetApp ONTAP is a storage operating system that provides a unified storage platform for organizations. It includes features such as data deduplication, compression, and tiering to optimize storage usage and reduce costs.

4.6.4.4 HPE 3PAR

HPE 3PAR is a storage array that provides high performance and reliability for organizations. It includes features such as data deduplication, compression, and tiering to optimize storage usage and reduce costs.

Choosing the right storage management software requires careful consideration of various factors such as the organization's storage requirements, budget, and IT infrastructure. Some of the key features to look for when choosing storage management software include:

1. Data backup and recovery
2. Data archiving
3. Data deduplication
4. Storage tiering
5. Storage virtualization
6. Compatibility with existing infrastructure
7. Scalability
8. Ease of use and management (Peters & Keane, 2015)

Storage management software is essential for organizations that require efficient and cost-effective storage of data. It provides various features such as data backup and recovery, data archiving, data deduplication, storage tiering, and storage virtualization to optimize storage usage and reduce costs. By choosing the right storage management software, organizations can improve performance, ensure data protection, and increase efficiency.

4.7 NETWORK MANAGEMENT SOFTWARE

Network Management Software (NMS) is a critical tool for managing complex networks. It is used to monitor and manage network infrastructure, troubleshoot network issues, and ensure optimal performance. NMS provides IT teams with a comprehensive view of the network, allowing them to quickly identify and resolve issues, and optimize network resources (Kim & Feamster, 2013). In this chapter, we will explore the different types of network management software and their features and benefits.

There are different types of network management software available in the market. They can be broadly classified into four categories: network monitoring tools, network performance analysis tools, network configuration management tools, and network security management tools (Figure 4.10).

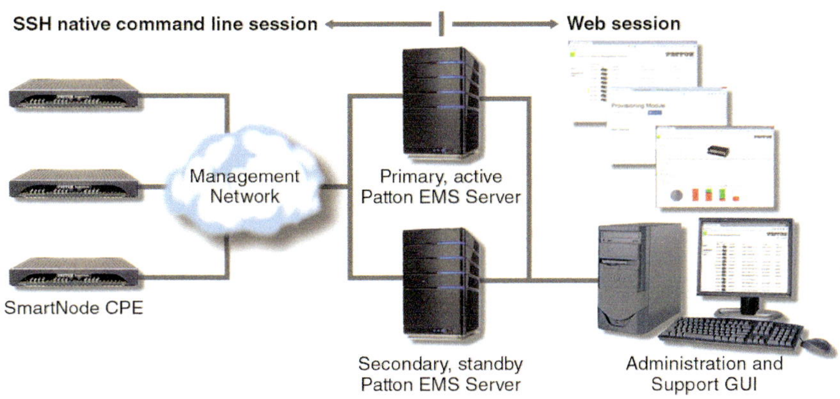

Figure 4.10. Flow diagram of Network Management Software (NMS) (Source: Patton, Creative Commons License).

4.7.1 Network Monitoring Tools

Network monitoring tools help IT teams to monitor the network infrastructure and detect issues in real-time. These tools allow IT teams to monitor network traffic, bandwidth usage, device health, and other network parameters (Ndiaye et al., 2017). Some popular network monitoring tools include Nagios, Zabbix, and PRTG. Network monitoring tools provide a centralized dashboard to view network data and alerts, making it easier for IT teams to quickly detect and resolve issues.

4.7.2 Network Performance Analysis Tools

Network performance analysis tools are used to identify and analyze network performance issues. These tools monitor network traffic, latency, packet loss, and other network parameters. They provide insights into the performance of the network and help IT teams to optimize network resources (Jansen et al., 2009). Some popular network performance analysis tools include SolarWinds and Paessler PRTG Network Monitor.

4.7.3 Network Configuration Management Tools

Network configuration management tools help IT teams to automate the configuration and management of network devices (Wickboldt et al., 2015). These tools enable IT teams to manage configurations for switches, routers, and other network devices in a centralized manner. They also help to ensure that configurations are standardized across the network. Some popular network configuration management tools include Ansible, Puppet, and Chef.

4.7.4 Network Security Management Tools

Network security management tools help IT teams to secure the network infrastructure from cyber threats. These tools include firewalls, intrusion detection systems, and anti-virus software (De Gante et al., 2014). They help to protect the network from unauthorized access, malware, and other security threats. Some popular network security management tools include Cisco Security Manager, Fortinet FortiManager, and Palo Alto Networks Panorama (Figure 4.11).

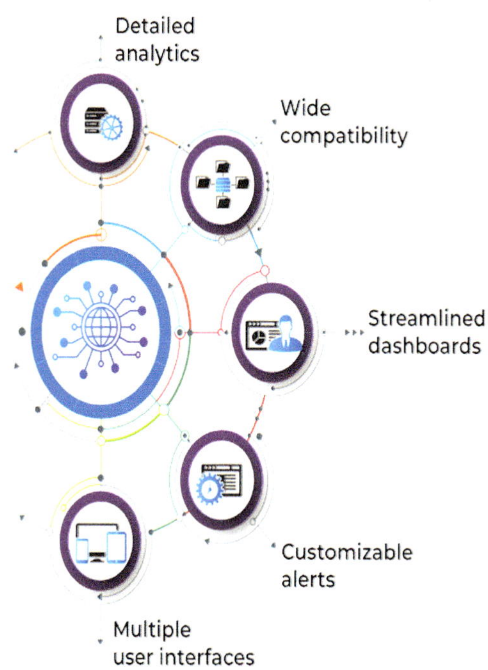

Figure 4.11. Image of key functionalities of network management tool (Source: Spiceworks, Creative Commons License).

4.7.5 Features and Benefits of Network Management Software

The features and benefits of network management software vary based on the type of tool.

4.7.5.1 Real-time Monitoring

Network management software provides real-time monitoring of network infrastructure and alerts IT teams about any issues, allowing them to quickly resolve them before they escalate (Haggerty & Seetharaman, 1998).

4.7.5.2 Centralized Management

Network management software provides a centralized dashboard to manage and monitor network devices, making it easier for IT teams to manage large networks.

4.7.5.3 Analytics and Reporting

Network management software provides analytics and reporting capabilities that help IT teams to identify trends, diagnose issues, and optimize network performance (Hespanha et al., 2007).

4.7.5.4 Automation

Network management software provides automation capabilities that help IT teams to automate routine tasks, such as configuration management and network device provisioning, saving time and reducing the risk of errors (Figure 4.12).

Figure 4.12. Illustration of automation (Source: Telecom Tv, Creative Commons License).

4.7.5.5 Security

Network management software includes security features that help IT teams to secure the network infrastructure from cyber threats (Velasco et al., 2019).

Network management software is a critical tool for managing complex networks. It provides IT teams with real-time monitoring, centralized management, analytics, automation, and security features, helping them to optimize network performance and ensure the network is secure. By using network management software, IT teams can reduce downtime, increase productivity, and improve the overall performance of their network infrastructure.

4.8 PERFORMANCE MANAGEMENT SOFTWARE

Performance Management Software (PMS) is a tool that helps organizations to manage, monitor, and improve employee performance (Diaconescu et al., 2004). It provides a framework for setting goals, tracking progress, providing feedback, and evaluating performance. In this chapter, we will explore the features and benefits of performance management software.

Performance management software is a crucial tool for organizations that want to optimize employee performance and achieve their strategic goals. It helps organizations to align employee goals with organizational objectives, identify areas for improvement, and provide feedback to employees (Figure 4.13).

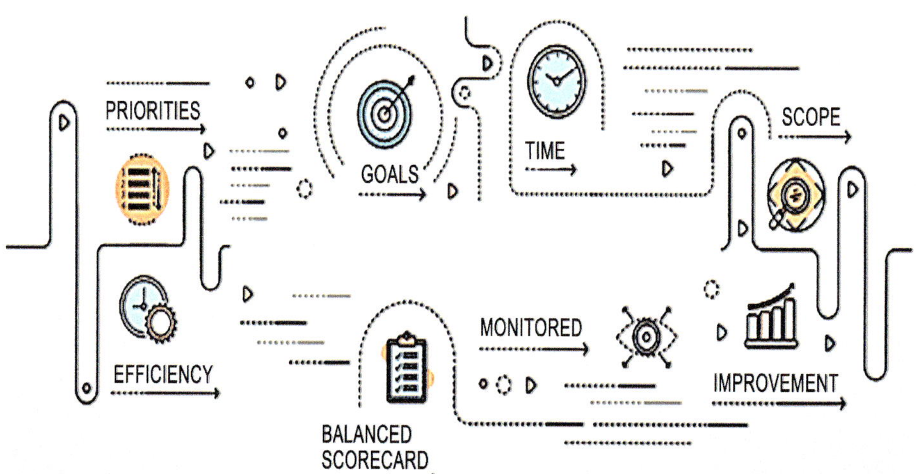

Figure 4.13. Diagram of performance management software (Source: Software testing help, Creative Commons License).

4.8.1 Features of Performance Management Software

Performance management software comes with a range of features that help organizations to manage employee performance effectively. Some of the key features of performance management software are discussed below.

4.8.1.1 Goal Setting

Performance management software provides a platform for employees and managers to set and track goals (Aguinis, 2009). It helps to align employee goals with organizational objectives, ensuring that everyone is working towards the same goal.

4.8.1.2 Performance Evaluation

Performance management software enables managers to evaluate employee performance using a range of criteria, such as productivity, quality of work, and customer satisfaction (Purna Sudhakar et al., 2011). It provides a standardized framework for evaluation, making it easier for managers to assess employee performance objectively.

4.8.1.3 Feedback Management

Performance management software provides a platform for managers to provide feedback to employees on their performance (Moynihan, 2008). It enables managers to provide constructive feedback, which helps employees to identify areas for improvement and develop their skills.

4.8.1.4 Performance Analysis

Performance management software provides analytics and reporting capabilities that help organizations to analyze employee performance data (Andres, 2002). It helps to identify trends, patterns, and areas for improvement, which can be used to develop strategies to improve employee performance.

4.8.2 Benefits of Performance Management Software

Performance management software offers a range of benefits to organizations. Some of the key benefits of performance management software are discussed below.

4.8.2.1 Increased Productivity

Performance management software helps to increase productivity by setting clear goals and expectations for employees (Ganesh & Gupta, 2010). It enables managers to provide feedback and support to employees, which helps them to improve their performance.

4.8.2.2 Improved Communication

Performance management software provides a platform for managers and employees to communicate effectively. It enables managers to provide feedback and support to employees, which helps to improve communication and collaboration in the workplace.

4.8.2.3 Enhanced Employee Engagement

Performance management software helps to enhance employee engagement by providing a platform for employees to set and track continue from here their goals, receive feedback, and develop their skills (Uraon & Gupta, 2020). It enables employees to take ownership of their performance and development, which can lead to increased job satisfaction and motivation.

4.8.2.4 Better Performance Evaluation

Performance management software provides a standardized framework for performance evaluation, which helps managers to evaluate employee performance objectively (Van Dooren et al., 2015). It ensures that all employees are evaluated based on the same criteria, which helps to reduce bias and improve the accuracy of performance evaluations.

4.8.2.5 Improved Decision Making

Performance management software provides analytics and reporting capabilities that help organizations to analyze employee performance data. It enables managers to make data-driven decisions about employee development and resource allocation, which can lead to better business outcomes (Armstrong & Baron, 2005).

Performance management software is a powerful tool that can help organizations to manage, monitor, and improve employee performance. It provides a framework for setting goals, tracking progress, providing feedback, and evaluating performance. By using performance management software, organizations can increase productivity, improve communication, enhance employee engagement, and make better decisions about employee development and resource allocation.

4.9 CONFIGURATION MANAGEMENT SOFTWARE

Configuration Management Software (CMS) is a tool that helps organizations manage and maintain the configuration of their hardware, software, and other IT assets. It provides a centralized platform for tracking changes, managing versions, and ensuring that all assets are up-to-date and working correctly (Conradi & Westfechtel, 1998). In this chapter, we will explore the features and benefits of configuration management software.

Configuration management software is essential for organizations that want to manage and maintain their IT assets effectively. It helps to ensure that all assets are up-to-date, configured correctly, and working as intended. Configuration management software is especially critical in large organizations that have many IT assets and need to manage them efficiently.

4.9.1 Features of Configuration Management Software

Configuration management software comes with a range of features that help organizations manage their IT assets effectively. Some of the key features of configuration management software include:

- **Asset Discovery:** Configuration management software helps organizations discover all their IT assets. It scans the network and identifies all hardware, software, and other IT assets, including servers, routers, switches, and applications (Estublier, 2000).
- **Configuration Tracking:** Configuration management software tracks changes to IT assets and maintains a record of all configurations. It enables organizations to track changes and roll back to previous configurations if needed.
- **Version Control:** Configuration management software provides version control for IT assets. It enables organizations to manage multiple versions of software, scripts, and other IT assets, ensuring that the correct version is installed on each asset.
- **Reporting and Analytics:** Configuration management software provides reporting and analytics capabilities. It enables organizations to analyze IT asset data, identify trends, and make informed decisions about asset management and maintenance (Crnkovic et al., 2003).
- **Automation:** Configuration management software automates many IT asset management tasks. It can automatically deploy software, apply patches, and update configurations, reducing manual effort and ensuring that all assets are up-to-date and configured correctly (Figure 4.14).

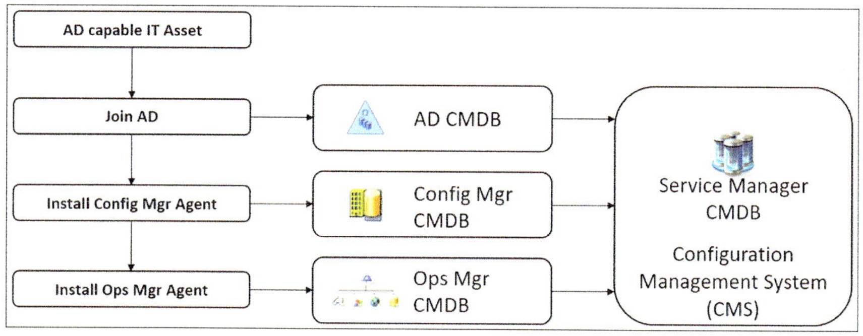

Figure 4.14. Schematic of Configuration Management Software (CMS) (Source: Pack Subscription, Creative Commons License).

4.9.2 Benefits of Configuration Management Software

Configuration management software offers a range of benefits to organizations. Some of the key benefits of configuration management software include:

- **Improved Efficiency:** Configuration management software improves efficiency by automating many IT asset management tasks. It reduces manual effort, enabling IT teams to focus on higher-value tasks (Bersoff, 1984).
- **Reduced Downtime:** Configuration management software helps to reduce downtime by ensuring that all IT assets are up-to-date and working correctly. It enables organizations to track changes and roll back to previous configurations if needed, reducing the risk of downtime due to configuration issues.
- **Improved Security:** Configuration management software helps to improve security by ensuring that all IT assets are up-to-date and configured correctly. It enables organizations to apply patches and updates quickly, reducing the risk of security breaches due to outdated software (Dart, 1991).
- **Compliance:** Configuration management software helps organizations to comply with regulatory requirements by ensuring that all IT assets are configured correctly and up-to-date. It enables organizations to track changes and maintain an audit trail, ensuring compliance with regulatory requirements (Babich, 1986).

Configuration management software is a critical tool for organizations that want to manage and maintain their IT assets effectively. It provides a centralized platform for tracking changes, managing versions, and ensuring that all assets are up-to-date and configured correctly. By using configuration management software, organizations can improve efficiency, reduce downtime, improve security, and ensure compliance with regulatory requirements (Hass, 2003).

4.10 VIRTUALIZATION SOFTWARE

Virtualization software is a tool that enables organizations to create and manage virtual machines (VMs) on physical servers. It allows multiple operating systems and applications to run on a single physical server, reducing hardware costs and improving server utilization (Dobrilovic & Stojanov, 2006). In this chapter, we will explore the features and benefits of virtualization software.

Virtualization software is critical for organizations that want to reduce hardware costs and improve server utilization. It enables organizations to create and manage multiple virtual machines on a single physical server, reducing the need for additional hardware.

4.10.1 Features of Virtualization Software

Virtualization software comes with a range of features that help organizations create and manage virtual machines effectively. Some of the key features of virtualization software are discussed below.

4.10.1.1 Hypervisor

Virtualization software includes a hypervisor that enables multiple virtual machines to run on a single physical server. The hypervisor provides a layer of abstraction between the physical hardware and the virtual machines, enabling them to share the physical resources of the server (Drepper, 2008).

4.10.1.2 Virtual Machine Management

Virtualization software provides tools for managing virtual machines, including creating, configuring, and deleting virtual machines (Pearce et al., 2013). It also provides tools for allocating resources to virtual machines, such as CPU, memory, and storage.

4.10.1.3 Live Migration

Virtualization software enables live migration of virtual machines between physical servers. It allows organizations to move virtual machines to different physical servers without downtime, enabling maintenance and upgrades to be performed without disrupting service (Jain & Paul, 2013).

4.10.1.4 Snapshots

Virtualization software provides the ability to take snapshots of virtual machines. Snapshots enable organizations to capture the current state of a virtual machine, including its configuration and data. Snapshots can be used to revert to a previous state if needed, such as after a software update or configuration change.

4.10.1.5 Resource Pooling

Virtualization software enables organizations to create resource pools that can be shared by multiple virtual machines (Xing & Zhan, 2012). Resource pooling enables organizations to allocate resources dynamically based on the needs of the virtual machines, improving resource utilization and reducing hardware costs (Figure 4.15).

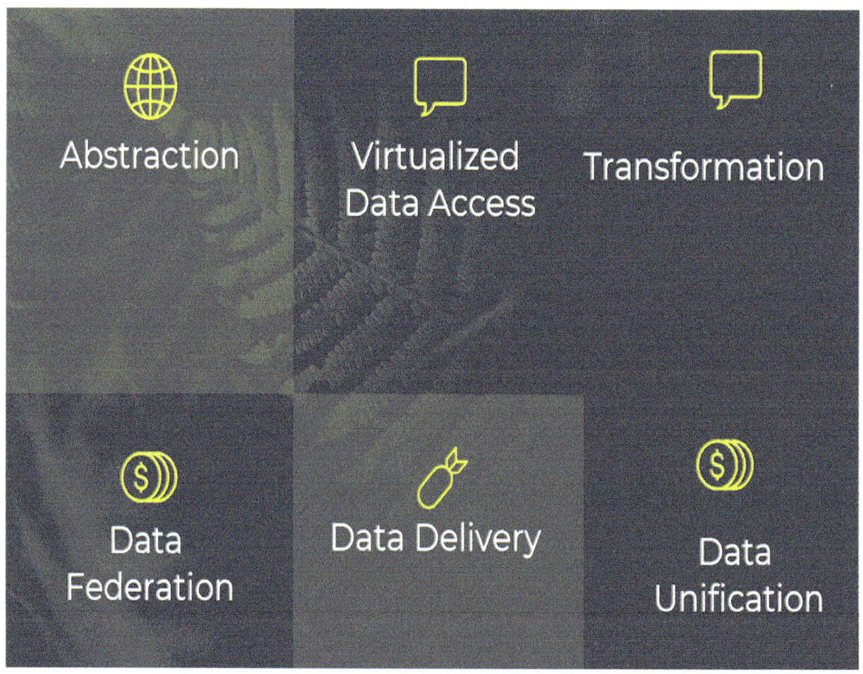

Figure 4.15. Schematic of top data virtualization software (Source: Predictive analytics, Creative Commons License).

4.10.2 Benefits of Virtualization Software

Virtualization software offers a range of benefits to organizations. Some of the key benefits of virtualization software include:

Reduced Hardware Costs: Virtualization software reduces hardware costs by enabling multiple virtual machines to run on a single physical server. It reduces the need for additional hardware, reducing capital and operational costs (Abels et al., 2005). Improved Server Utilization: Virtualization software improves server utilization by enabling multiple virtual machines to run on a single physical server. It maximizes the use of available resources, reducing wasted capacity and improving efficiency

Reduced Downtime: Virtualization software reduces downtime by enabling live migration of virtual machines between physical servers (Coogan et al., 2011). It allows organizations to perform maintenance and upgrades without disrupting service, reducing downtime and improving availability.

Improved Disaster Recovery: Virtualization software improves disaster recovery by enabling virtual machines to be replicated to other physical servers. It ensures that critical applications and data are available in the event of a hardware failure or other disaster. Virtualization software is a critical tool for organizations that want to reduce hardware costs, improve server utilization, and increase availability. It enables organizations to create and manage multiple virtual machines on a single physical server, reducing the need for additional hardware. By using virtualization software, organizations can improve efficiency, reduce downtime, and improve disaster recovery (Drutskoy et al., 2012).

4.11 METHODOLOGY FOR SELECTING A DATA CENTER MANAGEMENT TOOL

We reviewed the market for data center management software and analyzed options based on the following criteria:

i. Network, server, and application monitoring software.
ii. Monitoring automation with alerts for system performance problems.
iii. An easy-to-read dashboard with data interpreted into color-coded graphs and dials.
iv. Integration between tools that can provide seamless data sharing.
v. The option to centralize the monitoring of multiple sites in one location (Vaughan-Nichols, 2006).
vi. A free trial or demo package that allows the system to be evaluated before buying.
vii. Value for money from a comprehensive automated monitoring tool that will save the cost of staff.

4.12 BEST DATA CENTER MANAGEMENT SOFTWARE

With these selection criteria in mind, we identified a number of data center management tools, including both on-premises and SaaS options.

4.12.1 SolarWinds Network Performance Monitor

SolarWinds Network Performance Monitor (NPM) is a network monitoring tool that provides real-time visibility into network performance and helps organizations identify and resolve network issues quickly (Liu et al., 2021). In this chapter, we will explore the features and benefits of SolarWinds NPM.

SolarWinds NPM is a powerful tool for network monitoring and management. It provides real-time visibility into network performance and helps organizations identify and resolve network issues quickly. SolarWinds NPM offers a range of features that help organizations monitor and manage their networks effectively.

4.12.1.1 Features of SolarWinds NPM

SolarWinds NPM comes with a range of features that help organizations monitor and manage their networks effectively. Some of the key features of SolarWinds NPM are discussed below.

4.12.1.2 Network Mapping

SolarWinds NPM provides network mapping capabilities that help organizations visualize their network infrastructure. It provides a graphical representation of the network, enabling administrators to easily identify network devices, connections, and dependencies (Beloglazov et al., 2012).

4.12.1.3 Real-Time Monitoring

SolarWinds NPM provides real-time monitoring of network performance. It enables organizations to monitor network traffic, bandwidth utilization, and device availability in real-time, enabling administrators to identify and resolve network issues quickly.

4.12.1.4 Alerting and Notifications

SolarWinds NPM provides alerting and notification capabilities that help organizations stay informed about network issues. It enables administrators to set up alerts based on predefined thresholds and receive notifications via email, SMS, or other means when an issue is detected (Bhardwaj et al., 2010).

4.12.1.5 Performance Analysis

SolarWinds NPM provides performance analysis capabilities that help organizations identify and resolve performance issues (Lu et al., 2013). It enables administrators to track performance metrics over time, identify trends, and analyze network performance data to identify the root cause of issues.

4.12.1.6 Customizable Dashboards

SolarWinds NPM provides customizable dashboards that help organizations monitor the metrics that matter most to them. It enables administrators to create customized dashboards that display network performance metrics, alerts, and other information in real-time.

4.12.1.7 Benefits of SolarWinds NPM

SolarWinds NPM offers a range of benefits to organizations. Some of the key benefits of SolarWinds NPM are discussed below.

- Improved Network Performance: SolarWinds NPM helps organizations improve network performance by providing real-time visibility into network performance (Gholami & Akbari, 2015). It enables administrators to identify and resolve network issues quickly, reducing downtime and improving network availability.
- Increased Efficiency: SolarWinds NPM helps organizations increase efficiency by automating network monitoring tasks. It reduces the need for manual monitoring and enables administrators to focus on other critical tasks.
- Reduced Downtime: SolarWinds NPM helps organizations reduce downtime by enabling administrators to identify and resolve network issues quickly (Moore et al., 2005). It ensures that critical applications and services are available to users when they need them.
- Improved Security: SolarWinds NPM helps organizations improve security by providing visibility into network activity. It enables administrators to detect and respond to security threats quickly, reducing the risk of data breaches and other security incidents.

SolarWinds NPM is a powerful tool for network monitoring and management. It provides real-time visibility into network performance, helping organizations identify and resolve network issues quickly (Li et al., 2018). By using SolarWinds NPM, organizations can improve network performance, increase efficiency, reduce downtime, and improve security.

4.12.2 Paessler PRTG Network Monitor

Paessler PRTG Network Monitor is a comprehensive network monitoring tool that provides businesses and organizations with real-time insights into the health and performance of their network infrastructure.

4.12.2.1 Features of Paessler PRTG Network Monitor

Below are some of the key features and capabilities of PRTG Network Monitor:

- Network Device Monitoring: PRTG Network Monitor can monitor a wide range of network devices, including servers, routers, switches, and printers (Ahmed & Singh, 2012). It can provide detailed information about the status of these devices, such as CPU usage, memory usage, and network traffic.
- Application Monitoring: PRTG Network Monitor can also monitor a variety of applications running on your network, such as web servers, email servers, and databases. It can monitor the performance of these applications, as well as provide alerts if there are any issues.
- Network Traffic Analysis: PRTG Network Monitor can analyze network traffic in real-time, providing insights into the volume and type of traffic on your network. It can also help you identify potential bottlenecks and other issues that may be affecting network performance.
- Customizable Dashboards and Reports: PRTG Network Monitor provides customizable dashboards and reports that can be tailored to your organization's needs (Chang & Ramachandran, 2015). These dashboards and reports can provide real-time data on the health and performance of your network, as well as historical trends and other insights.
- Remote Monitoring: PRTG Network Monitor can monitor networks across multiple locations, making it ideal for organizations with distributed networks. It can also provide remote access to network devices and applications, allowing IT staff to troubleshoot issues from anywhere.

4.12.2.1.1. Advanced Alerting and Notification

PRTG Network Monitor provides advanced alerting and notification capabilities, allowing IT staff to receive alerts via email, SMS, or other channels when network issues arise. Alerts can be customized based on severity, time of day, and other criteria.

- Integration with Other Tools: PRTG Network Monitor can integrate with a variety of other tools, such as ticketing systems and network management platforms (Czarnul et al., 2019). This makes it easy to incorporate PRTG Network Monitor into your existing IT infrastructure.

Overall, PRTG Network Monitor is a powerful and flexible network monitoring tool that can provide organizations with the real-time insights they need to ensure the health and performance of their network infrastructure.

4.12.2.2 Benefits of Paessler PRTG Network Monitor

- Comprehensive Monitoring: PRTG Network Monitor provides a wide range of monitoring capabilities for network devices, applications, and traffic, allowing IT staff to gain real-time insights into the health and performance of their network infrastructure (Liu et al., 2016).

- Customizable Dashboards and Reports: PRTG Network Monitor provides customizable dashboards and reports that can be tailored to the specific needs of an organization (Sotomayor et al., 2009). This allows IT staff to focus on the most important data and metrics.
- Advanced Alerting and Notification: PRTG Network Monitor provides advanced alerting and notification capabilities, allowing IT staff to receive alerts via email, SMS, or other channels when network issues arise. This helps ensure that issues are addressed in a timely manner.
- Remote Monitoring: PRTG Network Monitor can monitor networks across multiple locations, making it ideal for organizations with distributed networks. This allows IT staff to troubleshoot issues from anywhere.
- Integration with Other Tools: PRTG Network Monitor can integrate with a variety of other tools, such as ticketing systems and network management platforms (Hammadi & Mhamdi, 2014). This makes it easy to incorporate PRTG Network Monitor into an organization's existing IT infrastructure.

4.12.2.3 Limitations of Paessler PRTG Network Monitor

- Complexity: PRTG Network Monitor can be complex to set up and configure, particularly for organizations with large and complex networks. This can require significant time and resources to properly implement and maintain.
- Cost: PRTG Network Monitor is a commercial product and can be expensive for organizations with limited budgets. The cost can vary depending on the number of sensors needed to monitor the network (Zheng et al., 2014).
- Resource Intensive: PRTG Network Monitor can be resource intensive, particularly when monitoring large and complex networks. This can require significant server resources, which may not be feasible for organizations with limited IT infrastructure.
- Lack of Native Cloud Support: PRTG Network Monitor does not natively support monitoring of cloud-based services, which can be a limitation for organizations with a significant cloud presence (Saha, 2014).
- Limited Mobile App Functionality: PRTG Network Monitor's mobile app has limited functionality compared to the desktop application, which may be a limitation for IT staff who need to monitor the network on the go.

4.12.3 ManageEngine OpManager

ManageEngine OpManager is a network monitoring and management tool that provides comprehensive insights into the performance and health of an organization's network infrastructure (Zhu et al., 2016). It offers a range of features and capabilities that can help IT staff proactively monitor and troubleshoot network issues.

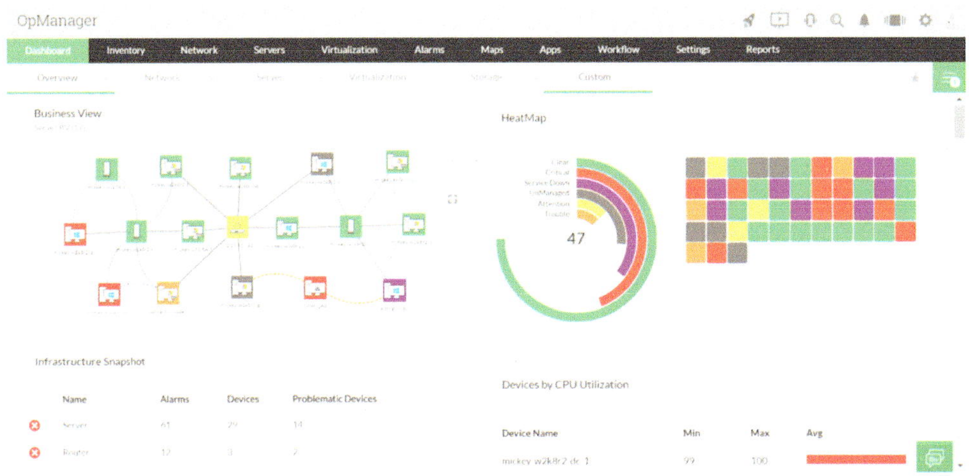

Figure 4.16. Picture of example of ManageEngine (Source: Science Direct, Creative Commons License)

4.12.3.1 Features of Manage Engine OpManager

Here are some key features of Manage Engine OpManager:

- Network Monitoring: Manage Engine OpManager can monitor a wide range of network devices, including servers, switches, routers, and firewalls. It provides real-time data on device availability, performance, and network traffic, which helps IT staff to identify and troubleshoot issues quickly (Li et al., 2014).
- Application Monitoring: Manage Engine OpManager can also monitor applications and services running on the network, including web servers, databases, and email servers. It provides detailed information on the performance of these applications, and alerts IT staff if there are any issues.
- Network Mapping and Visualization: Manage Engine OpManager provides a graphical representation of the network infrastructure, which helps IT staff to identify and troubleshoot issues more easily (Meisner et al., 2012). The network map also provides real-time data on device status, performance, and network traffic.
- Customizable Dashboards and Reports: Manage Engine OpManager provides customizable dashboards and reports that can be tailored to an organization's needs. These reports provide real-time data on network performance and health, which helps IT staff to make informed

decisions about network management and optimization (Whaiduzzaman et al., 2014).

- Advanced Alerting and Notification: Manage Engine OpManager provides advanced alerting and notification capabilities, which allows IT staff to receive alerts via email, SMS, or other channels when network issues arise. These alerts can be customized based on severity, time of day, and other criteria.
- Automation and Remediation: Manage Engine OpManager provides automation and remediation capabilities, which allows IT staff to automatically resolve common network issues. This helps to minimize downtime and improve network performance.
- Integration with Other Tools: Manage Engine OpManager can integrate with a variety of other tools, such as help desk software and configuration management tools (Rahmadani, 2022). This makes it easy to incorporate Manage Engine OpManager into an organization's existing IT infrastructure.

4.12.3.2 Benefits of Manage Engine OpManager

- Comprehensive Network Monitoring: Manage Engine OpManager provides comprehensive network monitoring capabilities, allowing IT staff to gain real-time insights into the performance and health of their network infrastructure.
- Customizable Dashboards and Reports: Manage Engine OpManager provides customizable dashboards and reports that can be tailored to an organization's specific needs (Mohammed Salih, 2005). This allows IT staff to focus on the most important data and metrics.
- Advanced Alerting and Notification: Manage Engine OpManager provides advanced alerting and notification capabilities, allowing IT staff to receive alerts via email, SMS, or other channels when network issues arise. This helps ensure that issues are addressed in a timely manner.
- Automation and Remediation: Manage Engine OpManager provides automation and remediation capabilities, allowing IT staff to automatically resolve common network issues. This helps to minimize downtime and improve network performance (Irvan & Rosyani, 2021).
- Integration with Other Tools: Manage Engine OpManager can integrate with a variety of other tools, such as help desk software and configuration management tools. This makes it easy to incorporate Manage Engine OpManager into an organization's existing IT infrastructure.

4.12.3.3 Limitations of Manage Engine OpManager

- Complexity: Manage Engine OpManager can be complex to set up and configure, particularly for organizations with large and complex networks. This can require significant time and resources to properly implement and maintain.

- Cost: ManageEngine OpManager is a commercial product and can be expensive for organizations with limited budgets (Gabdurahmanov & Trygg, 2016). The cost can vary depending on the number of devices being monitored and the features required.
- Resource Intensive: ManageEngine OpManager can be resource intensive, particularly when monitoring large and complex networks. This can require significant server resources, which may not be feasible for organizations with limited IT infrastructure.
- Limited Native Cloud Support: ManageEngine OpManager does not natively support monitoring of cloud-based services, which can be a limitation for organizations with a significant cloud presence.

Overall, ManageEngine OpManager is a powerful network monitoring and management tool that provides comprehensive insights into an organization's network infrastructure (Ganapathy, 2015). Its range of features and capabilities make it a valuable tool for IT staff who need to proactively monitor and troubleshoot network issues.

4.12.4 NLyte Software

Figure 4.17. Picture of example of NLyte (Source: Science Direct, Creative Commons License).

NLyte Software is a cloud-based platform that offers a wide range of solutions to help organizations streamline their business processes (Figure 4.16). It is designed to automate various business operations and improve operational efficiency. NLyte Software provides solutions for different industries including IT, healthcare, financial services, and more.

4.12.4.1 Features of NLyte Software

- Workflow automation: NLyte Software offers workflow automation solutions to streamline business processes and reduce manual work. It allows users to automate repetitive tasks, route documents, and approvals, and track progress in real-time.
- Document management: With NLyte Software, organizations can manage documents more efficiently (Mohyuddin & Dowland, 2007). It allows users to store, organize, and retrieve documents quickly and easily. The platform also provides advanced search capabilities to find specific documents quickly.
- Analytics and reporting: NLyte Software provides powerful analytics and reporting tools to help organizations make data-driven decisions. Users can create custom reports, charts, and dashboards to analyze data from various sources.
- Collaboration: NLyte Software offers collaboration tools to help teams work together more efficiently. It allows users to share documents, collaborate on projects, and communicate with team members in real-time.

4.12.4.2 Benefits of NLyte Software

- Increased efficiency: NLyte Software automates various business processes, which reduces manual work and increases efficiency. It helps organizations save time and money.
- Improved accuracy: The platform eliminates human error by automating repetitive tasks, reducing the risk of errors and ensuring accuracy (Ahmad et al., 2013).
- Better collaboration: NLyte Software provides collaboration tools that help teams work together more efficiently, which improves communication and productivity.
- Better decision making: NLyte Software provides powerful analytics and reporting tools, which help organizations make data-driven decisions.

4.12.4.3 Limitations of NLyte Software

- Limited customization: NLyte Software may not be fully customizable to meet the unique needs of every organization. Some businesses may need to modify their processes to fit the platform.
- Integration challenges: NLyte Software may face integration challenges

when working with other software systems used by organizations (Shittu et al., 2016). It may require additional time and resources to integrate the platform with existing software.

- Training requirements: Organizations may need to invest time and resources to train employees on how to use the NLyte Software platform effectively. This may impact productivity in the short term.
- Security concerns: As NLyte Software is cloud-based, organizations may have concerns about the security of their data. It is essential to ensure that the platform has adequate security measures in place to protect sensitive information (Thornton & Li, 2013).
- Cost: NLyte Software may have a high cost, especially for small businesses. It is essential to assess the platform's pricing structure and determine whether the benefits outweigh the cost.

Overall, NLyte Software is a cloud-based platform that offers various solutions to help organizations streamline their business processes. It provides workflow automation, document management, analytics and reporting, and collaboration tools. The platform helps organizations increase efficiency, improve accuracy, and make data-driven decisions. However, there may be limitations such as limited customization, integration challenges, training requirements, security concerns, and cost. Organizations need to evaluate these limitations and determine whether the platform is suitable for their business needs.

4.12.5 Kaseya VSA

Kaseya VSA is a remote monitoring and management (RMM) software solution designed for managed service providers (MSPs) and IT departments (Udanor & Oparaku, 2016). It offers a range of tools to manage and monitor IT infrastructure, including servers, workstations, and mobile devices, from a single dashboard.

4.12.5.1 Features Kaseya VSA

- Remote monitoring and management: Kaseya VSA provides a centralized dashboard to manage and monitor IT infrastructure remotely. It allows users to automate routine tasks, deploy software updates, and manage patches.
- IT asset management: The platform helps organizations track and manage IT assets, including hardware and software inventory, licenses, and warranties. It provides visibility into device status, usage, and performance (Islam, 2012).
- Network monitoring: Kaseya VSA includes network monitoring capabilities to detect and resolve issues before they impact end-users. It allows users to monitor network devices, bandwidth usage, and network security.

- Security management: The platform includes security management features to protect IT infrastructure from threats. It provides tools for antivirus management, patch management, and compliance reporting.

Backup and disaster recovery: Kaseya VSA provides backup and disaster recovery solutions to protect data and minimize downtime in case of a disaster.

4.12.5.2 Benefits Kaseya VSA

- Efficiency: Kaseya VSA helps organizations automate routine tasks, which reduces manual work and increases efficiency. It enables MSPs and IT departments to manage more endpoints with less effort.
- Visibility: The platform provides visibility into IT infrastructure, including hardware, software, and network devices. It allows users to track and manage assets effectively.
- Security: Kaseya VSA includes security management features to protect IT infrastructure from threats. It helps organizations stay compliant with industry regulations and security standards (Suhartono, 2012).
- Scalability: Kaseya VSA is a scalable solution that can grow with the organization's needs. It enables MSPs and IT departments to manage more endpoints as the organization expands.

4.12.5.3 Limitations Kaseya VSA

- Complexity: Kaseya VSA can be a complex solution to deploy and manage. It may require specialized IT skills and resources to configure and maintain the platform.
- Cost: Kaseya VSA may have a high cost, especially for small businesses. It is essential to assess the platform's pricing structure and determine whether the benefits outweigh the cost.
- Integration challenges: Kaseya VSA may face integration challenges when working with other software systems used by organizations. It may require additional time and resources to integrate the platform with existing software (Wang, 2010).

Kaseya VSA is a remote monitoring and management solution designed for managed service providers and IT departments. It provides remote monitoring and management, IT asset management, network monitoring, security management, and backup and disaster recovery solutions. The platform helps organizations increase efficiency, visibility, security, and scalability. However, there may be limitations such as complexity, cost, and integration challenges. Organizations need to evaluate these limitations and determine whether the platform is suitable for their business needs.

4.12.6 Device42

Device42 is an IT infrastructure management platform that provides a comprehensive view of an organization's IT infrastructure. It helps organizations manage their physical, virtual, and cloud-based infrastructure and applications in a single dashboard.

4.12.6.1 Features of Device42

- Inventory management: Device42 provides a centralized inventory management system that tracks all IT assets, including hardware, software, and network devices. It provides information on asset status, location, configuration, and relationships.
- Automated discovery: The platform offers automated discovery capabilities that scan and identify IT assets across an organization's infrastructure. It allows users to discover and map dependencies, identify unused or underutilized assets, and detect potential issues (Al-Fares et al., 2008).
- Application dependency mapping: Device42 provides application dependency mapping that helps organizations understand how applications are interconnected and which infrastructure components are critical to application performance.
- IP address management: The platform provides IP address management solutions that help organizations efficiently manage IP addresses and DNS records. It allows users to automate IP address assignments, track IP address usage, and detect conflicts.
- Reporting and analytics: Device42 provides reporting and analytics tools that enable users to create custom reports, charts, and dashboards. It provides insights into IT asset usage, performance, and cost.

4.12.6.2 Benefits of Device42

- Efficiency: Device42 helps organizations automate IT asset management tasks, which reduces manual work and increases efficiency. It enables IT teams to manage more assets with less effort.
- Visibility: The platform provides a comprehensive view of an organization's IT infrastructure, including hardware, software, and network devices. It enables IT teams to track and manage assets effectively.
- Reduced downtime: Device42 helps organizations detect potential issues before they impact end-users (Toosi et al., 2017). It provides insights into application and infrastructure performance, enabling IT teams to proactively address issues.
- Cost savings: The platform helps organizations optimize IT asset usage, identify unused or underutilized assets, and reduce maintenance costs.

4.12.6.3 Limitations of Device42

- Complexity: Device42 can be a complex solution to deploy and manage. It may require specialized IT skills and resources to configure and maintain the platform.

- Integration challenges: Device42 may face integration challenges when working with other software systems used by organizations. It may require additional time and resources to integrate the platform with existing software.
- Cost: Device42 may have a high cost, especially for small businesses. It is essential to assess the platform's pricing structure and determine whether the benefits outweigh the cost (Chahal & Harit, 2019).

Device42 is an IT infrastructure management platform that helps organizations manage their physical, virtual, and cloud-based infrastructure and applications. It provides inventory management, automated discovery, application dependency mapping, IP address management, and reporting and analytics tools. The platform helps organizations increase efficiency, visibility, reduce downtime, and cost savings. However, there may be limitations such as complexity, integration challenges, and cost. Organizations need to evaluate these limitations and determine whether the platform is suitable for their business needs.

4.12.7 Zabbix

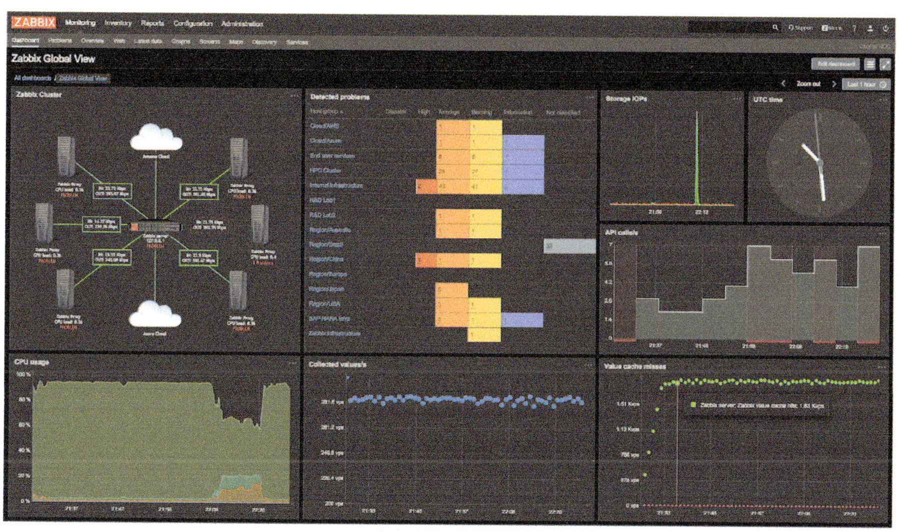

Figure 4.18. Picture of new components of Zabbix (Source: Zabbix LLC, Creative Commons License).

Zabbix is an open-source monitoring solution that provides real-time monitoring and alerting for IT infrastructure, applications, and services (Figure 4.17). It allows organizations to monitor network devices, servers, applications, and databases from a single dashboard (Duran & Aguilo, 2008).

4.12.7.1 Features of Zabbix

- Monitoring: Zabbix provides real-time monitoring of network devices, servers, applications, and databases. It supports a wide range of monitoring types, including SNMP, ICMP, JMX, SSH, and more.
- Alerting: The platform provides alerting and notification capabilities that send alerts to IT teams when issues occur. It allows users to configure alerts based on predefined conditions, such as threshold values, event correlation, and more.
- Dashboard: Zabbix provides a customizable dashboard that enables users to view and analyze data from various sources. It allows users to create custom dashboards, charts, and reports to visualize data in real-time (Helin, 2021).
- Capacity planning: The platform provides capacity planning features that help organizations plan and forecast infrastructure resources. It allows users to identify resource usage trends, forecast future resource requirements, and make informed decisions.
- Automation: Zabbix provides automation capabilities that allow users to automate repetitive tasks, such as server provisioning, configuration changes, and more.

ACTIVITY 4.1.

What steps would you take to diagnose the high CPU usage issue using Zabbix?

4.12.7.2 Benefits of Zabbix

- Efficiency: Zabbix helps organizations improve efficiency by automating repetitive tasks, reducing manual work, and providing real-time monitoring.
- Reliability: The platform provides reliable monitoring of IT infrastructure, applications, and services, which helps organizations detect and address issues proactively.
- Flexibility: Zabbix is highly customizable, allowing organizations to customize monitoring rules and configure alerts based on specific needs (Li et al., 2018).
- Cost-effective: Zabbix is an open-source solution that provides a cost-effective alternative to commercial monitoring solutions.

4.12.7.3 Limitations of Zabbix

- Complexity: Zabbix can be complex to set up and configure, especially for organizations with limited IT resources and skills.

- Resource-intensive: Zabbix can consume significant resources, including CPU, memory, and storage. It may require dedicated hardware or virtual machines to run the platform.
- Support: As an open-source solution, Zabbix may not provide the same level of support as commercial monitoring solutions (Velte et al., 2010). Organizations may need to rely on community support or hire external consultants to address issues.

Zabbix is an open-source monitoring solution that provides real-time monitoring, alerting, and automation capabilities for IT infrastructure, applications, and services. It helps organizations improve efficiency, reliability, and flexibility, and it provides a cost-effective alternative to commercial monitoring solutions. However, there may be limitations such as complexity, resource requirements, and support. Organizations need to assess these limitations and determine whether the platform is suitable for their business needs.

SUMMARY

The chapter explores various tools used for managing data centers. It discusses the benefits of data center management software, including improved efficiency, better resource utilization, and enhanced security. The chapter covers different types of management software, such as server management, storage management, and network management software. Additionally, it highlights the significance of configuration management software and virtualization software. The chapter concludes by outlining the process of selecting the best data center management tool, emphasizing the need to consider factors such as functionality, cost, and scalability.

REVIEW QUESTIONS

1. What are some common tools used for data center management, and what functions do they perform?
2. What are some of the benefits of using data center management software, and how do they improve efficiency and effectiveness?
3. What are the key differences between server management software, storage management software, and network management software, and how do they work together in a data center environment?
4. Why is configuration management software important in data center management, and what types of tasks can it help automate?
5. What is virtualization software, and how can it be used to optimize data center resources and increase flexibility?
6. What are some key factors to consider when selecting the best tool for data center management, such as scalability, interoperability, and ease of use?
7. How can data center management tools help improve security and compliance, and what features should be considered when evaluating these tools?
8. What are some common challenges associated with data center management, and how can tools such as performance monitoring software help address these challenges?
9. What are some emerging trends in data center management tools, such as artificial intelligence and machine learning, and how are they impacting the industry?
10. How can data center management tools be integrated with other IT systems and processes, such as DevOps and cloud computing, to improve overall performance and efficiency?

MULTIPLE CHOICE QUESTIONS

1. Which of the following is NOT a tool of data center management?

a) Virtualization software

b) Configuration management software
c) Network management software
d) Server management software

2. **Which of the following is NOT an advantage/benefit of data center management software?**
   a) Increased efficiency
   b) Reduced downtime
   c) Improved security
   d) Higher energy consumption
3. **Which of the following is NOT a type of management software?**
   a) Server management software
   b) Storage management software
   c) Database management software
   d) Network management software
4. **What is the significance of configuration management software?**
   a) It helps to manage the configuration of hardware devices in the data center
   b) It helps to manage the configuration of software applications in the data center
   c) It helps to manage the configuration of both hardware and software in the data center
   d) It has no significance in data center management
5. **Why is virtualization software important in data center management?**
   a) It helps to reduce hardware costs
   b) It helps to improve server performance
   c) It helps to improve scalability
   d) All of the above
6. **What is the process of selecting the best tool of data center management?**
   a) Conduct a needs assessment, identify potential tools, evaluate them, and select the best one
   b) Select the most expensive tool
   c) Choose the tool with the most features
   d) Ask other companies which tool they use

Answers to Multiple Choice Questions

1. (a) 2. (d) 3. (c) 4. (c) 5. (d) 6. (a)

REFERENCES

1. Abels, T., Dhawan, P., & Chandrasekaran, B. (2005). An overview of xen virtualization. Dell Power Solutions, 8, 109–111.
2. Aguinis, H. (2009). Performance management. Upper Saddle River, NJ: Pearson Prentice Hall, (Vol. 1, pp. 2–6).
3. Ahmad, T. T., Nordin, M. S., & Belio, A. (2013). The state of green computing knowledge among students in a Malaysian public university. Innovation, Communication and Engineering, 3(8), 831–842.
4. Ahmed, T., & Singh, Y. (2012). Analytic study of load balancing techniques using tool cloud analyst. International Journal of Engineering Research and Applications, 2(2), 1027–1030.
5. Alba, A., Alatorre, G., Bolik, C., Corrao, A., Clark, T., Gopisetty, S., ... & Traeger, A. (2014). Efficient and agile storage management in software defined environments. IBM Journal of Research and Development, 58(2/3), 5–1.
6. Al-Fares, M., Loukissas, A., & Vahdat, A. (2008). A scalable, commodity data center network architecture. ACM SIGCOMM Computer Communication Review, 38(4), 63–74.
7. Andres, H. P. (2002). A comparison of face-to-face and virtual software development teams. Team Performance Management: An International Journal (Vol. 1, pp. 2–7).
8. Armstrong, M., & Baron, A. (2005). Managing Performance: Performance Management in Action. CIPD Publishing (Vol. 1, pp. 1–7).
9. Babich, W. A. (1986). Software Configuration Management: Coordination for Team Productivity. Addison-Wesley Longman Publishing Co., Inc. (Vol. 1, pp. 2–6).
10. Beloglazov, A., & Buyya, R. (2010, May). Energy efficient resource management in virtualized cloud data centers. In 2010 10th IEEE/ACM International Conference on Cluster, Cloud and Grid Computing (Vol. 1, pp. 826–831). IEEE.
11. Beloglazov, A., Abawajy, J., & Buyya, R. (2012). Energy-aware resource allocation heuristics for efficient management of data centers for cloud computing. Future Generation Computer Systems, 28(5), 755–768.
12. Bersoff, E. H. (1984). Elements of software configuration management. IEEE Transactions on Software Engineering, 1, 79–87.
13. Bhardwaj, S., Jain, L., & Jain, S. (2010). An approach for investigating perspective of cloud Software-as-a-Service (SaaS). International Journal of Computer Applications, 10(2), 40–43.
14. Brooks, C., McFarlane, P., Pott, N., Trcka, M., & Tomaz, E. (2006). IBM Tivoli storage management concepts. IBM Redbooks, June (Vol. 1, pp. 2–6).
15. Brubeck, D. W., & Rowe, L. A. (1996). Hierarchical storage management in a distributed VOD system. IEEE Multimedia, 3(3), 37–47.
16. Cabrera, L. F., Andrew, B., Peltonen, K., & Kusters, N. (1998). Advances in Windows NT storage management. Computer, 31(10), 48–54.

17. Calheiros, R. N., Ranjan, R., Beloglazov, A., De Rose, C. A., & Buyya, R. (2011). CloudSim: a toolkit for modeling and simulation of cloud computing environments and evaluation of resource provisioning algorithms. Software: Practice and Experience, 41(1), 23–50.
18. Chahal, M., & Harit, S. (2019). Network selection and data dissemination in heterogeneous software-defined vehicular network. Computer Networks, 161(1), 32–44.
19. Chang, V., & Ramachandran, M. (2015). Towards achieving data security with the cloud computing adoption framework. IEEE Transactions on Services Computing, 9(1), 138–151.
20. Conradi, R., & Westfechtel, B. (1998). Version models for software configuration management. ACM Computing Surveys (CSUR), 30(2), 232–282.
21. Coogan, K., Lu, G., & Debray, S. (2011, October). Deobfuscation of virtualization-obfuscated software: a semantics-based approach. In Proceedings of the 18th ACM Conference on Computer and Communications Security (Vol. 1, pp. 275–284).
22. Crnkovic, I., Asklund, U., & Dahlqvist, A. P. (2003). Implementing and Integrating Product Data Management and Software Configuration Management. Artech House (Vol. 1, pp. 2–6).
23. Czarnul, P., Proficz, J., & Krzywaniak, A. (2019). Energy-aware high-performance computing: survey of state-of-the-art tools, techniques, and environments. Scientific Programming (Vol. 1, pp. 2–9).
24. Dart, S. (1991, May). Concepts in configuration management systems. In Proceedings of the 3rd International Workshop on Software Configuration Management (Vol. 1, pp. 1–18).
25. De Gante, A., Aslan, M., & Matrawy, A. (2014, June). Smart wireless sensor network management based on software-defined networking. In 2014 27th Biennial Symposium on Communications (QBSC) (Vol. 1, pp. 71–75). IEEE.
26. Diaconescu, A., Mos, A., & Murphy, J. (2004, May). Automatic performance management in component based software systems. In International Conference on Autonomic Computing, 2004. Proceedings (Vol. 1, pp. 214–221). IEEE.
27. Dobrilovic, D., & Stojanov, Z. (2006, October). Using virtualization software in operating systems course. In 2006 International Conference on Information Technology: Research and Education (Vol. 1, pp. 222–226). IEEE.
28. Drepper, U. (2008). The Cost of Virtualization: Software developers need to be aware of the compromises they face when using virtualization technology. Queue, 6(1), 28–35.
29. Drutskoy, D., Keller, E., & Rexford, J. (2012). Scalable network virtualization in software-defined networks. IEEE Internet Computing, 17(2), 20–27.
30. Duran, O., & Aguilo, J. (2008). Computer-aided machine-tool selection based on a Fuzzy-AHP approach. Expert Systems with Applications, 34(3), 1787–1794.
31. Estublier, J. (2000, May). Software configuration management: a roadmap. In

Proceedings of the Conference on the Future of Software Engineering (Vol. 1, pp. 279–289).

32. Gabdurahmanov, M., & Trygg, S. (2016). Analysis and Evaluation of Network Management Solutions (Vol. 1, pp. 2–6).
33. Ganapathy, A. (2015). AI Fitness Checks, Maintenance and Monitoring on Systems Managing Content & Data: A Study on CMS World. Malaysian Journal of Medical and Biological Research, 2(2), 113–118.
34. Ganesh, M. P., & Gupta, M. (2010). Impact of virtualness and task interdependence on extra-role performance in software development teams. Team Performance Management: An International Journal (Vol. 1, pp. 2–9).
35. Gholami, M., & Akbari, B. (2015, May). Congestion control in software defined data center networks through flow rerouting. In 2015 23rd Iranian Conference on Electrical Engineering (Vol. 1, pp. 654–657). IEEE.
36. Greenberg, A., Hamilton, J. R., Jain, N., Kandula, S., Kim, C., Lahiri, P., ... & Sengupta, S. (2009, August). VL2: A scalable and flexible data center network. In Proceedings of the ACM SIGCOMM 2009 Conference on Data Communication (Vol. 1, pp. 51–62).
37. Greenberg, A., Hamilton, J., Maltz, D. A., & Patel, P. (2008). The cost of a cloud: research problems in data center networks. ACM SIGCOMM Computer Communication Review, 39(1), 68–73.
38. Gupta, S. K., Gilbert, R. R., Banerjee, A., Abbasi, Z., Mukherjee, T., & Varsamopoulos, G. (2011, July). Gdcsim: A tool for analyzing green data center design and resource management techniques. In 2011 International Green Computing Conference and Workshops (Vol. 1, pp. 1–8). IEEE.
39. Haggerty, P., & Seetharaman, K. (1998). The benefits of CORBA-based network management. Communications of the ACM, 41(10), 73–79.
40. Hakiri, A., Gokhale, A., Berthou, P., Schmidt, D. C., & Gayraud, T. (2014). Software-defined networking: Challenges and research opportunities for future internet. Computer Networks, 75, 453–471.
41. Hammadi, A., & Mhamdi, L. (2014). A survey on architectures and energy efficiency in data center networks. Computer Communications, 40(1), 1–21.
42. Harmel, R. D., Smith, D. R., King, K. W., & Slade, R. M. (2009). Estimating storm discharge and water quality data uncertainty: a software tool for monitoring and modeling applications. Environmental Modelling & Software, 24(7), 832–842.
43. Hass, A. M. J. (2003). Configuration management principles and practice. Addison-Wesley Professional (Vol. 1, pp. 3–10).
44. Hazır, Ö. (2015). A review of analytical models, approaches and decision support tools in project monitoring and control. International Journal of Project Management, 33(4), 808–815.

45. Helin, M. (2021). Defining a Holistic Data Center Security Management Framework and Designing an Evaluation Tool, 3(1), 6–9.
46. Hernantes, J., Gallardo, G., & Serrano, N. (2015). IT infrastructure-monitoring tools. IEEE Software, 32(4), 88–93.
47. Hespanha, J. P., Naghshtabrizi, P., & Xu, Y. (2007). A survey of recent results in networked control systems. Proceedings of the IEEE, 95(1), 138–162.
48. Irvan, I., & Rosyani, P. (2021). Implementasi Sistem Monitoring Jaringan Kantor PT Mitra Solusi Infokom Menggunakan Manageengine Opmanager dengan Metode SNMP Protocol. Journal of Information System Research (JOSH), 3(1), 39–46.
49. Islam, A. T. F. (2012). A. Net Framework Approach for a Network Monitoring Tool. International Journal of Computer Applications, 55(10).
50. Jain, R., & Paul, S. (2013). Network virtualization and software defined networking for cloud computing: a survey. IEEE Communications Magazine, 51(11), 24–31.
51. Jammal, M., Singh, T., Shami, A., Asal, R., & Li, Y. (2014). Software defined networking: State of the art and research challenges. Computer Networks, 72(1), 74–98.
52. Jansen, S., Brinkkemper, S., & Finkelstein, A. (2009). Business Network Management as a Survival Strategy: A Tale of Two Software Ecosystems. Iwseco@ Icsr, 2009 (Vol. 1, pp. 2–6).
53. Jones, S., Cournane, S., Sheehy, N., & Hederman, L. (2016). A business analytics software tool for monitoring and predicting radiology throughput performance. Journal of Digital Imaging, 29(1), 645–653.
54. Kaczmarski, M., Jiang, T., & Pease, D. A. (2003). Beyond backup toward storage management. IBM Systems Journal, 42(2), 322–337.
55. Kim, H., & Feamster, N. (2013). Improving network management with software defined networking. IEEE Communications Magazine, 51(2), 114–119.
56. Lakshminarayanan, R., Kumar, B., & Raju, M. (2013). Cloud computing benefits for educational institutions. arXiv preprint arXiv:1305.2616, (Vol. 1, pp. 2–6).
57. Li, D., Shang, Y., & Chen, C. (2014, April). Software defined green data center network with exclusive routing. In IEEE INFOCOM 2014-IEEE Conference on Computer Communications (Vol. 1, pp. 1743–1751). IEEE.
58. Li, Y., Cai, Z. P., & Xu, H. (2018). LLMP: exploiting LLDP for latency measurement in software-defined data center networks. Journal of Computer Science and Technology, 33, 277–285.
59. Lim, K., Turner, Y., Chang, J., Santos, J. R., & Ranganathan, P. (2011). Disaggregated memory benefits for server consolidation. HP Laboratories, (Vol. 1, pp. 2–8).
60. Liu, J., Wang, S., Zhou, A., Kumar, S. A., Yang, F., & Buyya, R. (2016). Using proactive fault-tolerance approach to enhance cloud service reliability. IEEE Transactions on Cloud Computing, 6(4), 1191–1202.
61. Liu, W. X., Cai, J., Chen, Q. C., & Wang, Y. (2021). DRL-R: Deep reinforcement learning approach for intelligent routing in software-defined data-center networks.

Journal of Network and Computer Applications, 177, 102865.

62. Lomb, R., Emo, K. A., & VanDoorn, R. M. (1996). Storage management solutions for distributed computing environments. Hewlett Packard Journal, 47, 81–93.
63. Lu, X., Wang, H., Wang, J., Xu, J., & Li, D. (2013). Internet-based virtual computing environment: Beyond the data center as a computer. Future Generation Computer Systems, 29(1), 309–322.
64. Meisner, D., Wu, J., & Wenisch, T. F. (2012, April). Bighouse: A simulation infrastructure for data center systems. In 2012 IEEE International Symposium on Performance Analysis of Systems & Software (Vol. 1, pp. 35–45). IEEE.
65. Mohammed Salih, Y. M. (2005). Remote Network Management System (Doctoral dissertation, Sudan University of Science and Technology), (Vol. 1, pp. 2–9).
66. Mohyuddin, A., & Dowland, P. (2007). The art of network monitoring. Advances in Networks, Computing and Communications, 4(1), 91–100.
67. Moore, J. D., Chase, J. S., Ranganathan, P., & Sharma, R. K. (2005, April). Making Scheduling Cool: Temperature-Aware Workload Placement in Data Centers. In USENIX annual technical conference, General Track (Vol. 1, pp. 61–75).
68. Moreau, T. (2006). Server Management Tools for Trust Anchor Key Management Based on TAKREM. CONNOTECH Experts-conseils inc., Document, (C003595), (Vol. 1, pp. 2–6).
69. Moynihan, D. P. (2008). The Dynamics of Performance Management: Constructing Information and Reform. Georgetown University Press, (Vol. 1, pp. 4–6).
70. Ndiaye, M., Hancke, G. P., & Abu-Mahfouz, A. M. (2017). Software defined networking for improved wireless sensor network management: A survey. Sensors, 17(5), 1031.
71. Pearce, M., Zeadally, S., & Hunt, R. (2013). Virtualization: Issues, security threats, and solutions. ACM Computing Surveys (CSUR), 45(2), 1–39.
72. Peifeng, S., Chuan, S., & Xiang, Z. (2013). Intelligent server management framework over extensible messaging and presence protocol. China Communications, 10(5), 128–136.
73. Peng, H., & Wang, Y. (2010, August). WMIC-based technology server network management software design. In 2010 Second Pacific-Asia Conference on Circuits, Communications and System (Vol. 1, pp. 253–256). IEEE.
74. Peters, M., & Keane, M. (2015). Key reasons to use software-defined storage—and how to get started. ESG Inc., Milford, Connecticut, White Paper, (Vol. 1, pp. 2–6).
75. Purna Sudhakar, G., Farooq, A., & Patnaik, S. (2011). Soft factors affecting the performance of software development teams. Team Performance Management: An International Journal, 17(3/4), 187–205.
76. Putnam, A., Caulfield, A. M., Chung, E. S., Chiou, D., Constantinides, K., Demme, J., ... & Burger, D. (2015). A reconfigurable fabric for accelerating large-scale datacenter services. IEEE Micro, 35(3), 10–22.
77. Rahmadani, T. P. (2022). Analisis Pemantauan Access Point Local Arena Network

dengan Menggunakan OpManager: Analisis Pemantauan Access Point Local Arena Network dengan Menggunakan OpManager. Journal of Network and Computer Applications (ISSN: 2964–6669), 1(1), 9–18.

78. Rakhmonov, I. U., & Kurbonov, N. N. (2020). Analysis of automated software for monitoring energy consumption and efficiency of industrial enterprises. In E3S Web of Conferences (Vol. 216, p. 01178). EDP Sciences.
79. Ravandi, B., & Papapanagiotou, I. (2017, June). A self-learning scheduling in cloud software defined block storage. In 2017 IEEE 10th International Conference on Cloud Computing (CLOUD) (Vol. 1, pp. 415–422). IEEE.
80. Saha, B. (2014). Green computing. International Journal of Computer Trends and Technology (IJCTT), 14(2), 46–50.
81. Sehgal, N. K., & Ganguli, M. (2006, December). Applications of virtualization for server management and security. In 2006 IEEE International Conference on Industrial Technology (Vol. 1, pp. 2752–2755). IEEE.
82. Shende, S. B., & Chapke, P. P. (2015). Cloud database management system (CDBMS). Compusoft, 4(1), 1462.
83. Shittu, T. A., Gambari, A. I., & Thomas, A. O. (2016). Survey of education, engineering, and information technology students knowledge of green computing in Nigerian University. Journal of Education and Learning (EduLearn), 10(1), 70–77.
84. Sotomayor, B., Montero, R. S., Llorente, I. M., & Foster, I. (2009). Virtual infrastructure management in private and hybrid clouds. IEEE Internet Computing, 13(5), 14–22.
85. Suhartono, B. (2012). Sistem Monitoring Dan Availability Server Serta Perangkat Jaringan Dengan Menggunakan Aplikasi OpManager Dan Gammu. Jurnal IT, 6(1), 1–13.
86. Thornton, B., & Li, C. (2013, January). The applicability of network management systems in small businesses. In IEEE Conference Anthology (Vol. 1, pp. 1–7). IEEE.
87. Toosi, A. N., Qu, C., de Assunção, M. D., & Buyya, R. (2017). Renewable-aware geographical load balancing of web applications for sustainable data centers. Journal of Network and Computer Applications, 83(1), 155–168.
88. Udanor, C. N., & Oparaku, O. U. (2016). A Performance Evaluation of a Multi-Agent Mobile Learning System. International Journal of Interactive Mobile Technologies, 10(2), 2–7.
89. Uraon, R. S., & Gupta, M. (2020). Do HRD practices affect perceived market performance through operational performance? Evidence from software industry. International Journal of Productivity and Performance Management, 69(1), 85–108.
90. Van Dooren, W., Bouckaert, G., & Halligan, J. (2015). Performance Management in the Public Sector. Routledge, (Vol. 1, pp. 2–6).
91. Vaughan-Nichols, S. J. (2006). New approach to virtualization is a lightweight. Computer, 39(11), 12–14.
92. Velasco, L., Piat, A. C., Gonzlez, O., Lord, A., Napoli, A., Layec, P., ... & Casellas, R.

(2019). Monitoring and data analytics for optical networking: benefits, architectures, and use cases. IEEE Network, 33(6), 100–108.

93. Velte, A. T., Velte, T. J., Elsenpeter, R. C., & Elsenpeter, R. C. (2010). Cloud Computing: A Practical Approach, 2(1), 3–6.
94. Wang, G., Andersen, D. G., Kaminsky, M., Papagiannaki, K., Ng, T. E., Kozuch, M., & Ryan, M. (2010, August). c-Through: Part-time optics in data centers. In Proceedings of the ACM SIGCOMM 2010 Conference (Vol. 1, pp. 327–338).
95. Wang, H. (2010, January). From a mess to graphic maps: Visualization of large-scale heterogeneous networks. In 2010 Second International Conference on Computer Modeling and Simulation (Vol. 1, pp. 531–535). IEEE.
96. Waters, B. (2005). Software as a service: A look at the customer benefits. Journal of Digital Asset Management, 1, 32–39.
97. Weyns, D. (2017). Software engineering of self-adaptive systems: an organized tour and future challenges. Handbook of Software Engineering, 2(1), 1–6.
98. Whaiduzzaman, M., Gani, A., Anuar, N. B., Shiraz, M., Haque, M. N., & Haque, I. T. (2014). Cloud service selection using multicriteria decision analysis. The Scientific World Journal, (Vol. 1, pp. 2–6).
99. White, T., Calvert, D., & Litkey, J. (2005, June). Design of an Autonomic Element for Server Management. In Second International Conference on Autonomic Computing (ICAC'05) (Vol. 1, pp. 147–158). IEEE.
100. Wickboldt, J. A., De Jesus, W. P., Isolani, P. H., Both, C. B., Rochol, J., & Granville, L. Z. (2015). Software-defined networking: management requirements and challenges. IEEE Communications Magazine, 53(1), 278–285.
101. Xing, Y., & Zhan, Y. (2012). Virtualization and cloud computing. In Future Wireless Networks and Information Systems (Vol. 1, pp. 305–312). Springer Berlin Heidelberg.
102. Ying, Z., & Yong, S. (2009, May). Cloud storage management technology. In 2009 Second International Conference on Information and Computing Science (Vol. 1, pp. 309–311). IEEE.
103. Zheng, K., Wang, X., Li, L., & Wang, X. (2014, April). Joint power optimization of data center network and servers with correlation analysis. In IEEE INFOCOM 2014-IEEE Conference on Computer Communications (Vol. 1, pp. 2598–2606). IEEE.
104. Zhu, H., Liao, X., de Laat, C., & Grosso, P. (2016). Joint flow routing-scheduling for energy efficient software defined data center networks: A prototype of energy-aware network management platform. Journal of Network and Computer Applications, 63(1), 110–124.

CHAPTER 5

VIRTUALIZATION AND CLOUD COMPUTING

UNIT INTRODUCTION

The managers and directors of IT units are now at a crossroads due to an astonishing revolution in how such units work. First, there is stress on IT teams to provide better customer service and be quicker to support controversial business goals. On the contrary, IT teams are scrutinized to lower their spending, "do a lot more with a lot less," and show an ROI from optimizing programs that are as favorable as feasible.

By reflecting more on their virtualization strategies, smart IT directors have started to reconcile both opposing viewpoints. Virtualization was eventually developed to transform complete information centers into flexible, dynamic, service-based architectures. Virtualization was initially thought of as a technique to improve and update the usage of physical servers. These designs can now advance concerning corporate goals and competition (Xing & Zhan, 2012) (Figure 5.1).

IT has an excellent experience with data center virtualization. The economic benefits are amazingly significant. Efficient server, storage, and network resource sharing results in significantly cheaper capital expenditures and running expenses. Silos of inadequate application is avoided. The data center can now complement various applications effectively, execute them more quickly, and maintain greater service levels thanks to virtualization.

Given that cloud computing is expected to arrive soon, IT businesses must contend with some other revolutionary environment: How to establish a private cloud network that has a number of the identical efficiencies and economies promoted by third-party cloud services or the best way to utilize data center automation as a launching pad to reach third-party cloud services. (For additional data, see the Best Minds white paper "IT and the Cloud: Purchase, Build or Both?" for further details about converting your virtual vibrant data center into a cloud service).

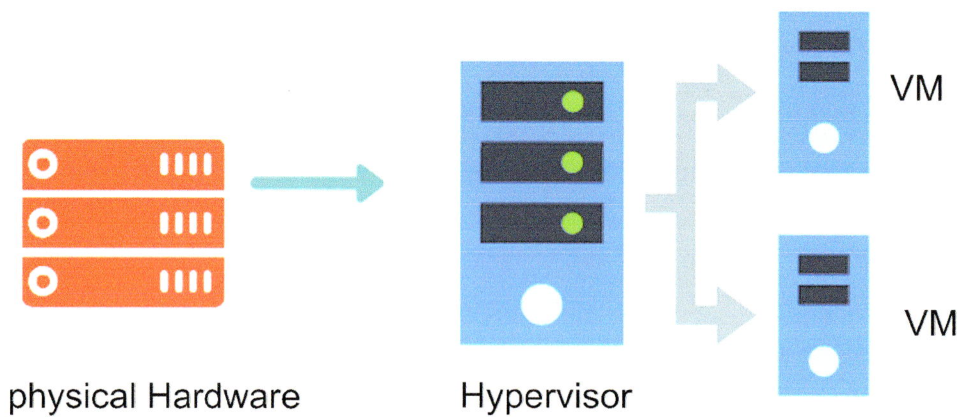

Figure 5.1. Illustration of virtualization (Source: Martin Evans, Creative Commons License).

While data center virtualization might be the most advantageous option for some businesses, some go much further with data center virtualization and create a highly autonomous and uniform "cloud model."

In any case, IT needs to improve its effectiveness and adaptability to keep up with the organization's growing business needs while also being strategically important. As virtualization grows, it also runs the danger of losing operational difficulties.

Initially, virtualization was used to increase the efficiency of physical servers. A highly dynamic, service-centered design is now applied to whole data centers, accelerating business goals and competition (Jain & Choudhary, 2016).

Learning Objectives

At the end of this chapter, reader will be able to understand:

1. The importance of virtualization and cloud computing
2. The significance of datacenter virtualization
3. The advantages of virtualization and cloud computing
4. Different types of virtualization

Key Terms

1. Cloud Computing
2. Cloud Maturity
3. Microsoft® Hyper-V
4. Amazon Web Services (AWS)
5. Vendor Lock-In
6. Microsoft's Azure
7. Google Cloud Platform (GCP)

5.1 NEED FOR VIRTUALIZATION AND CLOUD COMPUTING

Information technology departments are typically cost centers for businesses. It offers the assistance essential for rising sales and earnings, but its activities nonetheless weigh on the financial side of the worksheet. IT executives and managers are constantly challenged to provide the organization with more resources and services while spending less on capital investments and operational costs. They encounter the following difficulties (Gajbhiye & Shrivastva, 2014).

Remember

Server virtualization in data center management involves creating multiple virtual machines on a single physical server, which provides more efficient resource utilization and greater flexibility but requires careful planning and management to prevent performance issues and security risks.

5.1.1 Low Utilization

The historically low consumption of programs operating on physical servers—often as minimal as 5–10%—has been brought to light by server virtualization. IT is stressed to maximize material assets, such as internal systems and storage, due to the enormous increase in programs and support systems (Rashid & Chaturvedi, 2019).

5.1.2 Energy and Environmental Costs

A data center must use a great deal of energy for the devices to be powered and kept cool. Energy expenses can account for a sizable portion of IT expenditure, and energy costs often rise yearly. More power is absent in some locations. More demand to save energy is placed on IT units because some businesses adopt the "green" working principle and ask them for additional services (Berl et al., 2010).

5.1.3 Complex Operations

Application-centric data center designs may result in network design divisions. These asset arrays restrict resource sharing, are inefficient and duplicated, and increase the complexity of the diverse areas that must be handled.

5.1.4 Lack of Agility

It requires time to set up, install, update, verify, and launch a new business program. In the meantime, practically all smartphone users are familiar with quickly installing and downloading software.

Business owners know that new distribution models can drastically cut the time needed to provision apps, improving their ability to compete and bottom line. Businesses cannot be unable to waste time creating brand-new networks each time a new tool is required. A significant IT problem is providing applications much more effectively compared to the past (Sriram, 2022).

5.1.5 Fiscal Impact

Even cost areas like IT are required to immediately recover their expenses in the age of Return on Investment. This is particularly challenging given the usual low system efficiencies and the fact that most of the IT budget is set aside for underutilization. Companies could expect good capital margins with operational advantages as they make small efforts toward data center virtualization (Atiewi et al., 2018) (Figure 5.2).

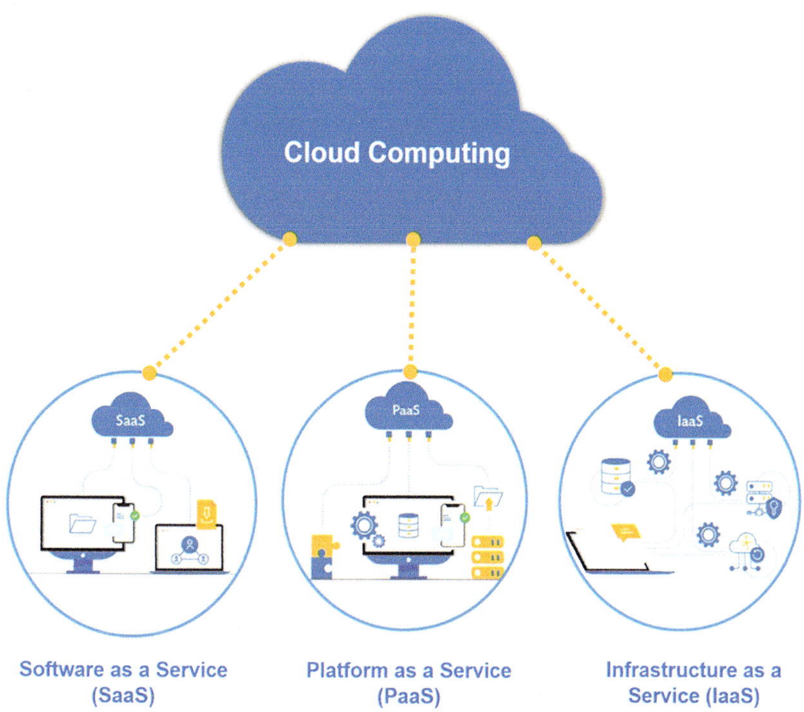

Figure 5.2. Schematic of cloud computing (Source: Development Asia, Creative Commons License).

5.2 LATEST FRONTIER OF DATACENTER VIRTUALIZATION

Even cost areas like IT are required to immediately recover their expenses in the period of Return on Investment. With the usual low system efficiencies and the fact that most of the IT cost is set aside for underutilization, this is particularly challenging. Companies could expect good capital margins with operational advantages as they make small efforts for data center virtualization (Gavrilovska, 2016).

5.3 DEFINING DIFFERENT TYPES OF VIRTUALIZATION

5.3.1 Virtualization

With the help of this technology, many logical units can "virtually" share a single physical unit or service. Conversely, virtualization technology can make it possible for several physical units or assets to look and function as a single "virtual" or logical unit or asset (Chiueh & Brook, 2005).

5.3.2 Server Virtualization

Software is often used to virtualize servers to maximize a server's material assets. A software-based "hypervisor" (like VMware or Microsoft® Hyper-V) divides a physical server into several virtual servers during server virtualization. Virtual machines are another name for virtual servers. Generally, each virtual server runs with its own unique set of resources and native operating system. Moreover, each virtual server can run one's stack of programs independently of other virtual servers and applications running on the same base machine (Daniels, 2009).

5.3.3 Data Center Virtualization

Enables the consolidation and optimization of other important physical resources within the data center by extending the idea of server virtualization. This continues with:

1. Server virtualization
2. Network virtualization
3. Storage virtualization

The connection between the services provided and the underlying physical hardware required to perform them is abstracted by data center virtualization.

Every asset is combined into a single virtual resource "pool." Organizations can transcend virtualization "silos" by integrating and organizing each virtual pool with the others. More efficiencies and benefits are generated as a consequence (Salagrama & Bibhu, 2022).

5.4 ADVANTAGES OF DATA CENTER VIRTUALIZATION

The administration of storage, server, and network functions occurs in a virtualized data center. The architecture that results has the following qualities or advantages:

1. Dynamic, efficient, and agile.
2. More efficient resource sharing (thanks to virtual pooling).
3. Reduced complexity now means fewer things to manage.
4. Deeper gains in the degree of consolidation, better resource planning and sharing, and simplified management of a unanimous infrastructure.

This last category of benefits offers the highest increases in effectiveness and production. Innovations in virtualized network management and integrated infrastructures can result in such advantages. These technologies bring higher virtualization management features and better integration that help enterprises construct and exploit virtual resources at several levels simultaneously—from computation to storage, networking, and security and management of assets (Challa, 2012).

The chance is to transition from isolated virtualization—where some apps use virtualized servers, and others use virtual storage—to a more integrated virtualization approach. Thus, network techniques, servers, and storage are all integrated.

Data center virtualization enables you to develop systems that can accommodate all (or the majority of) apps rather than creating separate infrastructures to meet the requirements of particular applications. You can gain management skills from programs you can't have from hardware by extracting them from material assets. They would comprise:

1. The competencies required to migrate from one physical server to another without disruption.
2. Increased availability for applications during hardware failure.
3. Resource scheduling and load balancing across existing infrastructure.
4. Improved backup and disaster recovery.
5. Increased performance, scale, and security.
6. Integration with storage and network infrastructures.

Did you Know?

According to a report by MarketsandMarkets, the global advanced data center virtualization market size is projected to grow from $5.69 billion in 2021 to $10.26 billion by 2026, at a compound annual growth rate (CAGR) of 12.5% during the forecast period.

The outcome is a framework that can run most or even all IT programs. Because the platform offers reliability, efficiency, and security, fewer applications need to be built with those features. The infrastructure that results is far more adaptable and dynamic (Duan & Yang, 2017).

5.5 ADVANCED-DATA CENTER VIRTUALIZATION

The transition to data center virtualization is a long-term access and process—a journey—one of the most crucial things to remember. Most businesses cannot instantly switch from their current architectures and procedures to a fluid virtual data center. As a result, you must prepare, divide your plan into manageable steps, and consider its benefits.

In the Happiest Minds white paper "IT and the Cloud: Purchase, Create or Both," a thorough, five-phase cloud maturity model explains the shift from integration to virtualization and, eventually, cloud computing. (Barabash et al., 2011).

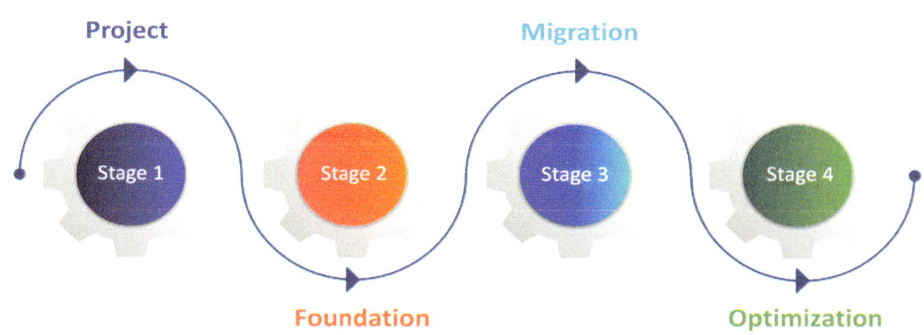

Figure 5.3. Image of Cloud Maturity Stages (Source: Veritis, Creative Commons License).

5.6 CLOUD COMPUTING IN DATA CENTER MANAGEMENT

A shared pool of reconfigurable computing assets (such as storage, networks, servers, services, and applications) which may be quickly deployed and removed with little administration work or service provider involvement, is made possible by the cloud computing concept. Cloud computing has completely transformed how businesses run their IT network and programs. Many advantages of cloud computing include cost reductions, flexibility, mobility, and improved security.

When mainframe computers were initially launched in the 1960s, cloud computing existed. The idea of distributed systems arose in the 1990s, allowing many groups to collaborate on computing resources. Amazon established Amazon Web Services (AWS) in the early 2000s, and it is regarded as the original cloud computing platform. Cloud computing is already a commonplace and crucial technology for companies of all sizes (Gang, 2010).

Any organization's IT network revolves around data centers, and cloud computing has become a crucial component of data center administration. Cloud computing offers a scalable and adaptable platform for managing workloads, software, and data storage. Businesses can quickly supply and deploy computing resources with cloud computing, making them more adaptable and reactive to shifting business requirements. Cloud computing also provides cost benefits by eliminating the requirement for significant upfront hardware and infrastructure investments and enabling a pay-as-you-go model for computing resource sharing. Also, cloud computing offers improved data security and confidentiality, essential for any firm dealing with sensitive data (Yin et al., 2013).

TIPS

When working with Google Cloud Platform (GCP) in data center management, it's important to take advantage of GCP's built-in security features such as identity and access management (IAM) roles, network security controls, and encryption options.

5.7 ADVANTAGES OF CLOUD COMPUTING

In terms of managing data centers, cloud computing has various benefits.

5.7.1 Scalability

Administrators of data centers can rapidly and easily increase or decrease their network in response to changing demand thanks to cloud computing. This eliminates the necessity of expensive hardware expenditures by allowing them to add or remove assets without physically updating or replacing hardware (Singh & Malhotra, 2012).

5.7.2 Cost Savings

Administrators of data centers can save money by utilizing cloud computing instead of managing their infrastructure and hardware. This covers renting physical space, paying for electricity, purchasing, upkeep, and upgrading hardware (Nayar & Kumar, 2018).

5.7.3 Flexibility

Data center operators may swiftly adjust to shifting business needs thanks to cloud computing without making large-scale infrastructure upgrades. This implies they don't need to make a big hardware expenditure to add new software, services, or customers to their data center.

5.7.4 Improved Efficiency

The capacity for automating common processes provided by cloud computing allows data center operators to manage architecture with less manual labor. As a result, the personnel working in the data center can concentrate on more crucial jobs, including enhancing security and efficiency or introducing new services (Jeevitha & Athisha, 2021).

5.7.5 Improved Reliability

Data center administrators can depend on their network to be accessible when required because cloud computing providers often guarantee high availability and dependability. This is particularly crucial in sectors like healthcare and finance, where downtime may be expensive or harmful (Li et al., 2020).

5.7.6 Enhanced Security

In the interest of safeguarding their infrastructure and their clients' data, cloud computing vendors frequently make significant investments in security precautions. To provide a better level of security than many organizations can accomplish by themselves, this can incorporate capabilities like multi-factor identification, encryption, and intrusion prevention system.

With increased flexibility, agility, and cost savings than conventional data center management approaches, cloud computing provides data center administrators with a robust array of resources for controlling their network more successfully (Sudha & Monica, 2012).

5.8 CHALLENGES OF CLOUD COMPUTING

Although cloud computing has many benefits for managing data centers, it also comes with several difficulties.

5.8.1 Security

Privacy is a significant concern in cloud computing since data center administrators must ensure their programs and data are secure from outside attacks. In a cloud context, where data is frequently dispersed across various places and systems, this cannot be easy to safeguard. To guarantee that their data and applications are appropriately secured, data center administrators must work collaboratively with cloud services and implement mechanisms like multi-factor authentication, encryption, and intrusion detection/prevention (Ali et al., 2015).

5.8.2 Compliance

Strict regulatory standards for the security and confidentiality of data exist in many different businesses, like HIPAA in the healthcare sector or GDPR in the European Union. Data center administrators must ensure that their cloud architecture complies with these criteria, which can be challenging given that cloud services may be active across several legal systems, each with its own set of rules (Yimam & Fernandez, 2016).

5.8.3 Vendor Lock-In

Data center executives may find it challenging to move their applications and data to a different cloud provider because of the use of innovative systems or architectures by some cloud services. This can lead to vendor lock-in, reducing mobility and gradually raising expenses.

5.8.4 Complexity

Cloud computing may be complicated and challenging, especially as businesses expand their network. Data center administrators must be very knowledgeable about cloud architectures and services and capable of managing and keeping an eye on various cloud service providers.

5.8.5 Cost Management

While cloud computing can save expenses in some instances, it can also raise costs if it is not used properly. To guarantee optimal effectiveness, data center administrators must closely monitor consumption and expenditure throughout their cloud infrastructure and improve their setups (Lee & Mautz, 2012).

5.8.6 Availability and Uptime

The dependability and reliability levels that cloud providers normally give vary depending on the provider and the particular services in use. Data center administrators must ensure that their cloud network is planned and set up for optimal reliability and that they have backup plans in place in case of service interruptions or outages. Therefore, when controlling their architecture, data center administrators must carefully weigh the benefits and drawbacks of cloud computing. They may build plans to guarantee that their information and applications are appropriately safeguarded, their expenses are reduced, and their infrastructure is built for optimal performance and durability by recognizing these concerns and collaborating effectively with cloud services (Ahuja & Mani, 2012).

5.9 CLOUD COMPUTING PROVIDERS

Numerous cloud computing service providers would provide services for managing data centers.

5.9.1 Amazon Web Services (AWS)

The popular cloud computing network AWS provides various data center management services, such as storage, computation, and networking (Figure 5.4). AWS's versatility, dependability, and security aspects are well known, and numerous businesses employ it.

Figure 5.4. Picture of Amazon Web Services (AWS) (Source: Amazon.com, Creative Commons License).

5.9.2 Microsoft Azure

Microsoft's Azure cloud computing system offers a variety of data center management solutions, such as storage, computation, and networking services. Azure is renowned for its extensive security and compliance capabilities and for being compatible with Microsoft's services and products.

5.9.3 Google Cloud Platform (GCP)

GCP is a Google cloud computing system offering various data center management services, such as storage, computation, and networking. In addition to its versatility, dependability, and security characteristics, GCP is also recognized for its sophisticated machine-learning abilities. IBM Cloud is a cloud computing framework that IBM offers. It offers various data center management services like storage, computation, and network sites. The powerful statistics, information management, privacy, and regulatory features of IBM Cloud are well-known (Bisong & Bisong, 2019) (Figure 5.5).

Figure 5.5. Illustration of google cloud platform (Source: Stallyons, Creative Commons License).

5.9.4 Oracle Cloud

Oracle Cloud is a cloud computing platform that offers several data center management services, such as networks, computing, and storage services. The compliance and safety aspects of Oracle Cloud are well recognized, as well as its sophisticated database management abilities. These service companies provide a broad spectrum of information center management services, from basic computing and storage services to sophisticated machine learning and reporting tools. Organizations can select the supplier that best suits their unique requirements and standards based on aspects like cost, stability, privacy, and efficiency (Elbahri et al., 2019).

ACTIVITY 5.1

As a data center manager, your organization is planning to migrate some of its applications to the cloud to improve agility and reduce costs. However, you also need to ensure that the transition to cloud computing and virtualization does not compromise security, compliance, or performance. What are some key considerations and best practices that you would recommend to ensure a smooth and secure migration to the cloud, and how would you monitor and manage the performance and availability of your virtualized workloads in the cloud?

SUMMARY

Virtualization and cloud computing are important technologies that have revolutionized the way organizations manage their IT infrastructure.

The importance of virtualization lies in its ability to allow multiple operating systems and applications to run on a single physical server, thereby optimizing resource utilization and reducing costs. Cloud computing, on the other hand, enables organizations to access computing resources such as servers, storage, and applications over the internet, making it more convenient and cost-effective than traditional IT infrastructure. The advantages of virtualization and cloud computing include improved resource utilization, scalability, flexibility, and cost savings. These technologies also enable organizations to respond more quickly to changing business needs and to reduce downtime and outages.

There are different types of virtualization including full virtualization, para-virtualization, and hardware-assisted virtualization. Full virtualization involves the creation of a virtual machine that emulates a complete hardware environment, while para-virtualization allows multiple operating systems to run on a single physical server by sharing the same kernel. Hardware-assisted virtualization, on the other hand, uses hardware features to support virtualization, making it more efficient and scalable.

REVIEW QUESTIONS

1. Why is virtualization and cloud computing considered important in today's IT industry?
2. What are the key benefits of datacenter virtualization, and how does it differ from traditional server setups?
3. What are the advantages of virtualization and cloud computing in terms of scalability, resource utilization, and cost savings?
4. Can you distinguish between the various types of virtualization, such as server, storage, and network virtualization, and explain how they are used in the cloud computing environment?
5. How do virtualization and cloud computing impact the way businesses manage their IT infrastructure and deliver services to customers, and what are some of the challenges they may face in this context?

MULTIPLE CHOICE QUESTIONS

1. Which of the following is not a reason for the importance of virtualization and cloud computing?

a) Cost reduction

b) Improved scalability

c) Increased security
d) Increased physical hardware usage

2. Which of the following best describes the significance of datacenter virtualization?

a) It allows for greater flexibility in server management and allocation.
b) It allows for more efficient cooling and power usage in datacenters.
c) It reduces the need for IT staff to physically maintain servers.
d) It allows for faster processing speeds for datacenter applications.

3. Which of the following is not an advantage of virtualization and cloud computing?

a) Improved disaster recovery capabilities
b) Increased hardware dependency
c) Enhanced resource utilization
d) Increased mobility for applications and data

4. Which type of virtualization allows for multiple operating systems to run simultaneously on a single physical machine?

a) Network virtualization
b) Storage virtualization
c) Application virtualization
d) Server virtualization

5. Which type of cloud deployment model involves a private cloud hosted and managed within an organization's own infrastructure?

a) Public cloud
b) Hybrid cloud
c) Community cloud
d) Private cloud

Answers to Multiple Choice Questions

1. (d) 2. (a) 3. (b) 4. (d) 5. (d)

REFERENCES

1. Ahuja, S. P., & Mani, S. (2012). Availability of services in the era of cloud computing. *Network and Communication Technologies*, *1*(1), 1–2.
2. Ali, M., Khan, S. U., & Vasilakos, A. V. (2015). Security in cloud computing: Opportunities and challenges. *Information Sciences*, *305*, 357–383.

3. Atiewi, S., Abuhussein, A., & Saleh, M. A. (2018, September). Impact of virtualization on cloud computing energy consumption: Empirical study. In *Proceedings of the 2nd International Symposium on Computer Science and Intelligent Control* (Vol. 1, pp. 1–7).
4. Barabash, K., Cohen, R., Hadas, D., Jain, V., Recio, R., & Rochwerger, B. (2011, September). A case for overlays in dcn virtualization. In *Proceedings of the 3rd Workshop on Data Center-Converged and Virtual Ethernet Switching* (Vol. 1, pp. 30–37).
5. Berl, A., Gelenbe, E., Di Girolamo, M., Giuliani, G., De Meer, H., Dang, M. Q., & Pentikousis, K. (2010). Energy-efficient cloud computing. *The Computer Journal*, *53*(7), 1045–1051.
6. Bisong, E., & Bisong, E. (2019). An overview of google cloud platform services. *Building Machine Learning and Deep Learning Models on Google Cloud Platform: A Comprehensive Guide for Beginners*. *1*(1), 7–10.
7. Challa, N. R. (2012, October). Hardware based i/o virtualization technologies for hypervisors, configurations and advantages-a study. In *2012 IEEE International Conference on Cloud Computing in Emerging Markets (CCEM)*. IEEE. (Vol. 1, pp. 1–5).
8. Chiueh, S. N. T. C., & Brook, S. (2005). A survey on virtualization technologies. *Rpe Report*. *42*, 11–21.
9. Daniels, J. (2009). Server virtualization architecture and implementation. *XRDS: Crossroads, The ACM Magazine for Students*, *16*(1), 8–12.
10. Duan, J., & Yang, Y. (2017). A load balancing and multi-tenancy oriented data center virtualization framework. *IEEE Transactions on Parallel and Distributed Systems*, *28*(8), 2131–2144.
11. Elbahri, F. M., Al-Sanjary, O. I., Ali, M. A., Naif, Z. A., Ibrahim, O. A., & Mohammed, M. N. (2019, March). Difference comparison of SAP, Oracle, and Microsoft solutions based on cloud ERP systems: A review. In *2019 IEEE 15th International Colloquium on Signal Processing & Its Applications (CSPA)*. IEEE. (Vol. 1, pp. 65–70).
12. Gajbhiye, A., & Shrivastva, K. M. P. (2014, September). Cloud computing: Need, enabling technology, architecture, advantages and challenges. In *2014 5th International Conference-Confluence The Next Generation Information Technology Summit (Confluence)*. IEEE. (Vol. 1, pp. 1–7).
13. Gang, C. (2010, November). Data center management plan in cloud computing environment. In *2010 3rd International Conference on Information Management, Innovation Management and Industrial Engineering*. IEEE. (Vol. 4, pp. 393–396).
14. Gavrilovska, A. (2016, March). Virtualizing the edge of the cloud: the new frontier. In *Proceedings of the12th ACM SIGPLAN/SIGOPS International Conference on Virtual Execution Environments* (Vol. 1, pp. 1–1).

15. Jain, N., & Choudhary, S. (2016, March). Overview of virtualization in cloud computing. In *2016 Symposium on Colossal Data Analysis and Networking.* IEEE. *(CDAN)* (Vol. 1, pp. 1–4).
16. Jeevitha, J. K., & Athisha, G. (2021). A novel scheduling approach to improve the energy efficiency in cloud computing data centers. *Journal of Ambient Intelligence and Humanized Computing*, *12*, 6639–6649.
17. Lee, L. S., & Mautz Jr, R. D. (2012). Using cloud computing to manage costs. *Journal of Corporate Accounting & Finance*, *23*(3), 11–15.
18. Li, C., Song, M., Zhang, M., & Luo, Y. (2020). Effective replica management for improving reliability and availability in edge-cloud computing environment. *Journal of Parallel and Distributed Computing*, *143*, 107–128.
19. Nayar, K. B., & Kumar, V. (2018). Cost benefit analysis of cloud computing in education. *International Journal of Business Information Systems*, *27*(2), 205–221.
20. Rashid, A., & Chaturvedi, A. (2019). Virtualization and its role in cloud computing environment. *International Journal of Computer Sciences and Engineering*, *7*(4), 1131–1136.
21. Salagrama, S., & Bibhu, V. (2022, February). Study of IT and Data Center Virtualization. In *2022 2nd International Conference on Innovative Practices in Technology and Management (ICIPTM)*. IEEE. (Vol. 2, pp. 274–278).
22. Singh, A., & Malhotra, M. (2012). Agent based framework for scalability in cloud computing. *International Journal of Computer Science & Engineering Technology (IJCSET)*, *3*(4), 41–45.
23. Sriram, G. S. (2022). Edge computing vs. Cloud computing: an overview of big data challenges and opportunities for large enterprises. *International Research Journal of Modernization in Engineering Technology and Science*, *4*(1), 1331–1337.
24. Sudha, M., & Monica, M. (2012). Enhanced security framework to ensure data security in cloud computing using cryptography. *Advances in Computer Science and Its Applications*, *1*(1), 32–37.
25. Xing, Y., & Zhan, Y. (2012). Virtualization and cloud computing. In *Future Wireless Networks and Information Systems.* Springer Berlin Heidelberg. (Vol. 1, pp. 305–312).
26. Yimam, D., & Fernandez, E. B. (2016). A survey of compliance issues in cloud computing. *Journal of Internet Services and Applications*, *7*, 1–12.
27. Yin, J., Sun, P., Wen, Y., Gong, H., Liu, M., Li, X., ... & Lin, C. (2013, August). Cloud3DView: An interactive tool for cloud data center operations. In *Proceedings of the ACM SIGCOMM 2013 conference on SIGCOMM* (Vol. 1, pp. 499–500).

CHAPTER 6

IMPORTANCE OF POWER AND COOLING MANAGEMENT

UNIT INTRODUCTION

The action or process of ensuring that cooling, power, and space are efficiently delivered at the correct date and in the proper quantity to manage IT loads and procedures is referred to as data center basic infrastructure capacity planning. The following are critical success elements for good power and cooling capacity management:

1. Giving precise capacity projections.
2. Having the adequate capacity to satisfy corporate requirements (Wang et al., 2010).

Determining the cooling and power capabilities at the rack level is necessary for accurate capacity predictions and effective capacity provisioning. Nowadays, it is uncommon to possess this skill. Data center operators frequently lack the knowledge necessary to efficiently deploy new equipment only at the rate demanded by the company and have a difficult time responding to straightforward inquiries like:

1. Where should I place the next server in my data center to avoid affecting the use of the equipment already there?
2. Where is the ideal place to install the suggested IT equipment regarding power and cooling accessibility?

3. Would installing new equipment negatively affect my safety margins, including redundancy and backup time?
4. Would I still have backup cooling or electricity in case of a problem or maintenance?
5. Can I install new hardware, like blade servers, utilizing my current cooling and power system (Stillwe et al., 2011)?
6. Is it necessary to distribute my blade servers for dependable performance?
7. When would I need more capacity due to the limitations of my present power and cooling system?

It's typical to be unable to respond to such straightforward inquiries. The safety margins may enable effective operation with a basic awareness of the system's general efficiency for data centers that are drastically over-designed. A minor but bearable amount of downtime might be experienced due to the accessibility being compromised by this ignorance. Oversizing offers a safety net until the available capacity matches the capacity consumed, even if it is neither economically nor environmentally effective. Yet, three reasons are now stressing data centers, revealing the shortcomings of current operational techniques in the process (Choudhury et al., 2012):

1. IT equipment with extreme density.
2. They need to reduce the total cost of ownership (TCO) to use data center resources better.
3. And the update cycle of IT equipment, change happens rapidly.

This causes pressure data centers to function more predictably (Nathuji & Schwan, 2007) (Figure 6.1).

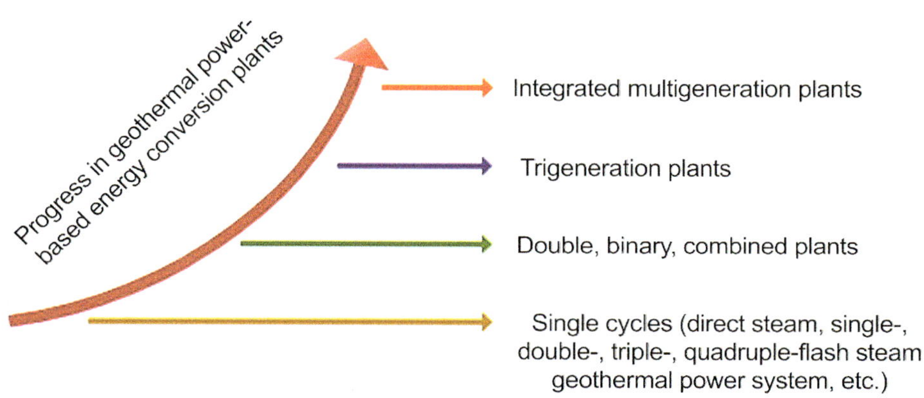

Figure 6.1. Illustration of power and cooling management (Source: Science Direct, Creative Commons License).

Learning Objectives

At the end of this chapter, the reader will be able to understand:

1. The importance of power and cooling management
2. The significance of high density IT equipments
3. The concept of capacity supply and system level capacities
4. The process of managing capacity
5. The mechanism of monitoring power and cooling for IT devices

Key Terms

1. Spare Capacity
2. Idle Capacity
3. Safety Margin Capacity
4. Stranded Capacity
5. Power Distribution Units (PDU)
6. Excess Capacity
7. Capacity Management

6.1 HIGH-DENSITY IT EQUIPMENT

Highly dense IT equipment consumes over 8 kW per rack enclosure. Servers' racks that are fully loaded might need anywhere between 6 kW and 35 kW of power. Yet, most data centers built today can only support less than 4 kW of electricity per rack. As was already said, increasing numbers of users are adding denser equipment than intended for their data centers, placing stress on cooling and power systems and potentially leading to overheating, overloads, and lack of resilience, which can result in downtime. Improved knowledge is needed by data center managers to effectively deploy this technology in both new and current data centers (Patrick et al., 2000).

6.2 TOTAL COST OF OWNERSHIP

Most organizations cannot support data centers that are grossly overdesigned or oversized. Significant capital and operating expenses are wasted. If a capacity was correctly managed, it is believed that such a typical data center of today could accommodate up to 30% more IT technology utilizing the identical facility for cooling and power capacity (Ellram, 1993). Compared to a system in which the capacity is adequately managed, the average data center cannot completely utilize its existing cooling and power capability, which lowers system effectiveness while raising electrical energy usage by 20% or more. Tools for capacity management may optimize power and cooling facilities and reduce electricity usage (Ellram, 1995) (Figure 6.2).

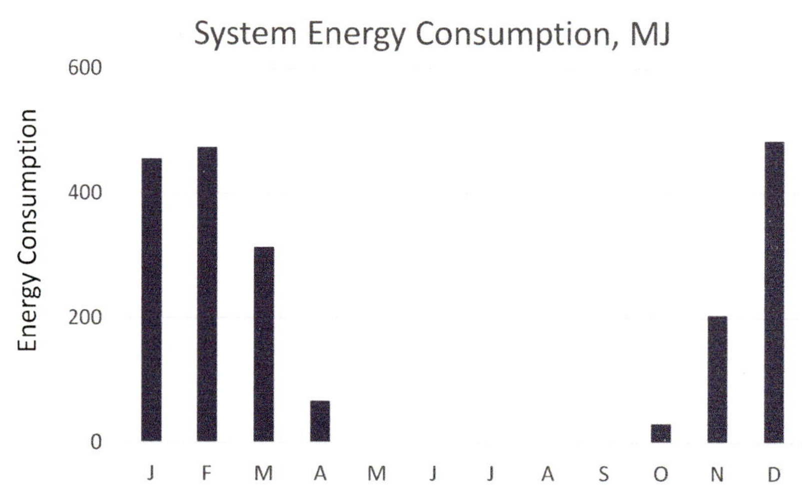

Figure 6.2. Graphically representation of Electrical energy usage (Source: Ramadas Narayanan, Creative Commons License).

6.3 RAPID PACE OF CHANGE

A common data center's IT equipment is continually evolving. Equipment refresh periods are often less than three years, and technology is added or deleted regularly. Additionally, IT systems' cooling and power needs fluctuate from minute to minute due to virtualization and power control capabilities offered by IT equipment providers (Keeling, 2008). The traditional "try to see if it works" approach to IT equipment deployment is no longer practical, with overheating being a common effect. To meet all these problems, capacity management solutions should provide real-time resource planning in a cost-effective, easy-to-use, easy-to-install, pre-engineered manner (Levinthal, 1998).

TIPS

For maximizing system-level capacities is to ensure that all components are properly integrated and optimized for efficient performance.

6.4 CAPACITY SUPPLY AND DEMAND

A systematic approach to capacity planning is essential to easily answer users' fundamental capacity questions. This ability to measure demand and supply for electricity and cooling is the core of capacity planning (Dooley, 2013).

While knowing the demand and supply for energy and cooling at the facility or room levels is helpful, it cannot give enough accurate data to address inquiries regarding deploying certain IT equipment. On the other hand, it is unnecessarily comprehensive and challenging to provide data on the demand and supply for energy and cooling just at the level of IT devices. This study applies the rack level as a practical and efficient level for power and cooling performance measurement and budgeting (Howlett, 2015).

The model of this chapter discusses measures the demand and supply for cooling and electricity so a group that provides in four significant ways:

1. As-configured maximum potential demand.
2. Current actual demand.
3. As-configured potential supply.
4. Current actual supply.

This data enables a thorough description of cooling and power conditions in a data center only at the rack level. Figure 6.3 uses descriptions from the text below to provide visual support (Yahdjian et al., 2015).

6.4.1 Power and Cooling Maximum Potential Demand

Current servers' power control mechanisms can result in two to one or more power variations during routine operation. All peak values brought on by this variation in the rack are represented by the highest "as configured" cooling and power requirements. Trending may be utilized to create this data now of configurations; the IT equipment could report data directly or be obtained in other ways (Ondeck et al., 2015).

Remember

Effective power and cooling management is crucial for maintaining the longevity and efficiency of your electronic devices, as well as reducing energy costs and minimizing the risk of equipment failure.

For capacity management, knowing that the maximum cooling and power requirement is always higher or equivalent to the real power and cooling need is essential (Laine et al., 2019).

6.4.2 Current Power and Cooling Actual Demand

It represents the energy used and heat produced at every rack at a given moment. The ideal way to achieve that is to measure the electrical power usage in real-time now at the rack level. Almost all devices have a power consumption equivalent to their heat output in watts. Some equipment, such as power distribution units (PDU), uninterruptible power systems (UPS), VoIP routers, and air conditioners, could be mathematically calculated to have a heat output in watts different from the electricity consumed. Rack power may be calculated by adding the reported power required by the collection of IT equipment in a rack, which may be measured mostly by power supply or through the IT equipment directly (Mutschle et al., 2021).

6.4.3 Power and Cooling Maximum Potential Supply

The quantity of energy and cooling that its existing infrastructure device may theoretically send to a rack level is called the as-configured power and cooling, full potential supply. Usually greater or equivalent to the real power plus cooling supply is the potential cooling and power supply (Ondeck et al., 2015). The system deteriorates if the maximum possible delivery for any specified load exceeds the power provided. It may be brought on by several things, including:

1. Blocked cooling system air filters.

2. They are reduced outside heat rejection capabilities because of harsh weather circumstances.
3. A power module failure in a modular UPS.

It is an essential function of a capacity planning system to identify when the actual supply differs from the value obtained or to diagnose the cause of system restrictions that hinder the implementation of the design supplies (Flum et al., 2019).

6.4.4 Current Power and Cooling Actual Supply

The design of a data center's cooling and power system, the present real capabilities of the major power and cooling sources, and the effects on some other loads' available resources are all used to calculate the actual cooling and power delivery at a rack (Pan et al., 2017).

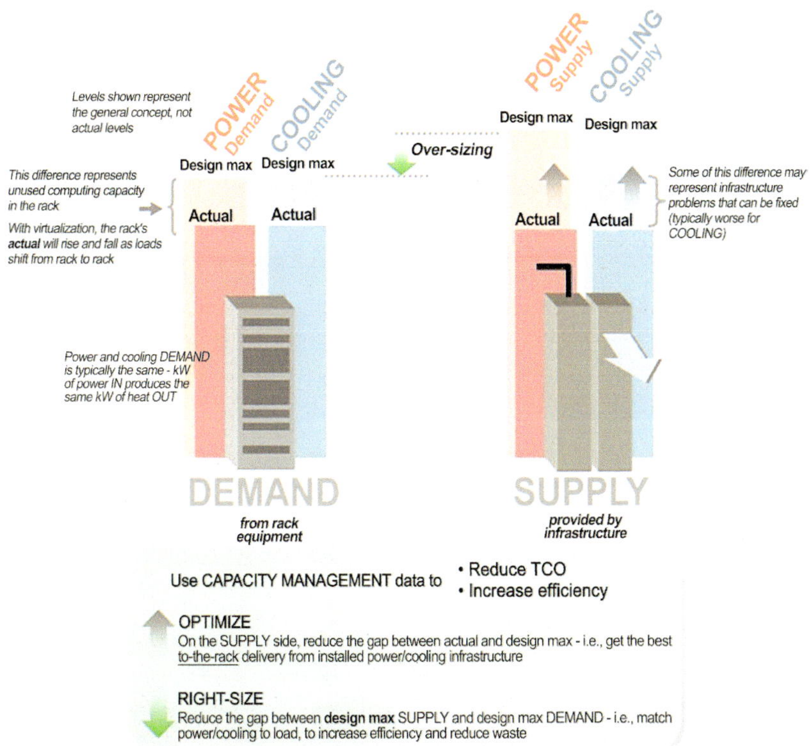

Figure 6.3. Diagram of supply and demand (Source: Schneider Electric, Creative Commons License).

Understanding the branch circuit capacity accessible to the rack, which is limited by the accessibility of unutilized power from upstream sources like PDUs and UPS, allows one to determine the real power source at a specific rack. In certain circumstances, a power system's architecture or configuration further restricts the available capacity. For instance, the design could include two power feeds or a flexible system that may not be filled (Ji et al., 2021) (Figure 6.3).

6.5 SYSTEM-LEVEL CAPACITIES

The air distribution design plays a significant role in establishing the basic cooling supplies at a rack, which is often more complicated than estimating the power source. Airflow is often given to an approximated grouping of racks, where it disperses among the racks depending on the drawing of the fans in the IT apparatus, unlike with the power design, in which wires restrict the flow of electricity. Due to this, specialized computer models are needed to calculate the available air volume, which is more complicated. The cooling supplies at a rack are more defined and may thus be calculated with greater precision in situations where the supplies or air circulation are immediately ducted to racks (Bond et al., 2001).

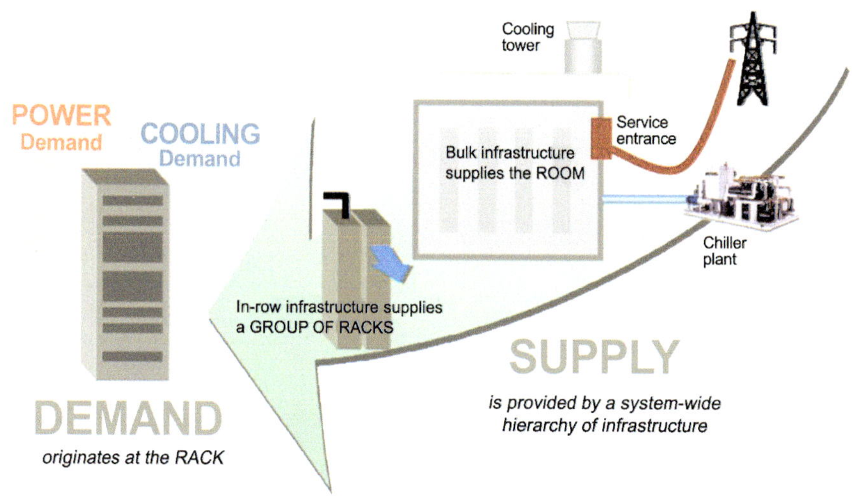

Figure 6.4. Diagram of the sources of supply and demand (Source: White paper 115, Creative Commons License).

As seen in Figure 6.4, the rack determines the need for cooling and electricity. Any supply discussed in the preceding part must also be recognized and measured at the rack. On the other hand, the cooling and power supply system is set up hierarchically rather than rack by rack, with supply equipment like UPSs, PDUs, and air conditioner units groups of racking. Bulk supply equipment like cooling systems and entry to the power service also serve as capacity supply sources which must be enough to meet demand. Hence, the cooling and power supply capacity should be measured at the rack and aggregate levels in line with the supplied equipment (Smith & Freeman, 2002).

Supply should constantly be more than or equivalent to demand to keep the data center from failing. It must be accurate at every rack and supply device providing rack clusters (Zhou et al., 2018). Thus, there is always extra capacity anywhere (if the total supply exceeds or exceeds the overall demand). For capacity planning reasons, excess capacity can take one of four main forms:

a) Spare capacity.
b) Idle capacity.
c) Safety margin capacity.
d) Stranded capacity (Gouveia et al., 2022).

The next sections explain each category of excess capacity, and Figure 6.5 provides illustrations.

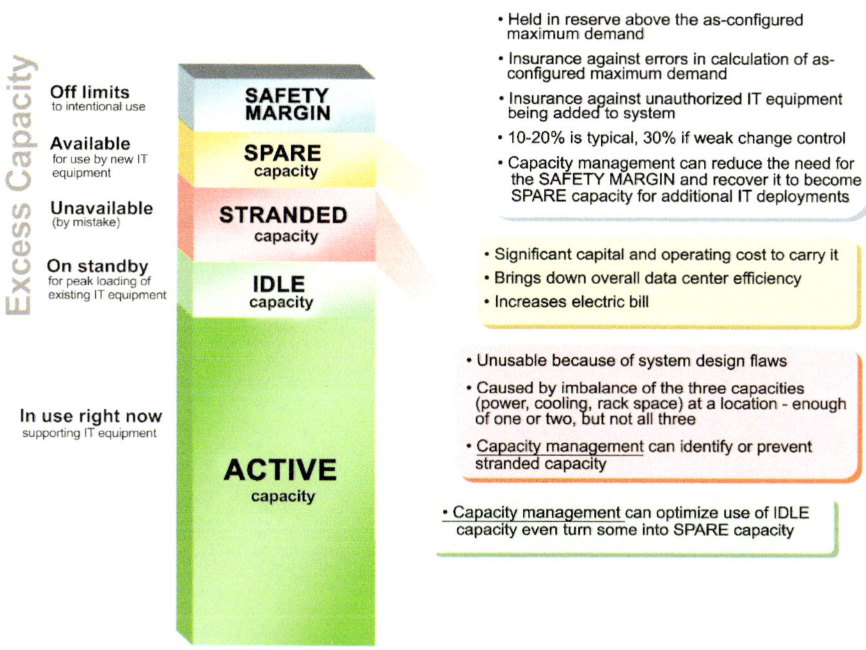

Figure 6.5. Illustration of types of excess capacity (Source: Schneider Electric, Creative Commons License).

6.5.1 Spare Capacity

Extra capacity is the real space available which is currently available and can be used "right now" for additional IT hardware. The cost of purchasing and maintaining the cooling and power facilities is a large portion of the capital and operational expenses associated with maintaining spare capacity. Also, a data center's operational efficiency is always lower, and its power consumption is higher when spare capacity exists (Xiong & Mason, 1999).

Some forms of spare capacity, including spare utilities connection capacity, are cost-effective in an efficient and effective organization and structure for a growing and evolving data center. Yet, to satisfy escalating demand, power and cooling devices must ideally only be built if and when necessary (Liu et al., 2005).

A capacity management system should understand and quantify growth plans to be effective (Shahriar et al., 2018).

6.5.2 Idle Capacity

Idle capacity is the spare supply currently held in reserve to fulfill the maximum formatted potential demand for cooling or power. This idle ability cannot supply the installation of new IT equipment because the existing IT devices may require it during peak load (Bulow et al., 1985).

A major issue in IT technology is idle capacity, which is brought on by automated virtual machine mobility and power control features. If power-managed IT technology shifts to increased power modes, the idle capacity should be kept up (Wu et al., 2014).

6.5.3 Safety Margin Capacity

Safety margin capacity is designed for excess capacity kept on hand, and the maximum possible power or cooling needs as configured.

Figure 6.6. Graphical representation of Safety margin capacity. (Source: Valentin, Creative Commons License).

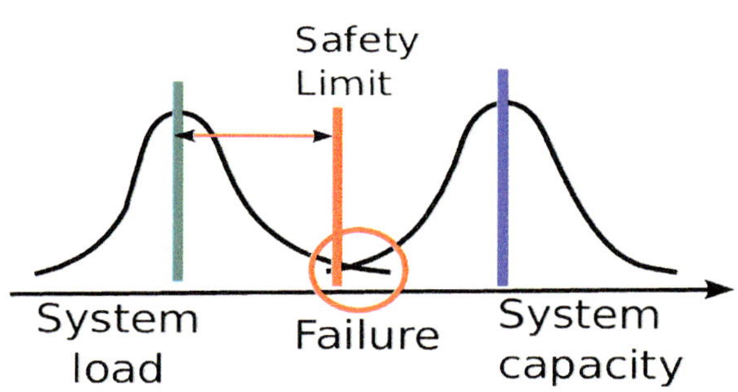

A system can continue to function by including a safety margin even if minor mistakes are made when calculating the maximum possible power and cooling request or if some unapproved IT equipment is introduced. To loose change standard operating procedures in data centers, up to 30% security margins may be used instead of the usual range of 10% to 20%. Its capacity is unavailable for IT deployments (Harrison et al., (2001) (Figure 6.6).

6.5.4 Stranded Capacity

Stranded capacity represents the capacity that is not accessible to IT loads owing to system architecture or design. Stranded capacity denotes an absence of any of the following capabilities:

i. Floor and rack space
ii. Power
iii. Power distribution
iv. Cooling
v. Cooling distribution (Farfan & Breyer, 2017).

All five ingredients must be present in adequate quantity for certain IT equipment. Nevertheless, these pieces are usually never accessible in the specific capacity proportion required to meet a given IT demand. There are always sites with rack space but still no available cooling or areas with electricity but no accessible rack capacity. Stranded capacity is an ability of one kind that is not used as one of the remaining four capacities described above has been utilized to its full capacity. Stranded capacity is undesired and can severely impede a data center's efficiency. Sadly, many data centers have substantial stranded capacity difficulties, with notable instances including (Kozlov & Lohman, 1999):

i. An air conditioning unit has appropriate capacity but low air dispersion to the IT load.
ii. A power distribution unit (PDU) has enough capacity but no open breaker locations.
iii. There is still floor space available, but no electricity.
iv. The air conditioners are in the wrong place.
v. Certain PDUs are overcrowded, while others are underutilized.
vi. Some parts are extremely hot, while others are frigid (Auger et al., 2021).

Based on the condition and the design of the cooling and power systems, it may be difficult to employ stranded capacity, or just minimal expenditures may be required to liberate stranded capacity for effective use. The use of stranded capacity has a cost. Removing a portion of the system or adding new cooling and power equipment is frequently essential (Jain et al., 1976). Since it is hard to explain to consumers or management why a data center, for instance, with 1 MW of power rating as well as cooling capacity, cannot cool this same new blade servers while it is only able to operate at 200 kW of load capacity, stranded capacity constitutes an extremely frustrating capacity management issue for operators of data centers.

In addition to identifying and emphasizing stranded capacity, a good capacity management system aids customers in preventing its creation in the first place (Oshiro & Fujimori, 2021).

6.6 MANAGING CAPACITY

The foundation for calculating the demand and supply of cooling and electricity has been developed in the earlier sections (Bradley & Glynn, 2002).

One may imagine a system for managing water cooling capacity based on measurements made by personnel and calculations made on paper; in fact, several data centers utilize a primitive version of this approach. Nevertheless, with the development of virtualization and IT technology, which constantly modifies its power and cooling requirements, utilizing connected power and cooling instruments paired with combined cooling and power capacity management solutions represents the sole realistic and practicable approach (Figure 6.7).

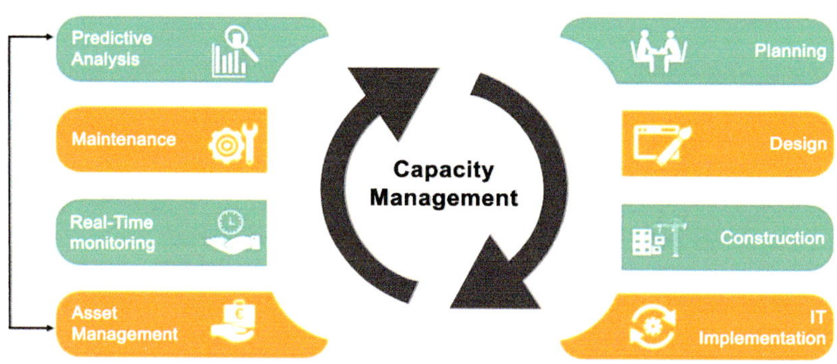

Figure 6.7. Illustration of capacity management (Source: NovelVista, Creative Commons License).

Such a technology would, within the user's eyes, offer the following features (Wu et al., 2005):

a) Presentation of capacity data
b) Setting the capacity plan
c) Alerting on violations of the capacity plan

d) Modeling proposed changes (Ahmadi, 1997).

6.6.1 Presentation of Capacity Data

The following levels should illustrate the data center's current demand and supply situations, including stranded capacity, spare capacity, and other capacity factors discussed previously in this paper (Burrows et al., 2000).

6.6.1.1 Room Level

Different capabilities of the entire space and the supply and demand at the bulk level. Focus primarily on the chiller, UPS, generator, cooling tower, and service entry equipment at the plant level (Li et al., 2012).

6.6.1.2 Row Level

Demand and supply for cooling and power related to rows or other logic zones inside the data center. Row-oriented cooling systems and power transmission technology, like PDUs, are frequently used together. Very useful for planning while rack-level information regarding the layout of certain racks is unknown (De Vitiis et al., 2020).

6.6.1.3 Rack Level

Demand and supply for cooling and power related to a particular rack or cabinet. This amount of information is necessary to diagnose issues or evaluate the effects of the deployment of IT devices. Perhaps connected to cooling systems and rack-level distributing circuits (Shah et al., 2008).

6.6.1.4 Organization Level

Executives need knowledge of both the usage and capacity utilization of the firm data centers as the emphasis on energy-efficient computing grows, and operations at data centers are required to lower their energy budget drastically (Tharenou et al., 2007).

The information mentioned above will be shown in a hierarchy drill-down model by good capacity management software and a visual showing the data center structure. Figures 6.8 and 6.9 show the room-level perspective and the organizing view, respectively (Gillespie & Dietz, 2009).

Did you Know?

High-density IT equipment can generate a significant amount of heat. This heat must be managed effectively to prevent damage to the equipment and ensure optimal performance.

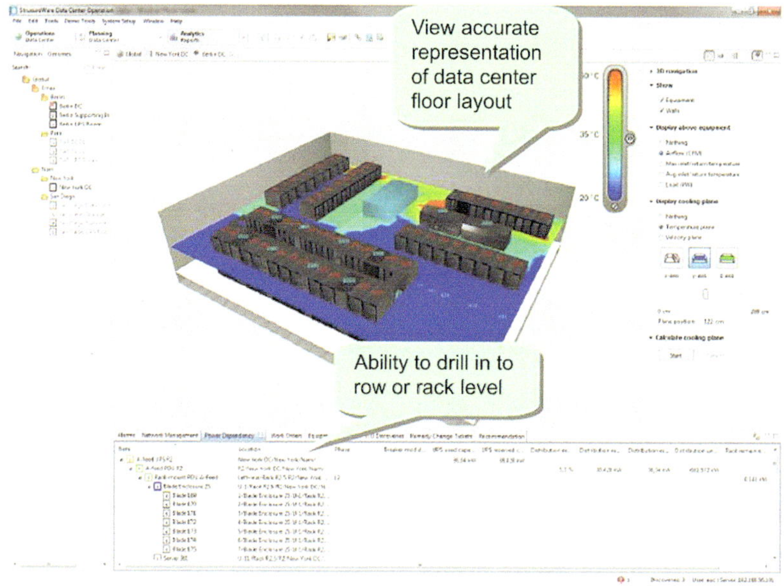

Figure 6.8. An illustration of how the Schneider Electric StruxureWare Data Center Operation program may be used to explore data center layout views (Source: White paper 115, Creative Commons License).

Figure 6.9. Image of Vizor app presenting organizational-level capacity metrics for mobile and iPad usage is an example view utilizing Schneider Electric StruxureWare Data Center Operation. (Source: White paper 115, Creative Commons License).

6.6.2 Setting the Capacity Plan

The data center's design process must include creating a capacity plan. After being deployed in the data center, the cooling and power equipment limits and, in some ways, "becomes" the demand side of a capacity plan. It is feasible to establish a production schedule that could adapt to IT expansion plans to minimize capacity expenditure and maximize electrical efficiency thanks to today's scalable data center power and cooling technologies (Von Lanzenauer et al., 2002).

It's crucial to guarantee the right amount of capacity and sufficient capacity. Too frequently, ensuring adequate capacity is prioritized over properly scaling for IT requirements. Oversizing is a typical outcome, hurting water usage, energy use, capital spending, and service contracts (Garland et al., 2016).

Datacenter different tools and techniques must be incorporated into the data center infrastructure management (DCIM) system since they aid in creating capacity plans. The InfraStruXure Designer data center design tool and the StruxureWare for Data Centers DCIM package from Schneider Electric are two examples of such a collection of software products (Taylor & Letham, 2018).

6.6.3 Alerting on Violations of the Capacity Plan

When real conditions exceed the parameters of a capacity management strategy, notifications about capacity must be raised. Local, visual, or audio alerts, websites, emails, and other management system communications, can be used to convey these cautions.

With the occurrence of certain user-defined events, such as:

1. Power usage of installed equipment inside a rack that is more than the maximum amount allowed by the capacity management strategy for that rack, room, or row.
2. It reduced cooling or power capability at the row, room, or rack level due to the failure or deterioration of a cooling and power subsystem.
3. They are entering a state where they cannot deliver the redundancy stipulated within the capacity management strategy for cooling or electricity systems (Gunther, 2007).

A hardware malfunction did not cause several of these occurrences. Therefore typical monitoring systems would not have detected any of them. A capacity management system's notifications tend to be proactive or predictive. It should be noted in a real data center, the capacity planning system works with other monitoring software, including real-time temperature, security, water leak, and fault monitoring. StruxureWare Central from Schneider Electric is a monitoring system that provides combined real-time warnings and capacity management notifications (Hooper, 1996).

6.6.4 Modeling Proposed Changes

An efficient DCIM system must enable capacity analysis in real-world and fictitious scenarios and determine present circumstances. These situations might involve:

a) Simulating malfunctions, such as the loss of a few cooling or power units.

b) Comparing anticipated growth with actual capacity utilization.

c) Proposals for adding, removing, and moving equipment.

d) Using historical data to predict trends (Green, 1991).

These scenarios must be compared to the current capacity management strategy using DCIM's features. To increase electricity efficiency or reduce floor space usage, for instance, an effective model should direct the user toward the optimum scenario among the alternatives. Figure 6.10 illustrates how DCIM may assist with equipment modifications by ensuring that each site has enough space, power, and cooling to accommodate the addition of new IT technology (Snijders, 1996).

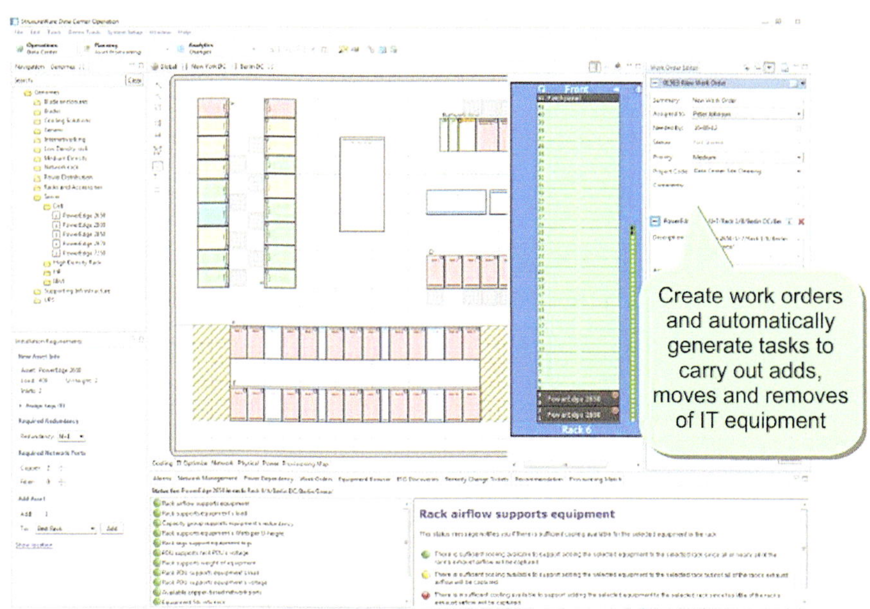

Figure 6.10. Image of example of the StruxureWare Data Center Operation (Source: Schneider Electric, Creative Commons License).

6.7 Monitoring Power and Cooling for IT Devices

Most of the time, a rack can be considered a power-guzzling black box that consumes electricity without knowing the IT equipment's number, kind, or position. If the power utilized at the rack level could be explicitly stated or monitored, the capacity planning system, as defined, only marginally depends on device-specific data. High-precision estimates of cooling needs may be made if the power usage is understood. There is no need for further information to verify that the cooling and power systems can accommodate the demand when such rack level numbers are within the parameters of the capacity plan. Consequently, capacity management provides numerous benefits to IT operations with the correct tools without requiring extensive inventory management of the IT assets. Nonetheless, there are benefits to knowing about the IT equipment in the rack or speaking with the IT equipment directly. These benefits consist of the following (Perpiñà et al., 2006):

a) Knowledge of the power user features of certain IT components
b) Understanding the devices' lowest and highest time-varying power characteristics
c) Being aware of unexpected needs for airflow or other uncommon fan operating modes
d) Use of U-space only at rack level (space capacity)
e) Ability to accurately analyze the impact of additions, deletions, or alterations.

ACTIVITY 6.1

As an IT manager of a large retail company, you have been asked to evaluate the current capacity of your company's e-commerce system. The company's online store has been growing rapidly over the past year, and the CEO is concerned that the current system might not be able to handle the increased traffic during the upcoming holiday season.

What specific factors would you consider when assessing the system-level capacities of your e-commerce platform? How would you go about identifying any potential bottlenecks in the system, and what steps would you recommend to ensure that the platform can handle the expected increase in traffic?

Capacity management software should understand the data to properly employ information acquired through precise inventory management (Jung et al., 2014).

Many small to medium-sized data centers lack the processes and structures, and the workforce is required to keep track of rack-related IT devices that allow inventory and change history. As a result, a capacity management solution cannot rely on the existence of such information but must be able to use it whenever it is available. Organizations may progress from basic capacity planning to an additional complete solution that includes modification and inventory control as they grow. Change management with capacity management interacts bidirectionally because change management relies heavily on capacity information management to calculate the effect of planned changes (Sun et al., 2013).

SUMMARY

The effective design and management of data centers depend heavily on capacity planning. The data center's complexity, scale, and density all increase the requirement for capacity management. There has been a description of a capacity management approach. It has been demonstrated that capacity planning, unlike conventional comprehensive inventory management systems, does not require precise information on the IT equipment at the rack level and involves less work to establish and maintain while still delivering most of the essential benefits. Capacity management, as this white paper outlines, could offer vital data center status insights that conventional monitoring methods do not. Newer DCIM software solutions offer the required features for effective and efficient capacity planning "out of the box" when paired with network power and cooling measurements.

REVIEW QUESTIONS

1. Why is power and cooling management important for IT systems?
2. What is the significance of high density IT equipment in power and cooling management?
3. How is capacity supply related to system level capacities in power and cooling management?
4. What are the key steps involved in managing capacity for power and cooling in IT systems?
5. What are some effective mechanisms for monitoring power and cooling in IT devices and systems?

MULTIPLE CHOICE QUESTIONS

1. Which of the following statements accurately reflects the importance of power and cooling management?

a) It has no significant impact on the overall performance of IT systems.
b) It can help reduce energy costs and improve system reliability.
c) It only affects large data centers and not smaller IT environments.
d) It is not a critical concern for IT administrators.

2. Why is the significance of high density IT equipment a key consideration in power and cooling management?

a) It can help reduce the overall energy consumption of IT systems.
b) It can lead to higher performance and productivity of IT systems.
c) It requires more power and cooling resources than traditional IT equipment.
d) It has no impact on the overall power and cooling requirements of IT systems.

3. **What is the concept of capacity supply and system level capacities in power and cooling management?**
   a) It refers to the total power and cooling resources available for IT systems.
   b) It is the ability to provide uninterrupted power and cooling to IT systems.
   c) It refers to the maximum amount of power and cooling that can be provided to individual IT components.
   d) It is the process of managing power and cooling requirements at the system level.
4. **What is the process of managing capacity in power and cooling management?**
   a) It involves adding more power and cooling resources to IT systems as needed.
   b) It requires regular monitoring and analysis of power and cooling usage.
   c) It involves balancing power and cooling resources across multiple IT components.
   d) It requires setting maximum limits on power and cooling usage for individual IT components.
5. **What is the mechanism of monitoring power and cooling for IT devices?**
   a) It involves physically checking the temperature and power usage of each device.
   b) It requires installing specialized software to track power and cooling usage.
   c) It involves relying on manufacturer specifications to estimate power and cooling requirements.
   d) It requires regular maintenance and cleaning of IT equipment.
6. **Which of the following is a benefit of effective power and cooling management?**
   a) Reduced energy costs
   b) Improved system reliability
   c) Increased system performance
   d) All of the above
7. **What is the main challenge associated with managing power and cooling for high-density IT equipment?**
   a) Identifying the specific power and cooling needs of each component
   b) Ensuring there is enough physical space to accommodate all equipment
   c) Balancing power and cooling requirements across multiple components
   d) Minimizing the risk of equipment failure due to overheating.

Answers to Multiple Choice Questions

1. (b) 2. (c) 3. (d) 4. (c) 5. (b)
6. (d) 7. (d)

REFERENCES

1. Ahmadi, R. H. (1997). Managing capacity and flow at theme parks. *Operations Research*, *45*(1), 1–13.
2. Auger, T., Trüby, J., Balcombe, P., & Staffell, I. (2021). The future of coal investment, trade, and stranded assets. *Joule*, *5*(6), 1462–1484.
3. Bond, L., Glover, S., Godfrey, C., Butler, H., & Patton, G. C. (2001). Building capacity for system-level change in schools: lessons from the Gatehouse Project. *Health Education & Behavior*, *28*(3), 368–383.
4. Bradley, J. R., & Glynn, P. W. (2002). Managing capacity and inventory jointly in manufacturing systems. *Management Science*, *48*(2), 273–288.
5. Bulow, J., Geanakoplos, J., & Klemperer, P. (1985). Holding idle capacity to deter entry. *The Economic Journal*, *95*(377), 178–182.
6. Burrows, R. F., Ray, J. G., & Burrows, E. A. (2000). Bleeding risk and reproductive capacity among patients with factor XIII deficiency: a case presentation and review of the literature. *Obstetrical & Gynecological Survey*, *55*(2), 103.
7. Choudhury, M. R., Hsieh, M. K., Vidic, R. D., & Dzombak, D. A. (2012). Corrosion management in power plant cooling systems using tertiary-treated municipal wastewater as makeup water. *Corrosion Science*, *61*, 231–241.
8. De Vitis, G. A., Foglia, P., & Prete, C. A. (2020). Row-level algorithm to improve real-time performance of glass tube defect detection in the production phase. *IET Image Processing*, *14*(12), 2911–2921.
9. Dooley, J. J. (2013). Estimating the supply and demand for deep geologic CO2 storage capacity over the course of the 21st century: a meta-analysis of the literature. *Energy Procedia*, *37*, 5141–5150.
10. Ellram, L. (1993). Total cost of ownership: elements and implementation. *International Journal of Purchasing and Materials Management*, *29*(3), 2–11.
11. Ellram, L. M. (1995). Total cost of ownership: an analysis approach for purchasing. *International Journal of Physical Distribution & Logistics Management*, *25*(8), 4–2
12. Farfan, J., & Breyer, C. (2017). Structural changes of global power generation capacity towards sustainability and the risk of stranded investments supported by a sustainability indicator. *Journal of Cleaner Production*, *141*, 370–384.
13. Flum, D., Burkhardt, M., Moog, D., Sossenheimer, J., Sanchez, J., & Abele, E. (2019). Tool for Simulation-Based Planning of Energy-Optimised Cooling Supply System Configuration for Manufacturing Facilities. In *Advances in Production Research: Proceedings of the 8th Congress of the German Academic* Association for Production Technology (WGP), Aachen, November 19–20, 2018 8 (pp. 510–521).
14. Garland, A., Ashton-Cleary, D., & Sinclair, R. (2016). Inpatient illness severity surveys provide essential data for planning capacity and managing patient flow in the acute hospital setting. *Journal of the Intensive Care Society*, *17*(3), 196–201.

15. Gillespie, N., & Dietz, G. (2009). Trust repair after an organization-level failure. *Academy of Management Review*, *34*(1), 127–145.

16. Gouveia, A. G., Viani, G. A., Bratti, V. F., Pavoni, J. F., Sullivan, R., Rosa, A. A., ... & Moraes, F. Y. (2022). System-Level Capacity of High-Dose Rate (HDR) Brachytherapy for Management of Cervical Cancer in an Upper-Middle Income Country: A Case Study From Brazil. *International Journal of Radiation Oncology–Biology–Physics*, *114*(3), 545–553.

17. Green, R. C. (1991). [Diversity, Continuity and Change in the History of the Bismarck Archipelago] The Lapita Cultural Complex: current evidence and proposed models. *Bulletin of the Indo-Pacific Prehistory Association*, *11*, 295–305.

18. Gunther, N. J. (2007). Going Guerrilla—A Case Study. *Guerrilla Capacity Planning: A Tactical Approach to Planning for Highly Scalable Applications and Services*, 199–211.

19. Harrison, J. F., Camazine, S., Marden, J. H., Kirkton, S. D., Rozo, A., & Yang, X. (2001). Mite not make it home: tracheal mites reduce the safety margin for oxygen delivery of flying honeybees. *Journal of Experimental Biology*, *204*(4), 805–814.

20. Hooper, N. (1996). Dynamic distribution planning techniques: progressive logistics optimization for manufacturers. *Logistics Information Management*, *9*(3), 27–35.

21. Howlett, M. (2015). Policy analytical capacity: The supply and demand for policy analysis in government. *Policy and Society*, *34*(3–4), 173–182.

22. Jain, S. R. H. S., Markham, R., Thomas, H. C., & Sherlock, S. (1976). Double-stranded DNA-binding capacity of serum in acute and chronic liver disease. *Clinical and Experimental Immunology*, *26*(1), 35.

23. Ji, F., Yang, S. H., Cao, X. D., & Yang, Y. B. (2021). Simulation of Multi-area Integrated Energy for Cooling, Heating and Power Based on Large Data Analysis. In *Advanced Hybrid Information Processing: 4th EAI International Conference, ADHIP 2020, Binzhou, China, September 26–27, 2020, Proceedings, Part I 4* (pp. 460–471).

24. Jung, S., Lee, J., Hyeon, T., Lee, M., & Kim, D. H. (2014). Fabric-based integrated energy devices for wearable activity monitors. *Advanced Materials*, *26*(36), 6329–6334.

25. Keeling, S. (2008). Time to branch out: the rapid pace of change in health care means nurse education needs urgent reform. *Nursing Standard*, *22*(32), 69–70.

26. Kozlov, A. G., & Lohman, T. M. (1999). Adenine base unstacking dominates the observed enthalpy and heat capacity changes for the Escherichia coli SSB tetramer binding to single-stranded oligoadenylates. *Biochemistry*, *38*(22), 7388–7397.

27. Laine, H. S., Salpakari, J., Looney, E. E., Savin, H., Peters, I. M., & Buonassisi, T. (2019). Meeting global cooling demand with photovoltaics during the 21st century. *Energy & Environmental Science*, *12*(9), 2706–2716.

28. Levinthal, D. A. (1998). The slow pace of rapid technological change: gradualism and punctuation in technological change. *Industrial and Corporate Change*, *7*(2), 217–247.

29. Li, Y., Fazio, P., & Rao, J. (2012). An investigation of moisture buffering performance of wood paneling at room level and its buffering effect on a test room. *Building and Environment*, *47*, 205–216.

30. Liu, Y., Tipper, D., & Siripongwutikorn, P. (2005). Approximating optimal spare capacity allocation by successive survivable routing. *IEEE/ACM Transactions on Networking*, *13*(1), 198–211.

31. Mutschler, R., Rüdisüli, M., Heer, P., & Eggimann, S. (2021). Benchmarking cooling and heating energy demands considering climate change, population growth and cooling device uptake. *Applied Energy*, *288*, 116636.

32. Nathuji, R., & Schwan, K. (2007). Virtualpower: coordinated power management in virtualized enterprise systems. *ACM SIGOPS operating systems review*, *41*(6), 265-278.

33. Ondeck, A. D., Edgar, T. F., & Baldea, M. (2015). Optimal operation of a residential district-level combined photovoltaic/natural gas power and cooling system. *Applied Energy*, *156*, 593–606.

34. Oshiro, K., & Fujimori, S. (2021). Stranded investment associated with rapid energy system changes under the mid-century strategy in Japan. *Sustainability Science*, *16*(2), 477–487.

35. Pan, H., Qi, L., Zhang, X., Zhang, Z., Salman, W., Yuan, Y., & Wang, C. (2017). A portable renewable solar energy-powered cooling system based on wireless power transfer for a vehicle cabin. *Applied Energy*, *195*, 334–343.

36. Patrick, R., Baldwin, S., & Williams, N. (2000). Application of direct bias control in high-density inductively coupled plasma etching equipment. *Journal of Vacuum Science & Technology A: Vacuum, Surfaces, and Films*, *18*(2), 405–410.

37. Perpiñ, X., Serviere, J. F., Saiz, J., Barlini, D., Mermet-Guyennet, M., & Millán, J. (2006). Temperature measurement on series resistance and devices in power packs based on on-state voltage drop monitoring at high current. *Microelectronics Reliability*, *46*(9–11), 1834–1839.

38. Shah, A., Patel, C., Bash, C., Sharma, R., & Shih, R. (2008, May). Impact of rack-level compaction on the data center cooling ensemble. In *2008 11th Intersociety Conference on Thermal and Thermomechanical Phenomena in Electronic Systems* (pp. 1175–1182). IEEE.

39. Shahriar, N., Chowdhury, S. R., Ahmed, R., Khan, A., Fathi, S., Boutaba, R., ... & Liu, L. (2018). Virtual network survivability through joint spare capacity allocation and embedding. *IEEE Journal on Selected Areas in Communications*, *36*(3), 502–518.

40. Smith, C. L., & Freeman, R. L. (2002). Using continuous system level assessment to build school capacity. *American Journal of Evaluation*, *23*(3), 307–319.

41. Snijders, T. A. (1996). Stochastic actor-oriented models for network change. *Journal of Mathematical Sociology*, *21*(1–2), 149–172.

42. Stillwell, A. S., Clayton, M. E., & Webber, M. E. (2011). Technical analysis of a river

basin-based model of advanced power plant cooling technologies for mitigating water management challenges. *Environmental Research Letters*, *6*(3), 034015.

43. Sun, M. J., Liu, S., & Wei, X. S. (2013). The Research of Automatic Monitoring Devices for Circulating Cooling Water. In *Advanced Materials Research* (Vol. 616, pp. 1940–1943).
44. Taylor, S. J., & Letham, B. (2018). Forecasting at scale. *The American Statistician*, *72*(1), 37–45.
45. Tharenou, P., Saks, A. M., & Moore, C. (2007). A review and critique of research on training and organizational-level outcomes. *Human Resource Management Review*, *17*(3), 251–273.
46. Von Lanzenauer, C. H., Eschen, E., & Pilz-Glombik, K. (2002). Capacity Planning in a Transitional Setting with Simulation-based Modeling: A Case Study. *International Transactions in Operational Research*, *9*(2), 125–139.
47. Wang, Z., Tolia, N., & Bash, C. (2010, April). Opportunities and challenges to unify workload, power, and cooling management in data centers. In *Proceedings of the Fifth International Workshop on Feedback Control Implementation and Design in Computing Systems and Networks* (pp. 1–6).
48. Wu, S. D., Erkoc, M., & Karabuk, S. (2005). Managing capacity in the high-tech industry: A review of literature. *The Engineering Economist*, *50*(2), 125–158.
49. Wu, Z., Sun, H., & Du, Y. (2014). A large amount of idle capacity under rapid expansion: Policy analysis on the dilemma of wind power utilization in China. *Renewable and Sustainable Energy Reviews*, *32*, 271–277.
50. Xiong, Y., & Mason, L. G. (1999). Restoration strategies and spare capacity requirements in self-healing ATM networks. *IEEE/ACM Transactions on Networking*, *7*(1), 98–110.
51. Yahdjian, L., Sala, O. E., & Havstad, K. M. (2015). Rangeland ecosystem services: shifting focus from supply to reconciling supply and demand. *Frontiers in Ecology and the Environment*, *13*(1), 44–51.
52. Zhou, Y., Panteli, M., Moreno, R., & Mancarella, P. (2018). System-level assessment of reliability and resilience provision from microgrids. *Applied Energy*, *230*, 374–392.

CHAPTER 7

CHALLENGES IN DATA CENTER MANAGEMENT

UNIT INTRODUCTION

Data centers are an essential component of modern corporate infrastructure, allowing companies to store, analyze, and manage massive volumes of data. Yet, data center administration presents several issues that can negatively influence an organization's productivity, security, and economics. This article will examine a few of the most pressing issues confronting data center administration and offer potential solutions (Wierman et al., 2014).

Data security is likely the most pressing issue confronting data storage management today. User data, intellectual property, and financial data are all stored in data centers, making them ideal cyber-attack targets. A data breach may be devastating, resulting in financial loss, legal responsibility, and reputational harm. To defend their systems against cyber-attacks, data center administrators must deploy comprehensive security procedures such as firewalls, systems for intrusion detection, access restrictions, and encryption (Schmidt et al., 2005).

Power management is very difficult since data centers need a lot of energy to run. Data center downtime due to power outages or variations can cost businesses money and productivity, especially data. Managers of data centers need to make sure their power stations are dependable, redundant, and expandable to accommodate varying needs. To reduce energy use, they may install energy-saving technology like virtualization, power software solutions, and effective cooling systems.

Another significant obstacle for data center organizations is capacity planning. Data centers must ensure companies have enough storage and processing power to handle increasing data volumes without experiencing outages or performance deterioration. Predicting future data requirements, choosing the right infrastructure, and expanding resources as necessary are all parts of capacity planning. Data center administrators may use metrics and machine learning methods to predict capacity requirements (Kant, 2009).

A network of interconnected devices that gather and send data is known as the Internet of Things (IoT). IoT devices produce massive volumes of data, and data centers are required to store, analyze, and process this data. The infrastructure of data centers must accommodate the growing number of IoT devices and the data they produce. They must also put strong security measures in place to safeguard IoT devices from online dangers.

Mobile businesses further hamper data center administration. Data centers should offer dependable and secure access to information and apps from any place, given the prevalence of mobile gadgets and remote work. Data center managers must ensure that their architecture can support demands for remote access while ensuring the privacy and security of customer data. They could put virtual private networks (VPNs), two-factor identification, and other security measures in place to safeguard mobile devices (Soundararajan & Govil, 2010).

The real news is crucial for data-driven enterprises that must act quickly on data and insights. Data center managers must ensure that their architecture delivers good reporting features without sacrificing performance. They can use data analytics and visualization tools to give real-time insights into the operations of data centers.

Data center administrators must delicately strike a balance between cost control and efficiency. Successful businesses must manage expenditures, but they also need to maintain an effective and dependable infrastructure. Data center administrators can use automation, energy-efficient technology, and virtualization to cut expenses and boost efficiency (Krein, 2017).

For effective data center administration, monitoring with infrastructure visibility is essential. To find and fix problems before they become significant, data center administrators require a good awareness of the availability and performance of their equipment. They could use technologies for monitoring technology that offer real-time warnings and insight into an infrastructure's functionality.

Another significant issue facing network infrastructure management is security policy. To defend against cyberattacks, data centers need strong network security, like firewalls, encryption, intrusion detection systems, and access restrictions. Data center managers must ensure their network security methods are current and capable of thwarting cyber threats (Garimella et al., 2012). Critical elements that affect the overall effectiveness of the operations of data centers include availability and performance. Data center managers must ensure existing infrastructure is easily accessible and capable of meeting rising demands without deteriorating performance. They can use technologies like load balancing, cluster analysis, and others to spread out workloads and provide high availability.

Many difficulties with data center administration can affect an organization's productivity, security, and financial success. Data center administrators must establish strong security procedures, dependable power infrastructure, effective resource control, and efficient and effective strategy to address these issues. Give their consumers a smooth experience; businesses must also keep an eye on them again and optimize the operation and accessibility of their equipment. Datacenter management may overcome these difficulties and promote corporate achievement in the digital era with the appropriate strategies and technology in place (Koutitas & Demestichas, 2010).

Learning Objectives

At the end of the chapter, the reader will be able to understand:

1. The challenges required for data security
2. The Concept of the Internet of Things (IoT)
3. The significance of real-time reporting and the challenge related to it
4. The importance of Mobile enterprises and the challenge related to it
5. The challenges required for performance and availability

Key Terms

1. Data Security
2. Firewall
3. Cyber Threat
4. Power Management
5. Data Center Infrastructure Management (DCIM)
6. Mobile Device Management (MDM)
7. Mobile Application Management (MAM)

7.1 DATA SECURITY

Data security prevents unwanted access, theft, alteration, and the destruction of sensitive and secret data. It is a crucial part of data technology for everyone, including corporations, governments, and private citizens (Denning & Denning, 1979). Using different safeguards for data includes data security.

7.1.1 Access Control

Access to data should be restricted to authorized individuals and allowed according to user responsibilities and privileges (Sandhu & Samarati, 1994) (Figure 7.1).

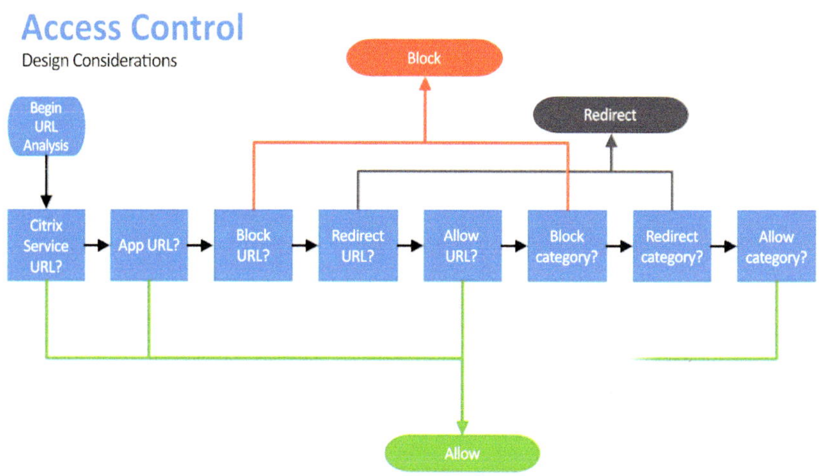

Figure 7.1. Example of data security (Source: Citrix, Creative Commons License).

7.1.2 Encryption

The data is converted into a secret code to protect unwanted access to confidential information (Davis, 1978).

7.1.3 Firewalls

A security system that monitors and restricts network traffic according to set security criteria (Bellovin & Cheswick, 1994) (Figure 7.2).

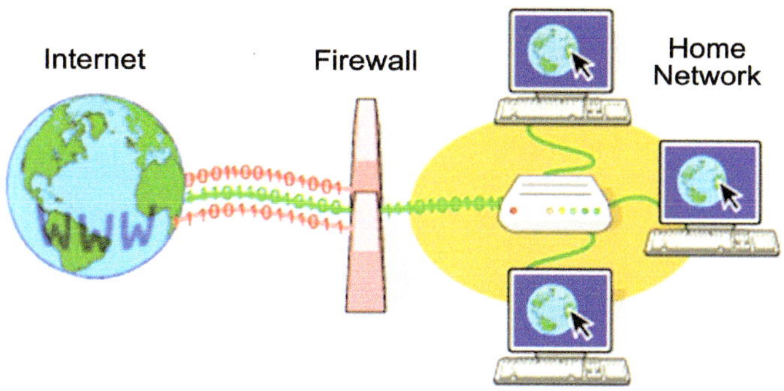

Figure 7.2. Diagram showing how a firewall operates (Source: How stuff works, Creative Commons License).

7.1.4 Antivirus and Anti-Malware

Software that can identify and eliminate harmful programs or files that might damage a network or machine (Potter & Day, 2009).

7.1.5 Backup and Recovery

Solutions for data backup to prevent data loss and allow data recovery in the event of system faults or calamities (Sharma & Singh, 2012). Because of the constantly shifting nature of cybersecurity risks, such as hacking, phishing malware, and ransomware assaults, data security issues develop. The following subheadings includes some typical difficulties in data security.

7.1.5.1 Increasing Sophistication of Cyber Threats

Attackers are always coming up with new ways to exploit weaknesses in data security devices due to the ongoing evolution of cyber threats (Choo, 2011).

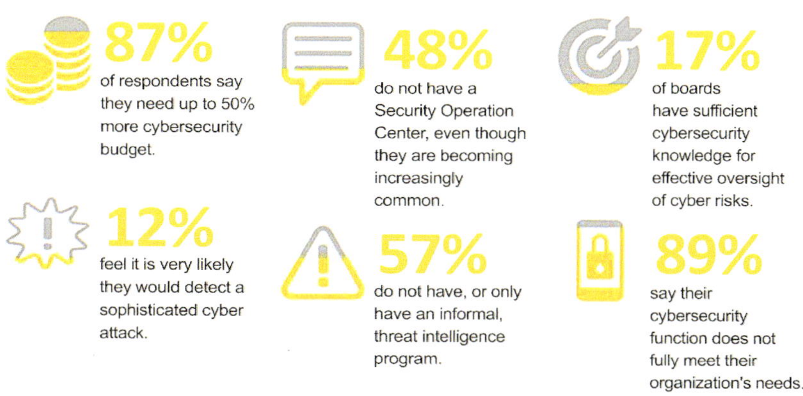

Figure 7.3. An example of a sophisticated cyber threat (Source: Help net security, Creative Commons License)

7.1.5.2 Insider Threats

Whether deliberate or accidental, illegal access by staff or subcontractors can threaten data security (Hunker & Probst, 2011).

7.1.6 Compliance with Data Protection Regulations

Companies must comply with complicated and difficult data protection rules, including the General Data Protection Regulation (GDPR) and the Health Insurance Portability and Accountability Act (HIPAA) (Kingston, 2017).

Did you Know?

The global capacity planning market is projected to reach USD 4.9 billion by 2024, with a compound annual growth rate (CAGR) of 11.4% from 2019 to 2024.

7.1.7 Integration of New Technologies

Emerging technologies, including the Internet of Things (IoT) like cloud computing, introduce new security concerns, such as safeguarding data transported over various networks and maintaining the security of information kept in the cloud (Choudhury & Harrigan, 2014).

7.1.8 Budget Constraints

Successfully implementing data security measures necessitates substantial expenditure, and many businesses may be constrained by financial restrictions that prevent them from investing in effective security technologies.

Data security is a recurring topic in networking in data centers' challenges. Security breaches may result in millions of dollars in stolen intellectual property, sensitive data breaches, and identity theft. Each data center administrator's first concern is risk assessment and protecting data stored and sent across the network (Moffitt, 1986).

7.2 POWER MANAGEMENT

Among the major issues facing data center operations is power control. Power failures or fluctuations could cause considerable downtime, leading to lost productivity, income, and data since data centers require a lot of energy. Making sure the electric grid is dependable, redundant, and scalable to meet the changing needs is part of power management. Datacenter administrators may overcome this problem by implementing energy-saving technology like power software solutions, virtualization, and effective cooling systems. They may also use renewable energy sources like solar and wind energy to power the operations of data centers. Data center administrators may increase the effectiveness and dependability of business operations, save energy costs, and enhance efficiency by tackling power management issues (Sinha & Chandrakasan, 2001) (Figure 7.4).

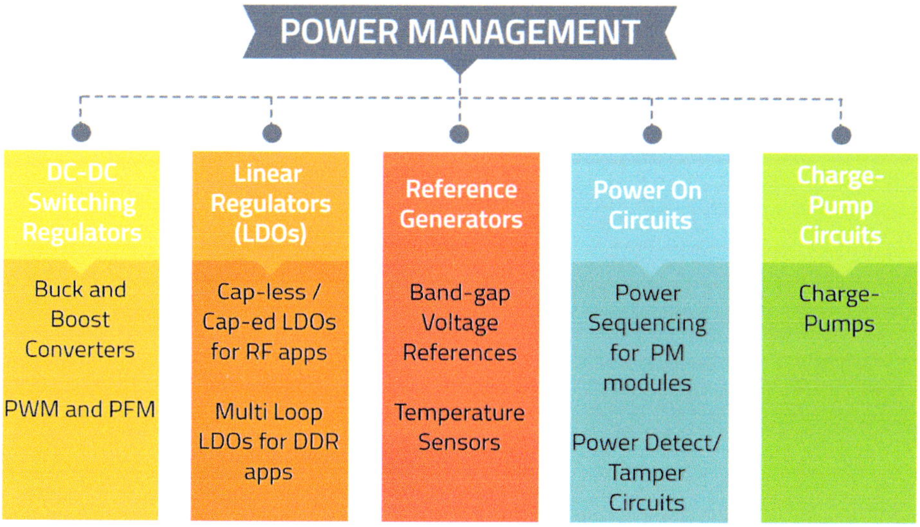

Figure 7.4. Diagram of the power management process (Source: Sankalp Semiconductor, Creative Commons License).

A variety of tasks are involved in managing power utilization in data centers.

7.2.1 Monitoring Power Usage

It's crucial to monitor how much electricity different parts of a data center are using. Servers, networking hardware, cooling systems, and power distribution units are all included (PDUs). Monitoring power utilization enables the detection of inefficiencies, and unusual energy consumption patterns, including improvement opportunities (Khan, 2001).

7.2.2 Power Distribution Management

PDUs are used in data centers to deliver power to different components. Power is supplied effectively and dependably to every element without overwhelming the system, thanks to good power transmission management (Pohjanheimo & Lakervi, 2000).

7.2.3 Cooling Management

A controlled working environment must be maintained by cooling systems since data centers produce a lot of heat. Effective cooling management ensures that cooling towers work as efficiently as possible, using less energy while upholding the desired temperature (Zapater et al., 2014).

7.2.4 Power Redundancy

To provide an uninterrupted supply of electricity, data centers should have back–up power systems set up. Uninterruptible power supply (UPS) or backup generators are examples of such backup power solutions (Gardner et al., 2017).

7.2.5 Power Efficiency Optimization

Virtualization, utilization monitoring, and consolidation are some approaches that may be utilized to improve power usage. Data centers may minimize the number of physical servers by using virtualized and consolidation, which reduces power usage. Utilization monitoring identifies new servers that may be decommissioned or repurposed to reduce total power usage (Isheden et al., 2012).

Power management within data centers is crucial for lowering energy costs, increasing dependability, and lowering environmental impact.

7.3 CAPACITY PLANNING

Ensuring peak performance necessitates running a data center at full capacity. Running out of capacity is a fatal obstacle. Thus, IT managers frequently put aside certain fault tolerance to ensure the data center's functioning. Managers are, therefore, increasingly favoring data center infrastructure management (DCIM) technologies as an effective strategy for handling capacity. DCIM systems may detect computing, storage, and cooling power while assisting in more effective data center management and achieving full capacity, hence keeping server farms at risk within limitations (Geng & Jiang, 2009).

Both beginners and specialists in data centers can relate to the difficulties of capacity management. Money is squandered if there is an excess or insufficient room or when there are too many or insufficient resources. Bad planning also wastes energy. The management of data center infrastructure is critical to resolving this issue. Management must have specified mechanisms to identify and track what is required and what is unnecessary (Eppen et al., 1989).

It is nearly hard to comprehend how much room, power, as well as cooling they have, anticipate when they will run out, choose one server that is appropriate for additional services, and determine precisely how often power is required to ensure uptime as well as availability inside a dynamic data center. To rapidly model and distribute space, control power, and control network connectivity with a DCIM solution is essential for finding hidden potential and controlling the capacity you already have (Figure 7.5).

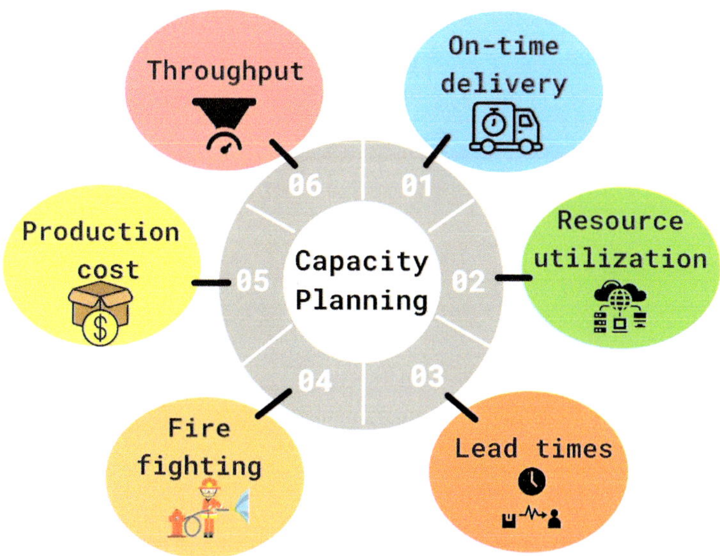

Figure 7.5. Example of capacity planning (Source: ERP information, Creative Commons License).

7.4 INTERNET OF THINGS (IOT)

Datacenter administration is further complicated by the capability to operate sensors remotely. Data centers need to boost bandwidth rates to process, save, and analyze data streams more favorably due to the expansion of the Internet of Everything and the enormous rise of data records. Control the volume of data; new data center techniques like edge computing should be implemented (Madakam et al., 2015).

The interconnected network with physical objects, including machines, cars, buildings, and other items, is called the Internet of Things (IoT). These objects have software, sensors, and connections that enable data exchange and online communication. That linked device network can completely transform how we conduct our lives and work by enabling the automation, control, and monitoring of many procedures and systems.

Nevertheless, managing the vast volumes of data these gadgets produce becomes increasingly difficult as the variety of linked devices increases. Data center managers can assist with this. The massive volumes of data IoT devices produce are processed, stored, and managed primarily through data centers (Gubbi et al., 2013).

Remember

As more and more devices become connected to the Internet of Things (IoT), it is important to ensure that proper security measures are in place to protect against potential cyberattacks.

Within the context of IoT, data center control presents three challenges.

7.4.1 Scalability

The amount of Internet of Things (IoT) devices and their data is growing exponentially. It implies that data centers must handle large volumes of data while being expandable enough to accommodate the increasing number of devices (McSherry et al., 2015).

7.4.2 Security

IoT devices are frequently vulnerable to computer hacking as well as cyberattacks. Safeguard the data such devices produce; information systems must have strong security mechanisms (Stewart, 2004).

7.4.3 Latency

IoT devices frequently need real-time data analysis; thus, there must be no lag or latency. Guarantee that IoT devices are operating effectively and that any reported problems are immediately fixed; data centers must be able to handle and always analyze information.

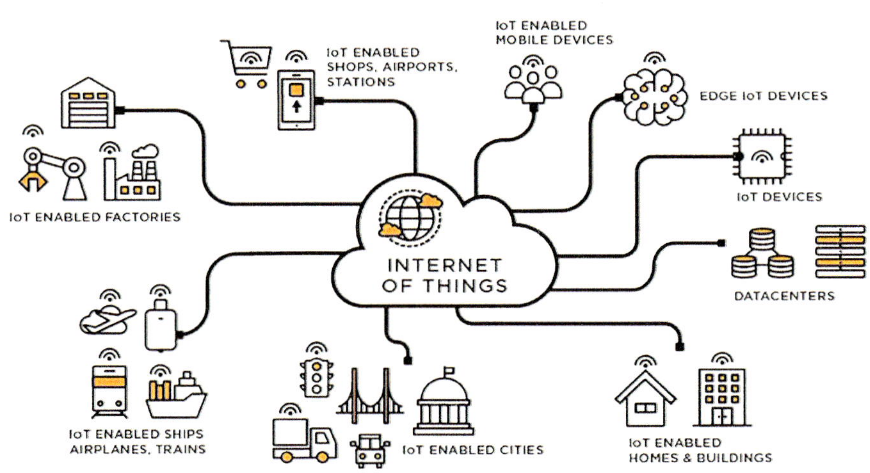

Figure 7.6. Schematic of Internet of Things (IoTs) (Source: Tibco, Creative Commons License).

The huge volumes of data created by connected devices, the necessity of scalability, the susceptibility of IoT devices against cyberattacks, and the demand for real-time data analysis make the web of things a big problem for data center administration (Rumble et al., 2011) (Figure 7.6).

7.5 MOBILE ENTERPRISE

Mobile computing and various personal devices further hampered data security within the data center. To avoid data leaking, company personnel must be watched and secured when individuals access vital corporate data on their devices. Furthermore, when remotely deleting the memory of mobile devices, tracing, and locking away or stealing devices, additional security is needed to prevent data breaches. Data centers should finally deal with the technological, organizational, and legal concerns that mobile corporate computing raises (Basole, 2007).

TIPS

In real-time reporting, prioritize accuracy and speed while ensuring the information is presented in a clear and concise manner.

And the use of mobile technological devices by organizations and businesses to enable their workers to work and access data from wherever at any time is referred to as mobile enterprise. Mobile Enterprise encompasses several applications and technology platforms, including mobile devices, mobile apps, mobile device management (MDM), including mobile application management (MAM). The desire for increased mobility and flexibility within the workforce has fueled the popularity of mobile devices related to workplace use in recent years. Mobile Enterprises, however, also pose significant management issues for data centers.

7.5.1 Network Performance

Wireless networks, which might be less dependable and have a lesser capacity than wired networks, are frequently used by mobile devices. It may result from performance problems and reduced access to data and processing (Sandström & Carlsson, 2008).

7.5.2 Scalability

The variety of mobile phones and apps businesses use can rapidly increase, making it challenging for data centers to meet the need for storage, computing power, and network bandwidth (Zamboni et al., 2019).

7.5.3 Device Management

Handling a large number of mobile devices, users, and applications may be a difficult and time-consuming task. It necessitates using mobile device management (MDM) with mobile application management (MAM) technologies to guarantee that devices and apps are safe, up to current, and correctly functioning (Rhee et al., 2012).

Data security, scalability, network performance, and device management are just a few of the important issues that Mobile Enterprise poses for data center administration. Strong security precautions, a dependable network infrastructure, effective devices, and application management technologies are necessary to address these difficulties (Pratt et al., 2014).

7.6 REAL-TIME REPORTING

The use of reports in the conventional method of IT monitoring has several drawbacks. Information can only reflect what has already occurred. When it is examined, patterns are recognized, and failures are forecast, it can be too late to implement the necessary corrections. Real-time reporting fills this gap by giving you real-time data, alarms, and notifications to manage errors promptly (Trigo et al., 2014).

With the advancements in data center technology, errors are inevitable. Potential problems include connections, network systems, cooling equipment, and applications. Routine system monitoring, including preventative data center management, is the key to resolving these issues.

You'll be more ready to face the future if you have a thorough understanding of the factors that contribute to technical errors and can see trends in the performance of your particular equipment. When things go wrong, you can make wise judgments if you understand your equipment more deeply (Zhang et al., 2015).

7.7 BALANCING COST CONTROLS WITH EFFICIENCY

The underlying paradox of data centers is between high efficiency and cheap cost. Datacenter administration calls for strict cost control and ensures the facility's effectiveness, creativity, and adaptability.

Green data centers are designed to be built sustainably; thus, businesses must closely regulate their data centers' power consumption and raise their awareness of their social and ecological duties. The physical constraints of servers, storage, and networking devices on applications could be lessened by existing virtualization technology. It may also achieve load balancing, address the inefficiency brought about by application setup web hosting, and effectively lower data center operational costs (Kraus et al., 2005). All data centers, by design, spend enormous quantities of energy in an incongruously inefficient way, according to a NY Times report. Online businesses often operate their facilities 24 hours a day at full capacity. Data centers can therefore squander 90% or more of the power they need from the grid.

Data center administrators may track energy usage, turn servers off at night, and find candidates for consolidating with a DCIM system. Environmental sensors may gather data to raise the temperature set point securely. Implementing an energy bill back scheme that promotes energy-efficient behavior could also benefit the business (Yang et al., 2021) (Figure 7.7).

Figure 7.7. Data Center Management Infrastructure Management Components Diagram (Source: Blue weave consultant, Creative Commons License).

According to Ciena.com, the power utilized to power cool the substantial amounts of technology needed accounts for up to 40% of a data center's operational expenditures. The quantity of energy data centers has been recognized to influence the environment negatively. Each manager's primary concern must be the energy consumption of data center control. Using energy monitoring systems to optimize your use may assist the environment and save money (Hu et al., 2019).

7.8 INFRASTRUCTURE MONITORING AND VISIBILITY

The challenge of obtaining comprehensive, real-time control and monitoring of remote networks remains one of the major pain issues for network engineers operating data center facilities (David et al., 2015).

While many manufacturers may provide different levels of remote device monitoring, maintaining a patchwork of various monitoring solutions is time-consuming and might result in coverage gaps. If a problem with a crucial piece of data center equipment is ignored for too long, it may even become a small problem that affects the entire organization. For instance, it may not first appear like a huge concern when a database server produces redundant or pointless logs. But your corporate applications, banking systems, and other systems can be affected if those logs build up to the point where the hard disk overflows and database functions stop working. As a result, it's critical to ensure that nothing slips through the gaps (Bickerstaff, 2022).

The constant monitoring and evaluation of the complete IT network is a key component of data center top management network monitoring and visibility, which aims to spot problems early on and solve them. It involves monitoring servers, network gadgets, storage systems, and other applications to ensure they operate properly (Bracs et al., 2016). Nevertheless, monitoring or visibility of the infrastructure provides several difficulties for data center operations.

7.8.1 Complexity

IT infrastructures for today are getting more and more complicated, requiring management, and monitoring of various layers of software and hardware components. Because of its complexity, it may be difficult to get a clear picture of the infrastructure, creating blind spots and complicating the effective troubleshooting of problems (Gray et al., 2010).

7.8.2 Data Overload

Data overload may be a major problem with the massive volumes of data produced by IT network monitoring applications. The enormous volume of data produced by these instruments can be difficult to assess and comprehend, resulting in missed alarms and serious problems (Woods et al., 2002).

7.8.3 Integration

Infrastructure monitoring and visualization technologies must relate to other IT management solutions to give a full perspective of the IT network. Integration may be difficult, particularly when integrating technologies from multiple providers (Steigenberger, 2017).

7.8.4 Scalability

Infrastructure control and visibility technologies must be adaptable enough to meet the increasing environmental demands as IT infrastructures evolve. It involves managing more data and expanding coverage throughout the infrastructure (Clarke & Dede, 2009).

7.8.5 Cost

Tools for monitoring and visibility of a company's IT infrastructure could be expensive, particularly when utilizing high-end solutions offering a complete picture of its IT infrastructure. Smaller firms may find it difficult to employ these technologies due to their high cost (Fankhauser, 2010).

In conclusion, monitoring and accessibility of infrastructure is a crucial component of data optimization, but it also comes with several difficulties, such as complexity, integration, data overload, scalability, and cost. It is necessary to address these difficulties by using technologies and tools that can offer a comprehensive perspective of the IT infrastructure and are scalable, affordable, and simple to use (Lee et al., 1996).

7.9 DATA CENTER NETWORK SECURITY

Critical infrastructure is not completely immune from cyberattacks simply because it is housed in a highly secure center. Managing company security rules and controls across or maybe more colocation sites is another typical data center management difficulty. It may be particularly challenging to use managed services and grant access to third-party suppliers or data center staff members (Knapp et al., 2011). A recent study found that granting third parties an excessive amount of access to sensitive information was the cause of 74% of breaches reported by corporations. You need a mechanism to uniformly apply corporate security policies across each remote infrastructure and confirm the legitimacy of each account trying to use data center services (Bari et al., 2012).

7.10 PERFORMANCE AND AVAILABILITY

The maximum performance and availability of the data center facilities must be maintained for your firm to operate as effectively as feasible. Operating regionally varied data centers without local employees or managed services at each site may be exceedingly difficult. If it fails in a data center 3,000 miles away, you need to restore a crucial switch quickly, so you don't have enough time to send an engineer to the opposite side of the nation to look at the issue (Jayasinghe et al., 2011).

Two crucial components of data center management include performance and availability, which relate to the capacity of the IT infrastructure to offer users dependable, responsive, and uninterrupted services. Performance describes the IT network's speed, effectiveness, and general reactivity, whereas availability describes the system's capacity to function and be reachable continuously.

However, ensuring optimal performance and availability presents several challenges for data center management, including:

7.10.1 Complexity

IT infrastructures nowadays are extremely complex, requiring a flawless interaction between several layers of software and hardware parts. It may be challenging to locate performance bottlenecks and conduct efficient troubleshooting because of the complex nature of the infrastructure (Logue et al., 2018).

7.10.2 Scalability

The IT infrastructure must be scalable enough to accommodate the rising load as user demands expand. It can be difficult to achieve scalability, particularly when employing outdated gear and software which might not be built to manage the needs of modern workloads.

7.10.3 Resiliency

Building resilience into the IT infrastructure, including redundant power sources, backup generators, and backup systems, is necessary to provide high availability. Yet, creating a highly robust infrastructure could be expensive, and many businesses would find it difficult to justify the expenditure.

7.10.4 Monitoring

It is crucial to keep track of the IT infrastructure's availability and performance to spot problems before they become serious. Nonetheless, monitoring may be difficult, particularly when working with several monitoring systems and significant volumes of data (Saito et al., 1999).

7.10.5 Cost

Investing in top-tier gear and software, which might be expensive, is frequently necessary to ensure the best availability and performance. For smaller firms that might not have the resources to invest in the newest technology, the cost may prove a major obstacle to its widespread use.

In conclusion, performance and availability are crucial components of data center operations, but they also pose several difficulties due to their complexity, resiliency, scalability, monitoring, and expense. Using technologies that are made for current workloads, including infrastructure resilience, and implementing effective tracking and control techniques are all necessary to address these difficulties (Wu et al., 2000).

The following are some precautions for these challenges.

7.10.6 Maintaining Availability and Uptime

You undoubtedly already know that the information saved on your server might be old-fashioned, incorrect, or lacking if you handle it with spreadsheets or other custom software. It might be difficult to map the energy chain or troubleshoot unanticipated outages (Lie et al., 1977).

Your asset information is kept in a single repository thanks to a DCIM solution. It makes it possible to preserve records consistently and accurately. It offers quick written and visual data to cut the time it takes to find assets and dependencies, thus reducing troubleshooting time (Nabi et al., 2016).

7.10.7 Reporting Reduced Operating Expenses

It is not sufficient to adopt solutions that save operational costs; you also need to demonstrate them. To remain competitive with third-party products, enterprise data center administrators must be able to gather performance and cost data and communicate their company's benefit, as per Uptime Institute. Data center executives may swiftly demonstrate to stakeholders that such a data center is progressing toward maximum operational efficiency by using a DCIM system with dashboards and reporting tools to collect data instantaneously across various dimensions (Enache & Srivastava, 2018).

7.10.8 Improving Staff Productivity

Facilities and IT employees must spend excessive time entering operations into spreadsheets for non-automated or manual systems. It consumes time that might be used for expanding service offerings and deciding on strategies for the data center. That assignment of specialists to perform additions, transfers, and adjustments is one laborious procedure that DCIM systems automate. This results in operational savings even while helping with provisioning and audits (McHugh, 2004).

Data center administrators may find it challenging to stay current with technological changes. In addition to making sure that their facilities are operating properly, managers must place a high priority on keeping up with trends. It may be a simple task for some. Some remedies are available despite unavoidable difficulties, and others may be avoided. Our data center service is prepared to outline several of the most prevalent issues administrators now deal with and offer suggestions for addressing them.

7.11 COOLING

As was already explained, every data center alone has a lot going on. If much technology is active, a surprising quantity of heat builds up. Systems start overheating whenever this heat can run unchecked, leading to server problems, system failures, and other issues. Managers may employ various data centers' cooling techniques, such as cooling water systems and air conditioning. The ideal cooling solution for a particular data center will rely on several variables (Ruhl, 1967).

ACTIVITY 7.1

Imagine you work for a healthcare company that handles sensitive patient data. Recently, one of your colleagues accidentally left their laptop in a coffee shop and it was stolen. The laptop contained unencrypted patient data, including names, addresses, and medical history.

What steps would you take to mitigate the potential data breach and protect the affected patients' information? How would you communicate the incident to the patients and stakeholders, and what measures would you put in place to prevent similar incidents from happening in the future?

SUMMARY

Data security, capacity planning, power management, the internet of objects, mobile enterprises, efficiency, real-time reporting, balancing price control and infrastructure monitoring, visibility, performance, data center network security, and accessibility are some of the challenges faced by data center management that are covered in this chapter. This chapter covers potential solutions to these problems, such as implementing strong security protocols, dependable energy infrastructure, effective capacity planning, efficient resource control, and analyzing and enhancing infrastructure efficiency. By tackling these issues, data center planning may help businesses succeed in the digital era.

REVIEW QUESTIONS

1. What are the challenges involved in ensuring data security in data center management?
2. Explain the concept of the Internet of Things (IoT) and its relevance to data center management.
3. Why is real-time reporting significant in data center management? What are the challenges involved in implementing it?
4. What is the importance of mobile enterprises in data center management? What are the challenges associated with it?
5. What are the challenges involved in ensuring performance and availability in data center management? How can they be addressed?

MULTIPLE CHOICE QUESTIONS

1. What is a major challenge in data center management related to security?

a) Difficulty in managing virtualized environments
b) Lack of redundancy and failover mechanisms
c) Data breaches and cyber attacks
d) Network congestion and bandwidth limitations

2. What is the Internet of Things (IoT)?

a) A cloud-based data center management system
b) A network of interconnected servers and storage devices
c) A system of connected devices that can exchange data with each other
d) A security protocol used in data center networks

3. **What is the significance of real-time reporting in data center management, and what is a major challenge related to it?**
   a) Real-time reporting enables faster decision-making, but it requires significant computing resources
   b) Real-time reporting provides better data accuracy, but it is difficult to implement and maintain
   c) Real-time reporting allows for proactive problem identification, but it can be challenging to integrate with existing systems
   d) Real-time reporting enables better resource utilization, but it requires specialized skills to implement and maintain
4. **Why are mobile enterprises important in data center management, and what is a major challenge related to it?**
   a) Mobile enterprises provide flexibility and agility, but they require more resources and infrastructure
   b) Mobile enterprises allow for remote management and monitoring, but they increase the risk of data breaches and cyber attacks
   c) Mobile enterprises enable better collaboration and communication, but they require more bandwidth and network resources
   d) Mobile enterprises offer better accessibility and productivity, but they require specialized skills and expertise to manage effectively
5. **What are the major challenges related to performance and availability in data center management?**
   a) Network congestion and bandwidth limitations
   b) Lack of redundancy and failover mechanisms
   c) Difficulty in managing virtualized environments
   d) All of the above

Answers to Multiple Choice Questions

1. (c) 2. (c) 3. (a) 4. (d) 5. (d)

REFERENCES

1. Bari, M. F., Boutaba, R., Esteves, R., Granville, L. Z., Podlesny, M., Rabbani, M. G., ... & Zhani, M. F. (2012). Data center network virtualization: A survey. *IEEE Communications Surveys & Tutorials*, *15*(2), 909–928.
2. Basole, R. (2007). Mobile enterprise readiness and transformation. *Encyclopedia of Mobile Computing and Commerce*, 481–486.

3. Bellovin, S. M., & Cheswick, W. R. (1994). Network firewalls. *IEEE Communications Magazine*, *32*(9), 50–57.
4. Bickerstaff, K. (2022). Living on with Sellafield: Nuclear infrastructure, slow violence, and the politics of quiescence. *Transactions of the Institute of British Geographers*, *47*(4), 955–970.
5. Bracs, M. A., Turner, I. L., Splinter, K. D., Short, A. D., Lane, C., Davidson, M. A., ... & Cameron, D. (2016). Evaluation of opportunistic shoreline monitoring capability utilizing existing "surfcam" infrastructure. *Journal of Coastal Research*, *32*(3), 542–554.
6. Choo, K. K. R. (2011). The cyber threat landscape: Challenges and future research directions. *Computers & security*, *30*(8), 719–731.
7. Choudhury, M. M., & Harrigan, P. (2014). CRM to social CRM: the integration of new technologies into customer relationship management. *Journal of Strategic Marketing*, *22*(2), 149–176.
8. Clarke, J., & Dede, C. (2009). Design for scalability: A case study of the River City curriculum. *Journal of Science Education and Technology*, *18*, 353–365.
9. David, N., Sendik, O., Messer, H., & Alpert, P. (2015). Cellular network infrastructure: The future of fog monitoring?. *Bulletin of the American Meteorological Society*, *96*(10), 1687–1698.
10. Davis, R. (1978). The data encryption standard in perspective. *IEEE Communications Society Magazine*, *16*(6), 5–9.
11. Denning, D. E., & Denning, P. J. (1979). Data security. *ACM Computing Surveys (CSUR)*, *11*(3), 227–249.
12. Enache, L., & Srivastava, A. (2018). Should intangible investments be reported separately or commingled with operating expenses? New evidence. *Management Science*, *64*(7), 3446–3468.
13. Eppen, G. D., Martin, R. K., & Schrage, L. (1989). OR practice—a scenario approach to capacity planning. *Operations research*, *37*(4), 517–527.
14. Fankhauser, S. (2010). The costs of adaptation. *Wiley Interdisciplinary Reviews: Climate Change*, *1*(1), 23–30.
15. Gardner, K., Harchol-Balter, M., Scheller-Wolf, A., Velednitsky, M., & Zbarsky, S. (2017). Redundancy-d: The power of d choices for redundancy. *Operations Research*, *65*(4), 1078–1094.
16. Garimella, S. V., Yeh, L. T., & Persoons, T. (2012). Thermal management challenges in telecommunication systems and data centers. *IEEE Transactions on Components, Packaging and Manufacturing Technology*, *2*(8), 1307–1316.
17. Geng, N., & Jiang, Z. (2009). A review on strategic capacity planning for the semiconductor manufacturing industry. *International Journal of Production Research*, *47*(13), 3639–3655.
18. Gray, M. W., Lukeš, J., Archibald, J. M., Keeling, P. J., & Doolittle, W. F. (2010). Irremediable complexity? *Science*, *330*(6006), 920–921.

19. Gubbi, J., Buyya, R., Marusic, S., & Palaniswami, M. (2013). Internet of Things (IoT): A vision, architectural elements, and future directions. *Future Generation Computer Systems*, *29*(7), 1645–1660.
20. Hu, T., Lan, J., Zhang, J., & Zhao, W. (2019). EASM: Efficiency-aware switch migration for balancing controller loads in software-defined networking. *Peer-to-Peer Networking and Applications*, *12*(2), 452–464.
21. Hunker, J., & Probst, C. W. (2011). Insiders and Insider Threats-An Overview of Definitions and Mitigation Techniques. *J. Wirel. Mob. Networks Ubiquitous Comput. Dependable Appl.*, *2*(1), 4–27.
22. Isheden, C., Chong, Z., Jorswieck, E., & Fettweis, G. (2012). Framework for link-level energy efficiency optimization with informed transmitter. *IEEE Transactions on Wireless Communications*, *11*(8), 2946–2957.
23. Jayasinghe, D., Pu, C., Eilam, T., Steinder, M., Whally, I., & Snible, E. (2011, July). Improving performance and availability of services hosted on iaas clouds with structural constraint-aware virtual machine placement. In *2011 IEEE International Conference on Services Computing* (pp. 72–79). IEEE.
24. Kant, K. (2009). Data center evolution: A tutorial on state of the art, issues, and challenges. *Computer Networks*, *53*(17), 2939–2965.
25. Khan, A. K. (2001). Monitoring power for the future. *Power Engineering Journal*, *15*(2), 81–85.
26. Kingston, J. (2017). Using artificial intelligence to support compliance with the general data protection regulation. *Artificial Intelligence and Law*, *25*(4), 429–443.
27. Knapp, K. J., Denney, G. D., & Barner, M. E. (2011). Key issues in data center security: An investigation of government audit reports. *Government Information Quarterly*, *28*(4), 533–541.
28. Koutitas, G., & Demestichas, P. (2010). Challenges for energy efficiency in local and regional data centers. *Journal of Green Engineering*, *1*(1), 1–32.
29. Kraus, T. W., Büchler, M. W., & Herfarth, C. (2005). Relationships between volume, efficiency, and quality in surgery—a delicate balance from managerial perspectives. *World Journal of Surgery*, *29*, 1234–1240.
30. Krein, P. T. (2017). Data center challenges and their power electronics. *CPSS Transactions on Power Electronics and Applications*, *2*(1), 39–46.
31. Lee, I., Lochhead, S., Ritter, J., & Zhao, Q. (1996). The costs of raising capital. *Journal of Financial Research*, *19*(1), 59–74
32. Lie, C. H., Hwang, C. L., & Tillman, F. A. (1977). Availability of maintained systems: a state-of-the-art survey. *AIIE Transactions*, *9*(3), 247–259.
33. Logue, D., Madigan, S. M., Delahunt, E., Heinen, M., Mc Donnell, S. J., & Corish, C. A. (2018). Low energy availability in athletes: a review of prevalence, dietary patterns, physiological health, and sports performance. *Sports Medicine*, *48*, 73–96.

34. Madakam, S., Lake, V., Lake, V., & Lake, V. (2015). Internet of Things (IoT): A literature review. *Journal of Computer and Communications*, *3*(05), 164.
35. McHugh, N. (2004). Improving staff member satisfaction and productivity through technology. *Aorn Journal*, *80*(3), 523–526.
36. Hunt, P. S., & Hartman, D. (2018). Meeting the measurements of inpatient staffing productivity. *Nursing Management*, *49*(6), 26–33.
37. McSherry, F., Isard, M., & Murray, D. G. (2015, May). Scalability! but at what cost?. In *HotOS* (Vol. 15, pp. 14–14).
38. Moffitt, R. (1986). The econometrics of piecewise-linear budget constraints: a survey and exposition of the maximum likelihood method. *Journal of Business & Economic Statistics*, *4*(3), 317–328.
39. Nabi, M., Toeroe, M., & Khendek, F. (2016). Availability in the cloud: State of the art. *Journal of Network and Computer Applications*, *60*, 54–67.
40. Paraskevopoulos, D., Karakitsos, E., & Rustem, B. (1991). Robust capacity planning under uncertainty. *Management Science*, *37*(7), 787–800.
41. Pohjanheimo, P., & Lakervi, E. (2000, January). Steady state modeling of custom power components in power distribution networks. In *2000 IEEE Power Engineering Society Winter Meeting. Conference Proceedings (Cat. No. 00CH37077)* (Vol. 4, pp. 2949–2954). IEEE.
42. Potter, B., & Day, G. (2009). The effectiveness of anti-malware tools. *Computer Fraud & Security*, *2009*(3), 12–13.
43. Pratt, A. K., Shah, N. S., & Boyce, S. W. (2014). Left ventricular assist device management in the ICU. *Critical Care Medicine*, *42*(1), 158–168.
44. Rhee, K., Jeon, W., & Won, D. (2012). Security requirements of a mobile device management system. *International Journal of Security and Its Applications*, *6*(2), 353–358.
45. Ruhl, R. C. (1967). Cooling rates in splat cooling. *Materials Science and Engineering*, *1*(6), 313–320.
46. Rumble, S. M., Ongaro, D., Stutsman, R., Rosenblum, M., & Ousterhout, J. K. (2011, May). It's Time for Low Latency. In *HotOS* (Vol. 13, pp. 11–11).
47. Saito, Y., Bershad, B. N., & Levy, H. M. (1999). Manageability, availability and performance in porcupine: A highly scalable, cluster-based mail service. *ACM SIGOPS Operating Systems Review*, *33*(5), 1–15.
48. Sandhu, R. S., & Samarati, P. (1994). Access control: principle and practice. *IEEE Communications Magazine*, *32*(9), 40–48.
49. Sandström, A., & Carlsson, L. (2008). The performance of policy networks: the relation between network structure and network performance. *Policy Studies Journal*, *36*(4), 497–524.
50. Schmidt, R. R., Cruz, E. E., & Iyengar, M. (2005). Challenges of data center thermal management. *IBM Journal of Research and Development*, *49*(4.5), 709–723.

51. Sharma, K., & Singh, K. R. (2012). Online data back-up and disaster recovery techniques in cloud computing: A review. *International Journal of Engineering and Innovative Technology (IJEIT)*, *2*(5), 249–254.
52. Sinha, A., & Chandrakasan, A. (2001). Dynamic power management in wireless sensor networks. *IEEE Design & Test of Computers*, *18*(2), 62–74.
53. Soundararajan, V., & Govil, K. (2010). Challenges in building scalable virtualized datacenter management. *ACM SIGOPS Operating Systems Review*, *44*(4), 95–102.
54. Steigenberger, N. (2017). The challenge of integration: A review of the M&A integration literature. *International Journal of Management Reviews*, *19*(4), 408–431.
55. Stewart, F. (2004). Development and security. *Conflict, Security & Development*, *4*(3), 261–288.
56. Trigo, A., Belfo, F., & Estébanez, R. P. (2014). Accounting information systems: The challenge of the real-time reporting. *Procedia Technology*, *16*, 118–127.
57. Wierman, A., Liu, Z., Liu, I., & Mohsenian-Rad, H. (2014, November). Opportunities and challenges for data center demand response. In *International Green Computing Conference* vol(1) (pp. 1–10).
58. Woods, D. D., Patterson, E. S., & Roth, E. M. (2002). Can we ever escape from data overload? A cognitive systems diagnosis. *Cognition, Technology & Work*, *4*, 22–36.
59. Wu, C. Y., Trombly, C. A., Lin, K. C., & Tickle-Degnen, L. (2000). A kinematic study of contextual effects on reaching performance in persons with and without stroke: influences of object availability. *Archives of Physical Medicine and Rehabilitation*, *81*(1), 95–101.
60. Yang, W., Wang, W., Wang, Y., Sun, R., Guo, J., Li, H., ... & Min, J. (2021). Balancing the efficiency, stability, and cost potential for organic solar cells via a new figure of merit. *Joule*, *5*(5), 1209–1230.
61. Zamboni, K., Schellenberg, J., Hanson, C., Betran, A. P., & Dumont, A. (2019). Assessing scalability of an intervention: why, how and who?. *Health Policy and Planning*, *34*(7), 544–552.
62. Zapater, M., Tuncer, O., Ayala, J. L., Moya, J. M., Vaidyanathan, K., Gross, K., & Coskun, A. K. (2014). Leakage-aware cooling management for improving server energy efficiency. *IEEE Transactions on Parallel and Distributed Systems*, *26*(10), 2764–2777.
63. Zhang, Y., Yin, Q., Yen, J., Li, J., Ying, H., Wang, H., ... & Cheng, J. (2015). Non-invasive, real-time reporting drug release in vitro and in vivo. *Chemical Communications*, *51*(32), 6948–6951.

CHAPTER 8

FUTURE TRENDS IN DATA CENTER MANAGEMENT

UNIT INTRODUCTION

Equipment used for information technology (IT) and the infrastructure required to support it, including power, fire systems, cooling, telecommunications, security, and automation, are all contained within data centers. These facilities are essential to the mission because they manage and save information safely and provide dependable access. They are dynamic, which enables the addition of the newest equipment, the upgrading of current equipment, the removal of outmoded parts, and the simultaneous use of both legacy and new equipment. An estimated 1% of the world's total electricity consumption is attributed to data centers. These are very energy-hungry facilities (Masanet et al., 2020).

The world is experiencing a pandemic, but the presence of data centers has, to some extent, lessened the severity of its effects. Data centers have made it possible for us to carry out many elements of our everyday lives in a digital format, which has aided in the development of a modern economy that is strongly dependent on technology. In response to COVID-19, Cybersecurity and Infrastructure Security Agency (CISA) has published guidelines on critical infrastructure workforce (Hoops et al., 2020). During the COVID-19 crisis, it has been determined that data centers are essential to society and play a mission-critical role. Because of our growing reliance on data centers and the anticipated growth of the industry, there is an immediate and pressing need to intelligently track and handle these facilities to enhance their efficiency, productivity, and long-term viability while simultaneously lowering the failure's risk. The inability to access data and services is one of the drawback of downtime for data center, and this causes both monetary and non-monetary losses.

Management automation of mission-critical facilities has greatly benefited from emerging technologies, and we are currently experiencing a quickening of the pace at which technological innovation is taking place. Emerging trends help us understand the potential new normal that will exist in the not too distant future since earlier tactics may not always be effective. We are now able to recognize patterns, predictions, and behaviors almost instantly, thanks to the advancements that have been made in simulation, robotics, intelligent monitoring, and artificial intelligence. The authors have highlighted the three biggest technological trends affecting automation of data center management and a decrease in human engagement based on their prior expertise. The first is data science-based intelligent monitoring and management systems; the second is simulation tools that incorporate digital twinning and artificial intelligence; and the third is robotics for automation process. Millions of data centers globally will be greatly affected by these advancements, which may even be disruptive (Figure 8.1).

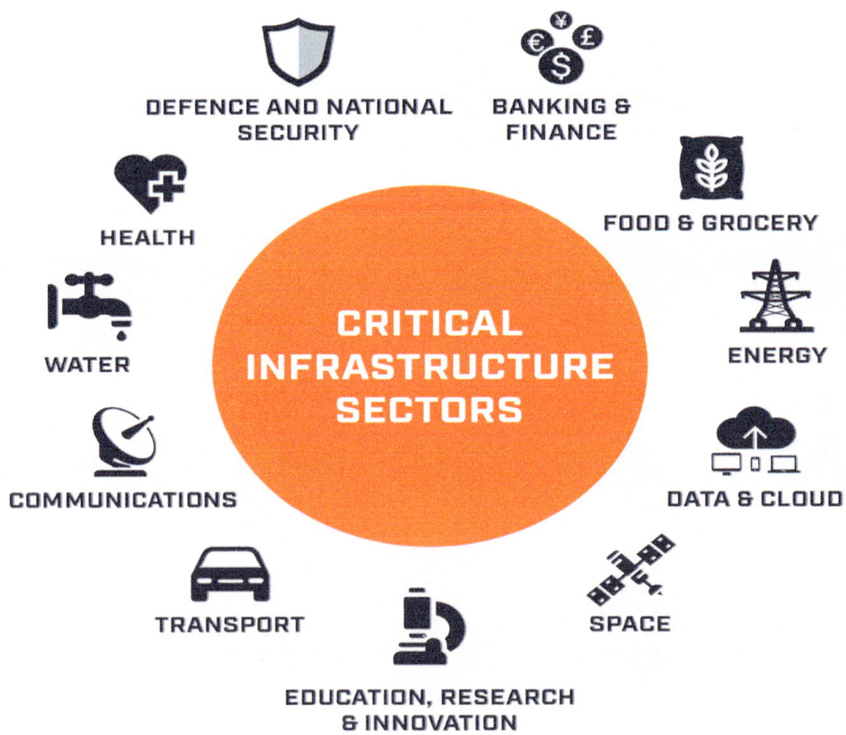

Figure 8.1. Illustration of infrastructure cyber security (Source: Huntsman, Creative Commons License).

Learning Objectives

At the end of the chapter, reader will be able to understand:

1. The working of intelligent monitoring systems
2. The concept of Artificial Intelligence (AI)
3. The importance of robotics in today's world
4. The significance of simulation tools and edge computing
5. The future aspects of data center management

Key Terms

1. Artificial Intelligence (AI)
2. Robotics
3. Resource Optimization
4. Edge Specific Monitoring Tool
5. Intelligent Monitoring Systems
6. Automation
7. Internet of Things (IoT)

8.1 LEGISLATION, BEST PRACTICES, AND STANDARDS

For the industry of data centers, both individuals and organizations from all over the world have made contributions to the development of standards and recommended procedures. Best practices and standards are a reliable source of guidance when it comes to the planning, construction, and management of data centers (Levy et al., 2019). This includes everything from performance guidelines to local and country codes. Although automation is still relatively novel idea in realm of data centers, the vast majority of standards and best practices have, in more recent iterations, incorporated automated real-time monitoring procedures (Levy & Subburaj, 2021). This is because automation is both relevant and widely implemented (Levy, 2020). Because of this, it is essential to recognize developing tendencies that affect these facilities, as legislation, best practices and standards are continuously evolving to accommodate new challenges and technologies. It is important to make this point clear (Celestine et al., 2021).

Some of the main publications used by professionals include the ANSI/TIA 942-B: Telecommunications Infrastructure Standard for Data Centers [3], the ANSI/BICSI-002: Data Center Design and Implementation Best Practices [4], the ISO/IEC 22237: Information technology - Data Centre

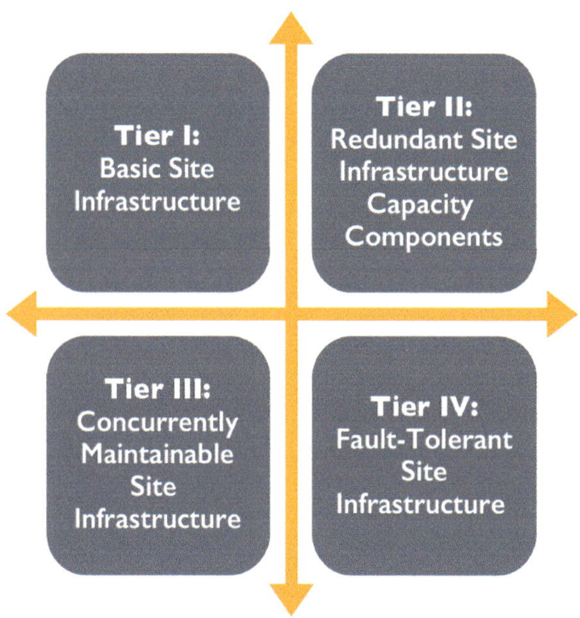

Figure 8.2. Schematic of Data Center Site Infrastructure Standard (Source: Cloud Gal, Creative Commons License).

Facilities and Infrastructures [5] [6] [7] [8] [9] [10] [11], the Data Center Site Infrastructure Standard [12], the ANSI/ASHRAE 90.4: Energy Standard for Data Centers [13], the ASHRAE Technical Committee 9.9 guidelines (Mastelic et al., 2014), the BICSI-009: Data Center Operations and Maintenance Best Practices [17], the Data Center Site Infrastructure Tier Standard: Operational Sustainability [18], the Data Centre Operations Standard (DCOS) [19], and the Singapore Standard SS 564 (Green Data Centers) (Mastelic et al., 2014).

In addition, different U.S. government entities have expressed concern about data centers, and have addressed them with legislation. Recent examples include the Energy Efficient Government Technology Act of 2019 [21], the 2019 update to the Data Center Optimization Initiative [22], and the 2016 U.S. Data Center Energy Usage Report (Dai et al., 2014). In an effort to be aligned with regulations, standards and best practices, automation is being used to improve data center management, making them more energy efficient and sustainable (DiMinico & Jew, 2006) (Figure 8.2).

8.2 INTELLIGENT MONITORING SYSTEMS

The need for monitoring systems and intelligent management that use data science is the first new development we will discuss (Brocklehurst, 2021). The sensing devices and Internet of Things (IoT) make it possible to collect data for mission-critical facilities (Shehabi et al., 2018). This enables information (such as, power, temperature, location, resource utilization and humidity, amongst other things) to be gathered in real-time and shared (Manganelli et al., 2021).

The first challenge is obtaining data in real time, which is especially difficult in existing data centers due to inadequate monitoring (Inker et al., 2016). When it comes to software tools or management platforms for data centers, several options are available. Depending on the priorities and requirements, one tool may be more suitable than another. Some examples of such tools are as follows:

a) DCIM (data center infrastructure management) technologies to monitor as well as control data center infrastructure;
b) BMS (building management systems) solutions for building monitoring and control;
c) EMS (energy monitoring systems) solution for monitoring and primarily controlling energy use;
d) CFD (computational fluid dynamics) a modelling program that can evaluate airflow for different equipment setups.

An innovative method for important IT equipment and data center infrastructure characteristics real time monitoring mentioned in Chew and Yan

(2022) and Arman et al. (2016). The system is anticipated to be dependable, sensor-based, low cost, wireless, low energy and noninvasive. It gives measurements in real-time which allow for building each parameter's data map. It measures many metrics across equipment and facility's physical space. The environmental/ motion sensing and power sensing device categories are highlighted in this data collection technique. In addition, this examines platform-level telemetry to collect data straight from the processor of IT equipment (Figure 8.3).

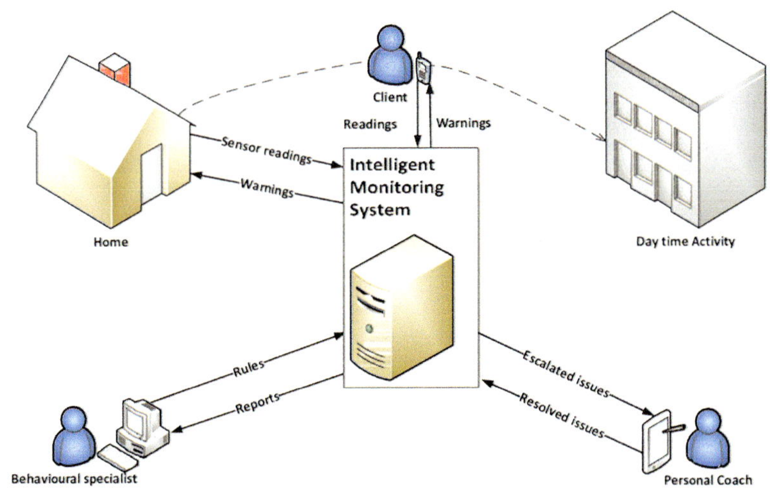

Figure 8.3. Diagram of intelligent monitoring system (Source: Hugo Velthuijsen, Creative Commons License).

Measurements include both the IT infrastructure and the related hardware. The majority of data center components, like dependable power sources, generators, automatic transfer switches, electrical panels, cooling systems and power distribution units, possess communication interfaces that enable the remote retrieval and transfer of real-time data using a common protocol, like Simple Network Management Protocol (SNMP) over TCP/IP. The motion and environmental characteristics such as, humidity, fire, temperature, relative airflow, water, air pressure difference, vibration, illumination, and security systems. It requires the sensory devices deployment over cabinets and physical space and measuring locations at varying heights to measure them. Each sensed parameter has its range. Environmental characteristics can be measured across a greater spectrum with the help of modern technology.

The cycle of an intelligent management and monitoring system for data centers is shown in Figure 8.4. Several sensing devices and equipment collect and transfer data to storage devices. Because data may be incomplete plus may contain errors, this strategy includes data cleansing. It is necessary to organize the huge amount of data collected so that it can easily merged, shared, maintained and analyzed. Metadata management system is highly recommended. Data processing is subsequent phase, which entails estimating various metrics and important indicators to comprehend how data centers act in current and forecast possible issues. The multidimensional data center's key performance and risk indicators are proposed in Cho and Woo (2020) and Levy and Hallstrom (2017) to thoroughly monitor data centers, including risk and performance. The recent incorporation of these indicators into data center best practices (Bilal et al., 2014). In Evans and Gao (2016), data center risk assessment has explored, as well as the use of automation to manage data center risk effectively. Then, prescriptive and predictive analytics are performed using data science. Finally, data science contributes to regulating many data center factors to increase sustainability, productivity, efficiency, and operations while decreasing risk.

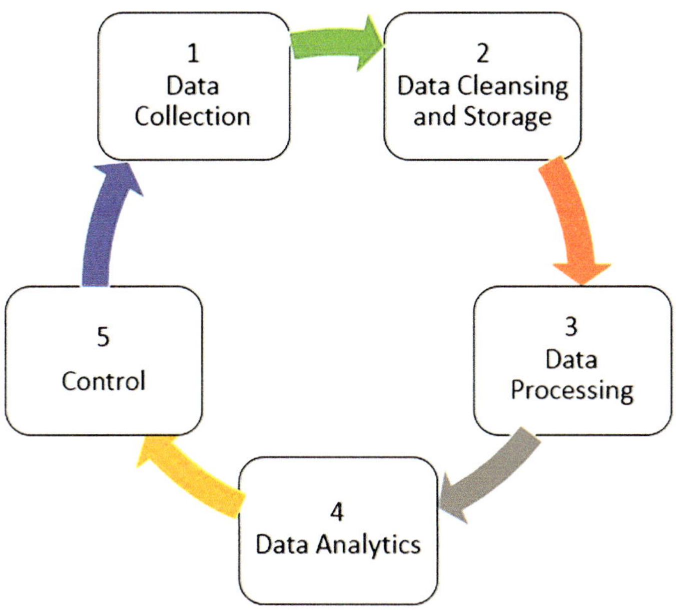

Figure 8.4. Illustration of intelligent management and monitoring system (Source: Science Direct, Creative Commons License).

Data science involves far more than technology; this is a discipline that collects, analyzes, normalizes, large amounts of data using techniques such as mathematics, data engineering, visualization, , statistics and advanced computing among others. With the help of the Internet of Things (IoT), sensor-based technology, and artificial intelligence (AI), data center industry is adopting data science across multiple processes to assist users in using this data appropriately and performing actions based on real-time data and prior knowledge. Good data center optimization plans incorporate each assets required to enable end-to-end resource management, facilitating the development of integrated strategy for risk mitigation and performance enhancement.

Assessing multilayer node and event entities determines the number of the intelligent data center monitoring system's parameters. This method increases our understanding of the actions occurring at a certain node. Due to higher number of nodes, one of the important benefits is that technique reduces cumulative number of incidents which could be a root cause.

Modern data centers aim to provide the highest level of operating stability and availability plus to detect unusual events and enhance energy efficiency easily. Intelligent monitoring comprises control of all sensing devices and technical components, event reporting, appropriate energy support, and data transmission to primary control element. The data from all distributed pieces are then used to provide central servers with real-time information. The objectives for system productivity, energy consumption, dependability and availability, and operational expenses must coexist harmoniously.

Intelligent monitoring systems needing continuous monitoring with automated intelligent warnings are difficult to establish. Operations and administration of a data center should be stable. To meet the increasing expectations of today's digital world, resources should be in approach. However, gathering and comprehending granular data isn't easy but monitoring results at a higher level has been possible. Monitoring technologies also provide a unique opportunity to collect data and investigate anomalies.

As the data center evolves, risk issues may increase without improved resource allocation, proactive monitoring, predictive maintenance, and scalability. Temperature, energy, power and humidity are only beginning of data center monitoring. Fire detectors, for example, are typically linked to a fire control panel. Nonetheless, they may be included in the monitoring tool to give management a motivation for early intervention and system integration.

All sensing devices must be tested and maintained automatically. Alarms do not prevent crises; data center operations should always include emergency planning. Quality of service concerns, efficiency of energy, scalability, latency, and service-level agreement assurance are some of major obstacle's clouds and hyper-scale data center designs face today. Virtualization of networks, servers and computing services adds complexity to managing the data center's architecture. Other significant issues include interconnection of IT resources to provide defined quality of service, energy efficiency, high bandwidth connectivity, a high oversubscription ratio and low bandwidth, and fault tolerance (Corrado et al., 2022).

8.3 SIMULATION TOOLS AND DIGITAL TWINS

While monitoring technologies of data center capture vast quantities of data and play a crucial role in their respective field of application, a problem occurs when these data are made actionable.

Hence, artificial intelligence is utilized to design algorithms to minimize risks (such as temperature, energy, and workloads) and improve the data center architecture. Hence, second developing trend is demand for simulation tools that incorporate digital twinning and artificial intelligence.

Simulation tools may be utilize artificial intelligence or based on theoretical models to extract information from data directly. In step-by-step method is provided for modeling a data center from the standpoint of cyber-physical systems, taking computational and physical components into account. Information from computer manufacturer is utilized to validate model.

By the theoretical model, simulations are generated of prior known scenarios in. Predictions without specified equations are examined in some paper using supervised machine learning methods (e.g., nonlinear regression, neural network and support vector machine).

To evaluate various operations in the data center, a training data set links input data to known output values and builds a model from data collected to forecast the outcomes for an unknown data set. To comprehend various scenarios for workloads, quality of service needs, IT resources, simulations and projections are employed.

Google has applied machine learning to increase efficiency and lower cooling demand and overall emissions in their data centers (Alam & Saddik, 2017). To build more effective and adaptive framework to comprehend dynamics and boost efficiency, they deployed a system of neural networks trained on various operational situations and parameters of the data centers.

The deep neural networks model was trained using historical data and real time data (such as power, temperatures, pump speeds and set points) gathered by thousands of sensing devices, which were then used to predict average power usage effectiveness (PUE), temperature, and pressure over the following hour. Predictions helped mimic suggested actions. With the lowest PUE indication, the machine learning system cut the energy needed for cooling by 40%.

A real-world example of how machine learning is used in data centers is shown in Table 8.1. Predictions are made using inputs and outputs in supervised learning. Data is examined to find unsupervised learning patterns, correlations, and relationships. Also, a list of permitted behaviors and restrictions is provided in reinforcement learning.

Table 8.1. Machine Learning Algorithms' Practical Applications (Source: E. Masanet, Creative Commons License)

Learning algorithm	Practical application
Supervised (labeled data)	Measurement and benchmarking. Modelled and simulated. Behavior forecasting. Optimization of resources. Thresholds and alarms. Customizing communication. Detection of fraud. Segmenting your clientele Recognition and Classification of images, texts and audio. Risk analysis. Proactive upkeep.
Unsupervised (unlabeled data)	Detection of intrusions. Recognizing similar items. Creation of a library of assets. Market research. Simulations and modelling. Forecast of behavior. Resource management. Detection of anomalies.
Reinforcement (unlabeled data)	Video recognition. Robotics. Simulations and modelling. Forecast of behavior. Resource management. Electronic twin. Navigation. Routes and resource deployment that are ideal.

A complicated digital representation of a physical object or apparatus known as a "digital twin" is linked by measured data such as vibration, power pressure, and temperature. The digital twin of a data center is a simulated 3D representation of actual data center that analyses current situation and suggests control actions to improve certain parameters through a feedback loop.

A digital twin of the data center is created using validation, calibration, and modeling. A site survey, data entry, physical observations, and engineering analysis are all part of the process. Digital twins represent actual objects or topics in digital world by using features, communication skills and data. Their simulated digital twins continuously adapt to changes in the physical data center in close to real-time. Sensing equipment gathers data in real-time, enabling monitoring of the facility and simulation of various scenarios. The digital twin makes forecasts based on assumptions about the behavior or change of various resources, allowing for more rational decision-making other than providing real time knowledge. Real-time remote tracking and administration, higher risk assessment, automatic maintenance, dependability, a more educated and effective technique of decision support, service personalization, improved reporting, and connectivity are a few advantages of the digital twin (Choi et al., 2011).

A reference model for digital twin architecture is put forth in to construct cloud-based cyber-physical systems. Use of cloud computing infrastructure can increase the scalability of the digital twin concept. Every physical object is somehow represented and related to a cloud-based digital twin object. If physical environment changes, a sensing gadget seeks to update present state to its digital twin. The system is separated into three operational modes: a deep integration of sensor-services fusion, a cyber-level digital twin services-fusion, and a physical-level sensors fusion mode. The computation, communication, and control characteristics were analytically modelled by the authors.

The implementation of this technology is fraught with difficulties. Digital twin performance depends on bidirectional real-time communication between physical resources and their digital twins to provide physical realism without compromise. Connectivity latency, huge data volume, spatial-temporal sensor data resolution, large data creation rate, high data accuracy, quick online storage, large data diversity, and data processing are significant challenges in achieving this. The model must adapt following the physical resource's ongoing evolution while maintaining backward compatibility. More clarity and interpretability of judgments made on digital twins will be necessary since many physical attributes on which digital twins can be imagined would require more security and safety. Furthermore, interpretable and physically consistent models are needed. The digital twin must also be presented to the user in a way different from the physical resource and easier and more logical to use.

8.4 EDGE COMPUTING

To reduce quantity of data that needs to be transported back to central data center, edge computing, a future trend in data center management, includes placing data processing closer to the data source. Due to the expansion of IoT devices and the rising demand for low-latency applications, this is becoming more common.

Here are some examples of how data center management is being altered by edge computing.

8.4.1 Distributed Architectures

Edge computing requires a new approach to data center management, focusing on distributed architectures that can support processing at the edge. This means that data center managers must design and deploy infrastructure optimized for edge computing, such as modular data centers, micro data centers, and edge-specific hardware and software.

8.4.2 Remote Management

Since data processing is scattered across several sites with edge computing, remote management solutions are crucial for data center management. Data center administrators no longer need to make frequent on-site visits because remote management solutions enable the monitoring and management of infrastructure from a single location.

8.4.3 Edge-Specific Monitoring Tools

New monitoring tools that are tailored for distributed architectures are needed for edge computing. These technologies must be able to track infrastructure health in real-time as well as performance, availability, and security across numerous locations.

8.4.4 Increased Bandwidth

Remember

Edge computing involves processing data locally on devices or servers near the source, rather than sending all the data to a centralized data center for processing.

High-speed communication between the edge locations and the main data center is necessary for edge computing. To ensure that data can be transported rapidly and reliably, data center managers must invest in high-speed networking technologies like 5G and SD-WAN.

Data centers are being planned, implemented, and managed differently due to the emerging data center management trend known as edge computing. Data center managers may ensure that their infrastructure can serve the expanding need for low-latency applications and IoT devices by focusing on distributed designs, remote management, edge-specific monitoring tools, and high-speed connectivity.

8.5 ARTIFICIAL INTELLIGENCE (AI)

Well, use of machine learning algorithms and other artificial intelligence (AI) technologies to automate repetitive processes and improve the efficiency of the data center is an emerging trend in data center management. AI can evaluate vast amounts of data, spot trends, and abnormalities, and offer suggestions for infrastructure improvement.

Here are a few examples of how AI is being applied to data center management.

8.5.1 Predictive Maintenance

AI can analyze data from sensors and other monitoring instruments to spot possible concerns before they develop into larger difficulties. This enables data center operators to perform proactive maintenance, cutting downtime and raising the infrastructure's overall resilience.

8.5.2 Resource Optimization

AI may evaluate how well the infrastructure functions and suggest improving resource use, such as modifying power and cooling levels following workload demands. Cost savings and increased energy effectiveness may result from this.

8.5.3 Security

Artificial intelligence (AI) can be used to identify possible security risks, such as DDoS attacks, and take appropriate measures to reduce the risk. AI may also track user activity and spot irregularities pointing to a security breach.

TIPS

Consider the ethical implications of the technology and ensure that it is being used in a responsible and transparent manner for working with artificial intelligence (AI)

8.5.4 Automation

Automation with artificial intelligence is possible for repetitive processes like server provisioning, software upgrades, and backup and recovery. This can increase productivity and cut expenses by allowing IT workers to concentrate on more strategic responsibilities.

Future data center management trends like artificial intelligence (AI) can completely change how data centers are run. AI can assist in enhancing the data center's overall effectiveness, dependability, and performance by automating repetitive processes, maximizing resource consumption, and enhancing security.

8.6 ROBOTICS

While IoT and fixed sensing devices have proven to be useful tools for monitoring data centers, facilities still need more mobile technologies to sufficiently automate monitoring and control. Use of robotics is the third emerging trend. A robot is responsible for automating particular process or repetitive task. Robots carry out duties that would otherwise be done by people, boosting efficiency and automating processes while decreasing human error.

Robots have been trained to roam data centers and gather pertinent environmental and asset data through a number of tests (Rosa et al., 2016). In a vision-based mobile robot with the ability to read the LEDs indicators is used to automate asset tracking, among other tasks with minimal human interaction. Encoding was done using a unique binary number. A data center monitoring system is proposed in using multiple robots patrolling the physical space. They all communicate with human administrator through wireless transmission. The system is made up of robots with transponders that enable them to locate themselves precisely in an indoor environment, an effective path with path adaptation, and minimal latency which requires that robot's route be modified based on server utilization, which is constantly fluctuating in a data center. Implemented in is an autonomous mobile robot equipped with a laser range sensor and an internal motion unit, capable of exploring physical space, monitoring, and performing measurements that can be communicated via a web interface. Robot determines the best path to avoid moving and static obstacles.

There have also been private sector research attempts for robots to watch over actual data centers. To monitor environmental factors and assets management in data center, IBM has equipped iRobot Create with extra sensing devices and connections, a portable computer, as well as a webcam, among other things. This system is explained in detail in. The self-driving robot travels over uncharted physical territory using the floor tiles of the data center and stops to estimate the size of any unobstructed tiles. Intelligent sampling is used to manage energy more effectively, track parameters, and find abnormalities at a lower cost than with traditional techniques (Figure 8.5).

Figure 8.5. Picture of robots (Source: Future skill prime, Creative Commons License).

Another approach takes into account cloud robotics is combination of robotics and cloud computing. It allows robots to take advantage of modern data centers' efficient storage, connectivity and processing tools. Furthermore, it excludes repair and upgrade costs and reduces reliance on custom middleware. Describes a cloud robotics platform for data centers' environmental monitoring. It is based on the Robot Operating System (ROS), a sophisticated robotics application framework and open-source software tool. Using a map already established in a data center to precisely track important measures, the mobile physical robot can independently navigate, identify, and carry out a list of measurements at various points specified by user through graphical user interface. The findings of a simulated experiment are presented in the work(Russo et al., 2016).

Another use for autonomous robots in data center security is where it is impractical to employ human staff around-the-clock. Furthermore, robots are dependable, adaptable, and vigilant. They generally include day/night cameras, multiple sensing devices, and artificial intelligence-enhanced capabilities. The robot's features include fever detection technology, collision avoidance, license plate monitoring, facial recognition, anomaly detection, and escalation, human communication, and advanced navigation with automatic door and elevator interaction. To protect its new data centers, a switch is using autonomous robots that have been augmented with artificial intelligence.

Software, digital, and non-physical robots are other terms for the same thing. Chatbots, for example, can converse with users on their smartphones or desktops. Open-domain dialogue study looks on a complementary strategy that uses a conversational neural model to create "chatbot" which can converse about almost anything that user desires in order to better handle wide range of conversational subjects.

Did you Know?

The global robotics market was valued at $62.75 billion in 2020 and is projected to reach $248.57 billion by 2027, growing at a CAGR of 20.8% during the forecast period.

Such advancements reflected in the 'sensibleness and specificity average,' a new human evaluation metric proposed for open-domain chatbots. This metric captures simple but important human communication qualities. Combating protection and prejudice in models is a critical priority (Lenchner et al., 2011). Nonphysical robots can extract business insight from large data sets for smart data center troubleshooting by improving user experiences and interactions.

There are a few drawbacks to using robotics in data center. First, because it is a new field, there will be a lot of trial and error before the technology is proven effective. Second, cost of implementing robotics with reduced risk is substantial. Finally, robotics technologies necessitate modern infrastructure and equipment to pair devices, and such solutions are not feasible for many existing data centers.

8.7 FUTURE RESEARCH

The landscape of global data center is changing. They are more automated, have less employees and require less labor as compared to older facilities. Outdated data centers are being updated with latest technologies to remain competitive. This paper investigated 3 key emerging trends in data center management automation:

a) Data science-based intelligent management and monitoring systems;

b) Simulation tools integrating digital twinning and artificial intelligence;

c) Robotics for process automation.

All of them are cutting-edge technologies that'll eventually contribute to highly efficient and effective use of unmanned data centers, a long-term objective that has gained urgency in light of the global pandemic.

Lack of suitable instrumentation is the biggest obstacle to using them in current data centers. However, latest technologies including, wireless communications, sensing devices and IoT and data from equipment have enabled many data centers to adopt these trends. Artificial intelligence is crucial in data analysis, providing insights humans cannot decipher. Robotics automation allows for the automation of processes, decreasing human error.

Although there will always be a need for humans, implementing these new trends will enable faster and more accurate decision-making. Data centers will considerably benefit from certain important upcoming technologies, even though they are not directly related to automation. One example is edge computing, that involves having resources close to data source and having data close to where it is needed to decrease data transport costs and latency due to end user's proximity. Another example is using innovative cooling technologies such as liquid cooling to improve efficiency. Among the others are advancements in storage technology such as expanding the availability of solid-state technology, cutting-edge data security and protection technologies using blockchain technology, and immersive experiences related to technologies like virtual reality (Kehoe et al., 2015).

ACTIVITY 8.1

A company that manufactures automobiles is considering implementing robotics in their production line to improve efficiency and reduce errors. They are interested in your expertise as a robotics consultant to answer the following questions:

1. What types of robots are most suitable for their production line?
2. How much would it cost to implement robotics in their production line, and what is the estimated return on investment?
3. What kind of training would be required for their employees to work with the new robots?

SUMMARY

The chapter "Future Trends in Data Center Management" discusses various technologies and concepts that are expected to play a significant role in the future of data center management. The chapter begins by discussing intelligent monitoring systems, which use machine learning and predictive analytics to identify potential issues before they become major problems. This technology allows data center managers to proactively address issues and minimize downtime. The concept of Artificial Intelligence (AI) is also discussed, as it is expected to play a significant role in data center management in the future. AI can automate routine tasks and provide insights into the performance of data center systems.

The chapter also highlights the importance of robotics in today's world and its potential to transform data center management. Robotic systems can perform tasks such as server maintenance and hardware replacement, freeing up human staff to focus on more complex tasks. Simulation tools and edge computing are also discussed as important technologies in data center management. Simulation tools allow data center managers to model and test different scenarios, while edge computing can improve the efficiency of data processing and reduce latency.

REVIEW QUESTIONS

1. How do intelligent monitoring systems work in data center management?
2. What is Artificial Intelligence (AI) and how does it relate to data center management?
3. Why is robotics important in today's world and how is it being utilized in data center management?
4. What is the significance of simulation tools and edge computing in data center management?
5. What are some future aspects of data center management and how are they likely to impact the industry?
6. How can data center managers best prepare for the changing landscape of technology and data center management trends?

MULTIPLE CHOICE QUESTIONS

1. What is the purpose of intelligent monitoring systems in data center management?

a) To replace human workers in data centers
b) To provide real-time insights and alerts on data center performance
c) To automate all data center management tasks
d) To store and process data in a data center

2. **What is Artificial Intelligence (AI) in data center management?**
   a) A set of manual procedures to manage data centers
   b) A process to design new data center hardware
   c) A set of tools that automate data center management
   d) A set of algorithms that mimic human intelligence to optimize data center operations
3. **What is the role of robotics in data center management?**
   a) To monitor and maintain data center hardware
   b) To process data in a data center
   c) To provide customer support for data center users
   d) To design and build data centers
4. **What is the significance of simulation tools in data center management?**
   a) To simulate data center operations and optimize resource utilization
   b) To provide virtual reality experiences of data center facilities
   c) To replace human workers in data centers
   d) To store and process data in a data center
5. **What is edge computing in data center management?**
   a) A process to manage data centers remotely
   b) A way to reduce latency by processing data closer to the source
   c) A way to store data in multiple data centers for redundancy
   d) A process to optimize data center cooling and power usage
6. **What is the future of data center management?**
   a) A shift towards more manual processes and less automation
   b) A focus on physical security and data center location
   c) A move towards more sustainable and eco-friendly data centers
   d) A decrease in the importance of data center management in the digital economy

Answers to Multiple Choice Questions

1. (b) 2. (d) 3. (a) 4. (a) 5. (b) 6. (c)

REFERENCES

1. Alam, K. M., & El Saddik, A. (2017). C2PS: A digital twin architecture reference model for the cloud-based cyber-physical systems. IEEE Access, 5, 2050–2062.
2. Arman, S., Smith, S. J., Sartor, D. A., Brown, R. E., Herrlin, M., Koomey, J. G., ... & Lintner, W. (2016). United states data center energy usage report. Lawrence Berkeley National Laboratory.3, 45–48.

3. Bilal, K., Malik, S. U. R., Khan, S. U., & Zomaya, A. Y. (2014). Trends and challenges in cloud datacenters. IEEE Cloud Computing, 1(1), 10–20.
4. Brocklehurst, F. (2021). International Review of Energy Efficiency in Data Centers, 1(1), 11–14.
5. Celestine, A. D. N., Sulic, M., Wieliczko, M., & Stetson, N. T. (2021). Hydrogen-Based Energy Storage Systems for Large-Scale Data Center Applications. Sustainability, 13(22), 12654.
6. Chew, M. Y. L., & Yan, K. (2022). Enhancing interpretability of data-driven fault detection and diagnosis methodology with maintainability rules in smart building management. Journal of Sensors, 3, 1–48.
7. Cho, J., & Woo, J. (2020). Development and experimental study of an independent row-based cooling system for improving thermal performance of a data center. Applied Thermal Engineering, 169, 114857.
8. Choi, W., Park, K. W., & Park, K. H. (2011, June). Scout: Data center monitoring system with multiple mobile robots. In The 7th International Conference on Networked Computing and Advanced Information Management. IEEE. (Vol. 1, pp. 150–155).
9. Corrado, C. R., DeLong, S. M., Holt, E. G., Hua, E. Y., & Tolk, A. (2022). Combining green metrics and digital twins for sustainability planning and governance of smart buildings and cities. Sustainability, 14(20), 12988.
10. Dai, J., Ohadi, M. M., Das, D., Pecht, M. G., Dai, J., Ohadi, M. M., ... & Pecht, M. G. (2014). Standards relating to data center. Optimum Cooling of Data Centers: Application of Risk Assessment and Mitigation Techniques, 2, 31–45.
11. DiMinico, C., & Jew, J. (2006). Telecommunications Infrastructure Standard for Data Centers ANSI/TIA. 942, 100–110.
12. Evans, R., & Gao, J. (2016). Deepmind ai reduces google data center cooling bill by 40%. DeepMind Blog, 20, 158.
13. Hoops, K., Johnson, T., Grossman, E. R., McCourt, A., Crifasi, C., & Benjamin-Neelon, S. E. (2020). Stay-at-home orders and firearms in the United States during the COVID-19 pandemic. Preventive Medicine, 141, 106–281.
14. Inker, L. A., Tighiouart, H., Coresh, J., Foster, M. C., Anderson, A. H., Beck, G. J., ... & Levey, A. S. (2016). GFR estimation using β-trace protein and β2-microglobulin in CKD. American Journal of Kidney Diseases, 67(1), 40–48.
15. Kehoe, B., Patil, S., Abbeel, P., & Goldberg, K. (2015). A survey of research on cloud robotics and automation. IEEE Transactions on Automation Science and Engineering, 12(2), 398–409.
16. Lenchner, J., Isci, C., Kephart, J. O., Mansley, C., Connell, J., & McIntosh, S. (2011, June). Towards data center self-diagnosis using a mobile robot. In Proceedings of the 8th ACM International Conference on Autonomic Computing (Vol. 2, pp. 81–90).
17. Levy, M. (2020, October). A novel framework for data center risk assessment. In 2020 11th IEEE Annual Ubiquitous Computing, Electronics & Mobile Communication

Conference (UEMCON). IEEE. (Vol. 1, pp. 0148–0154).

18. Levy, M., & Hallstrom, J. O. (2017, January). A new approach to data center infrastructure monitoring and management (DCIMM). In 2017 IEEE 7th Annual Computing and Communication Workshop and Conference (CCWC). IEEE. (Vol. 1, pp. 1–6).
19. Levy, M., & Subburaj, A. (2021, January). Emerging trends in data center management automation. In 2021 IEEE 11th Annual Computing and Communication Workshop and Conference (CCWC). IEEE. (Vol. 1, pp. 0480–0485).
20. Levy, M., Raviv, D., & Baker, J. (2019, January). Data center simulations deployed in MATLAB and Simulink using a cyber-physical systems lens. In 2019 IEEE 9th Annual Computing and Communication Workshop and Conference (CCWC). IEEE. (Vol.1, pp. 465–474).
21. Manganelli, M., Soldati, A., Martirano, L., & Ramakrishna, S. (2021). Strategies for improving the sustainability of data centers via energy mix, energy conservation, and circular energy. Sustainability, 13(11), 6114.
22. Masanet, E., Shehabi, A., Lei, N., Smith, S., & Koomey, J. (2020). Recalibrating global data center energy-use estimates. Science, 367(6481), 984–986.
23. Mastelic, T., Oleksiak, A., Claussen, H., Brandic, I., Pierson, J. M., & Vasilakos, A. V. (2014). Cloud computing: Survey on energy efficiency. Acm Computing Surveys (csur), 47(2), 1–36.
24. Quirk, D. (2022). Meeting Data Center Energy Compliance. ASHRAE JOURNAL, 64, 28–31.
25. Rosa, S., Russo, L. O., Farulla, G. A., Carlone, L., Antonini, R., Marco, G., & Bona, B. (2016). An application of laser-based autonomous navigation for data-center monitoring. In Intelligent Autonomous Systems 13: Proceedings of the 13th International Conference IAS-13. Springer International Publishing. (Vol. 1, pp. 95–107).
26. Russo, L. O., Rosa, S., Maggiora, M., & Bona, B. (2016). A novel cloud-based service robotics application to data center environmental monitoring. Sensors, 16(8), 1255.
27. Shehabi, A., Smith, S. J., Masanet, E., & Koomey, J. (2018). Data center growth in the United States: decoupling the demand for services from electricity use. Environmental Research Letters, 13(12), 124030.
28. Turner, W. P., Seader, J., & Renaud, V. (2014). Data Center Site Infrastructure Tier Standard. Topology, Uptime Institute, LLC.3, 2–3.
29. Wiboonrat, M. (2020, March). Human Factors Psychology of Data Center Operations and Maintenance. In 2020 6th International Conference on Information Management (ICIM). IEEE. (Vol. 1, pp. 167–171).

INDEX

Q

R

S

T